A Study In DIPLOMACY
the Story of Arthur Bliss Lane

A Study In DIPLOMACY

the Story of Arthur Bliss Lane

by

VLADIMIR PETROV

HENRY REGNERY COMPANY

CHICAGO

Copyright © 1971 by Vladimir Petrov. All rights reserved.
Published by Henry Regnery Company,
114 West Illinois Street, Chicago, Illinois 60610
Manufactured in the United States of America
Library of Congress Catalog Card Number: 70–143846

To my teacher,
Samuel Flagg Bemis

Books by the same author:
- "June 22, 1941": Soviet Historians and the German Invasion
- Money and Conquest: Alied Occupation Currencies in World War II
- What China Policy?
- My Retreat from Russia
- Soviet Gold

Contents

To the Reader

Studies of American foreign policy rarely focus on the men who conduct it. There are tomes on the institutional and organizational problems of the State Department; on the successes and failures of the United States in various parts of the world; on the arrogance of *Pax Americana*; on the interplay of the multitude of factors — economic, political, social, cultural, even anthropological — affecting policy-making and policy-implementation. On occasion, the collective foreign service officer and the foreign policy establishment find themselves stretched out under the magnifying glass of a psychoanalyst or an industrial efficiency expert. But the individual, the irreducible single unit in every development in this vast field, the live human being — his personality, his political and other predilections, his tastes and traits that affect policies and actions even in our age of government by committee and computerized fact finding — is somehow left out.

This omission is unfortunate, for in human affairs it is unnatural to divorce a creation from its creator. It is impossible to analyze and attempt to solve a major problem without taking into account the human element that formed it and the human resources available for its solution. Impersonal as the government appears to be, it is still the individual man who keeps the world spinning. But what do we know — aside from generalities — about the individuals who man the ship of state in the turbulent international seas? The memoirs that prominent personalities sometimes write, while certainly helpful, are inadequate. The authors tend to defend their records; besides, many extraneous considerations make their stories less than candid. Once in a great while there comes along a Robert Murphy or a Lord Moran, courageously, if somewhat indiscreetly, opening a view of the men in the "kitchen" of history making momentous decisions on the spur of the moment or moved by motives and circumstances that may appall an uninitiated person. But Murphys and Morans are few and far between, and even their accounts are by necessity fragmentary and incomplete.

Arthur Bliss Lane never rose to the top of the pyramid. A career diplomat, he was more concerned with implementation than with formulation of policy, much as he tried to influence his government's decisions. To the extent that he headed American embassies in several countries at times of acute crises affecting the fortunes of the United States, he was important. He was in Nicaragua when a democratic regime created by the Americans gave way to Somoza's dictatorship. He was in Yugoslavia when the United States, having parted from its interwar isolationism, joined forces with Great Britain in order to push Yugoslavia into the war against the Axis. He was in Poland after the war, vainly trying to save it for freedom and democracy even as his own government put it outside the perimeter of its vital interests.

But in the present context, the question whether Arthur Bliss Lane was "important" or not seems irrelevant, as is the question of how "typical" or how representative of the foreign policy establishment he was. A close look at any self-effacing state department bureaucrat, or at an ambassador attired in tails and striped pants, is certain to reveal unique individual characteristics that affect his official function; in Lane's case, not even a close look is required to see that he differed from others in many notable respects.

The uniqueness of each human being has always fascinated me. Thus leaving, for once, to others the search for syntheses and common denominators, I decided to concentrate my attention on one person. The product can hardly be called a "case study," for that would imply broad general findings based on a unique experience. It should probably be classified as a biography, except that I was more interested in Arthur Bliss Lane as diplomat and public servant than in his overall personality. By sheer chance, he witnessed and participated in many colorful and interesting developments. What matters more, he left his own indelible imprint on a number of memorable events that attracted, even if for a short while, the attention of the world.

In selecting Lane as the principal character for the present story, I also was moved by other more mundane considerations. He left a large collection of personal papers, and in my research, I could also utilize the official files of the State Department. There were still many people on the scene who had served with him, or were closely associated with him in different stages of his career, and who were willing, indeed anxious, to talk about him. Finally, I knew Arthur Bliss Lane personally. All this afforded an opportunity to reconstruct what should be regarded as the implementation of American policy in certain arbitrarily selected countries and times carried out by one man, with all his idiosyncrasies and his great and small struggles, both in the foreign capitals where he served and in his relations with his own government. Mainly in order to provide a reasonable perspective, I had to correlate Lane's role in a given situation with broader national and international developments that affected his thoughts and behavior, as well as with the pertinent decisions of his superiors in Washington who attempted to guide his official actions.

As the reader will see, this is neither a eulogy nor a critical analysis of the man; it is rather a recognition of the fact that whether in a leading or supporting role, Arthur Bliss Lane was always on stage, as indeed he had intended to be throughout his political lifetime.

Vladimir Petrov
Institute for Sino-Soviet Studies
George Washington University
Washington, D.C.

September 1970

Note on Sources

This book is based to a large extent on Arthur Bliss Lane's personal papers deposited with the Yale University Library and on unpublished State Department documents in the National Archives in Washington, D.C. Quotations from the papers of these two collections found in the text are not specifically attributed to one or to the other. Documents from the Roosevelt Library, the Princeton University Library, and the Manuscript Division of the Library of Congress are identified by source.

Most of the published documents quoted here come either from the *Foreign Relations of the United States* series or from *Documents on German Foreign Policy,* both published by the Government Printing Office, Washington, D.C., and referred to in the footnotes as FR and GFP, respectively. In important instances references to the appropriate secondary sources are also made in the footnotes.

During the many years of my on and off research for this book I talked and corresponded with a large number of people who either participated in the events that interested me or knew Arthur Bliss Lane with varying degrees of intimacy. In the latter group were many of his contemporaries in the Foreign Service of the United States, some of whom had served in the missions which he headed in the thirties and forties. These men helped me in assessing the evidence I had accumulated, and it was largely through them that I could reconstruct the evolution of Arthur Bliss Lane and his political views. It is next to impossible to measure their individual contributions to my work, but perhaps James C.H. Bonbright, Paul C. Daniels, Louis J. Fortier, Loy W. Henderson, Robert P. Joyce, and Karl L. Rankin were particularly informative in answering my queries.

Other contributors included George V. Allen, Willard L. Baulac, Charles E. Bohlen, William C. Bullitt, Homer M. Byington, Jr., V. Cavendish-Bentinck, Jan Ciechanowski, Peter Constan, Richard T. Davies, Roman Debicki, Allen W. Dulles, Elbridge Durbrow, Waldemar J. Gallman, Milan Gavrilovich, Joseph C. Grew, J.B. Hoptner, Outerbridge Horsey, Robert F. Kelley, Foy D. Kohler, Nicholas L. Knezevich, Ben Mandel, Stanislaw Mikolajczyk, Robert Murphy, Francis B. Stevens, H. F. Arthur Schoenfeld, Charles W. Thayer, Llewelyn E. Thompson, William S. Tonsek, Howard K. Travers, Peter Visher, Henry A. Wallace, John C. Wiley, Paul Zaleski and Peter B. Lane.

Finally, of immeasurable value to me were my numerous conversations with Mrs. Arthur Bliss Lane and her late husband's secretary of many years, Miss Iona McNulty. Thanks to them, I was able to locate many vital sources of information and to double-check data I had collected elsewhere. I must add that at no time did Mrs. Lane attempt to influence my treatment of the subject so close to her heart, or, indeed, as much as ask to read the manuscript. To her, as well as to all the others mentioned above, I express my sincere gratitude.

A Study In DIPLOMACY
the Story of Arthur Bliss Lane

I

Apprenticeship

Arthur Bliss Lane devoted thirty years of his life to the protection of American national interests in Europe and Latin America. He was a man of deep albeit changing convictions, with a strong and independent mind. While he believed in the discipline which held together the pyramid of the State Department, on more than one occasion he interpreted official policy more liberally than his superiors considered warranted, and in many instances he attempted, through forceful presentations of his views, to alter this policy. Although he had many close and devoted friends, his tenacity and his combative spirit did not make him very popular within the foreign policy establishment even when — or particularly when — his analyses of the situation were proven correct by subsequent developments.

Lane's disregard for the consquences of being controversial led to a premature termination of his career. In 1947, at the age of 53, he resigned as ambassador to Poland to be able "to speak and write openly, without being hampered by diplomatic convention" about the true conditions in Poland and about the failure of the United States to secure the fulfillment of the Yalta and Potsdam agreements regarding that country. He wrote a book entitled *I Saw Poland Betrayed* and several articles; he lectured all over the country; and for several years he was deeply involved in domestic politics as one of the early authorities on Cold War issues.

In spite of these unique features of his personality and his life, Arthur Bliss Lane was in one respect representative of a whole generation of American diplomats. He firmly believed that the foreign policy of the United States had to conform to the principles expressed in the Declaration of Independence and the Constitution of the United States, principles which he

1

held to be of universal value. Advancing the interests of the country was to him inseparable from advancing the cause of freedom and democracy. His criterion of good and evil left little room for equivocation; he had a single set of standards by which he judged the men he encountered and the events he witnessed. He had little tolerance for those who were prepared to compromise these principles for the sake of expediency. Although he accepted the frailty of human nature in private life he was inflexible in judging political decisions of statesmen.

At times, this rigidity caused Lane serious inner conflicts, for from experience and observation he knew that there often is more than one recognizable truth. He had good capacity for understanding local conditions in strange lands. He sympathized with the plight of ordinary men, and with the predicament of the governments of small nations striving to survive against great odds. But in times of crisis, when a clash of interests and policies required him to take a definite stand, he invariably chose positions conforming to his own basic beliefs and to his idea of what his mission as a representative of the United States in each situation had to be.

There were many men in the American foreign service in the period between the two great wars who more or less shared Lane's *weltanschauung*. Most of these men, however, abided by the discipline of the government service and the existing chain of command even when it meant compromising their convictions and their better judgment. Lane, particularly toward the end of his service, had less patience with his own government and more of a crusading spirit than was good for his career. He was aware of it, and accepted the consequences (if not always gracefully), preferring the satisfaction of remaining true to himself to long-range career or even policy considerations. Because of his seniority, he probably could have stayed as an American envoy in some foreign land longer than he actually did. But, having lost trust in the wisdom of the men who directed the policies of the United States, he chose resignation—and opposition. That, however, was at the end. Let us start with the beginning.

Arthur Bliss Lane entered the diplomatic service under most fortunate circumstances. He had a good family background. He received good schooling, which included the Ecole de l'Ile

de France in Liancourt, France, and Yale College. He excelled
in history, foreign languages, and sports. Immediately upon his
graduation from Yale in June, 1916, Thomas Nelson Page, a
prominent author serving as ambassador to Italy who was on a
visit to the United States, asked him to become his private
secretary. Lane accepted this position enthusiastically even
though it carried no salary with it: the family fortune, founded
by his grandfather, inventor and industrialist E. W. Bliss, was
sufficient to afford this luxury. Ambassador Page liked the
bright young man. He introduced Lane into the subtleties of
diplomacy and the rigorous demands of protocol, and helped
him to develop the clear and concise language of political
reporting which became one of the major strong points of the
young diplomat.

In the summer of 1917, Arthur Bliss Lane was officially
admitted to the Foreign Service. Two years later, he moved
from Rome to Warsaw to open, together with Hugh Gibson, the
first American legation in newly resurrected Poland. In the
spring of 1920 he joined the most important American mission
abroad, that in Great Britain, as private secretary to Ambassador John W. Davis, a future presidential candidate of the
Democratic Party and a man of immense ability and intelligence. Among Lane's tutors in politics and diplomacy were
such men as Joseph C. Grew, Charles Evans Hughes, Dwight
W. Morrow, J. Reuben Clark, and Josephus Daniels.

A young American, performing perhaps minor, but often
delicate assignments for his ambassador in major European
capitals, had ample opportunity to meet prominent men and
observe them closely. Kings and queens, cabinet ministers,
dukes and counts, foreign diplomats, and important traveling
Americans formed an ever-changing, fascinating environment.
Etiquette and diplomatic protocol, mixed with hard-headed
politics, were the way of life. In London, Ambassador Davis
put Lane in charge of the embassy's relations with the Court of
St. James, a most exacting job in view of the endless stream of
ambitious American matrons anxious to be presented to British
royalty. Under George S. McClellan Harvey, a prominent isolationist publisher and editor, who replaced Davis in 1921, Lane
began to learn the hard way how to handle newsmen—an art
which in time he developed to perfection.

Along with the development of indispensable diplomatic skills evolved Lane's world outlook. In some ways, he was a typical product of the liberal education of the Wilsonian era. A firm believer in the blessings of liberty and the democratic form of government, he carried these beliefs into the realm of foreign policies. Peace, justice, international law, and morality in accordance with the idealistic American concepts, formed the foundation for his judgments. Like so many ivy leaguers, he was a populist at heart, with a strong feeling for the underdog. Although sometimes it could not be helped, Lane disliked taking advantage of his social background. Not until many years later did his Florence-born wife, Cornelia Thayer Baldwin, whom he married in Italy in 1918, find out that he was a direct descendant of William Bradford, second governor of the Plymouth Colony.

Lane thought a great deal of Woodrow Wilson, whom he briefly escorted during the President's triumphant visit to Italy in 1919. He admired the pianist Paderewski, Poland's first prime minister, and Monsignor Achille Ratti, the Apostolic Nuncio in Warsaw, who later was elected Pope Pius XI. He made friends with many talented young Americans and Englishmen in London and Paris in the years following World War I who were destined to become prominent in politics and diplomacy. However, he never was carried away by an emotional attachment to anybody; hero-worship was alien to his nature. In colorful descriptions of various functions that he attended, which filled long and frequent letters to his parents, one searches in vain for signs of reverence and humility. Referring to the founder of the American Federation of Labor, for instance, the 22-year-old secretary of the embassy in Rome wrote: "Mr. Gompers is a fine chap—a big-hearted man with remarkably broad vision, who sees the big points and then fights for his principles with such ardor that he has risen from a Dutch-Jewish silk worker in the slums of London to be the second most powerful man in America, a man so much thought of that he has dined with the chiefs of state of all the allied countries." In spite of his admiration for Wilson, Lane happily related to his mother an episode in which he caught the president ignorant of one of the most burning contemporary political issues in Italy, adding: "You could have knocked me over with a straw: for he is an exceedingly cultured man and history is his forte. Well, I was not so surprised when I heard that Lloyd George interrupted a speaker in the Peace Conference one day to ask him what he meant by the Banat—and where it was. Somehow or other, it is pleasing to a small man to trap a great one on some point of knowledge and I crowed over it for days." This pleasure of trapping great men (and not so great) was to grow with the years, not always increasing Lane's popularity and sometimes creating difficulties in his relations with his fellow diplomats.

Lane's perception of the world, and of the United States' place in it, was essentially formed in the early years of his career against the background of the First World War. To him, the Central Powers were evil; despotic. The Allied and Associated Powers were their opposite. It was natural for good to triumph over evil in the war, but the peace had to be just. Lane knew by heart a passage from Wilson's address to Congress in January, 1917: "No peace can last or ought to last, which does not recognize and accept the principle that governments derive all their just powers from the consent of the governed, and that no right everywhere exists to hand peoples about from sovereignty to sovereignty as if they were property . . . every people should be left free to determine its own polity, its own way of development, unhindered, unthreatened, unafraid, the little along with the great and powerful." Nonetheless, Lane was pragmatic enough to recognize the limitations imposed by the dictates of the international balance of power. Unlike some idealistic Wilson worshipers at the Paris peace conference who became bitterly disillusioned with the president, he accepted as inevitable certain deviations from the latter's peace program. Lane saw nothing wrong in Italy's claims to the South Tirol or to the Dalmation Coast (he wrote approvingly of Ambassador Page's efforts to convince the President to yield to the Italian demands); in his view, high principles did not necessarily apply to an enemy.

The experience of those years had one lasting and perhaps most important effect on Lane's world outlook: it convinced him that the United States was destined to perform an important mission in the world. It had participated in the great war not out of selfishness or greed but in order to secure for humanity a just and durable peace. He was proud that with all its dilutions and modifications the peace settlement which emerged out of the Paris conference was still essentially an American peace based on Wilson's Fourteen Points. Wilson himself was a leading world statesman, idolized by millions of Europeans whose destinies seemed to be in his hands. Although the United States shared the glory of victory over the wicked Central Powers with the French and British Empires, unlike its allies it was moved by noble and humanitarian motives; its power and promise were great enough to check the ambitions of the imperialists and expansionists. He might have had reservations about his emotional president, but he regarded as a tragic mistake the withdrawal of the United States into isolation under the succeeding Harding administration.

During this first sojourn in Europe, Lane encountered the phenomenon of nationalism, so new to him, which engulfed Central and Eastern Europe and which plagued the sessions of the Peace Conference and the Supreme Council. He watched its manifestations with mixed feelings, approving in principle but finding it not quite to his personal liking. His observations in Poland were particularly instructive. Like most foreign diplomats, he was much more at ease with the cosmopolitan Polish aristocracy than with the aroused masses. Yet he felt the need to understand the masses. Warsaw did not impress him as a very interesting or attractive city; in a letter to his mother he termed the Polish capital "decidedly primitive." But he watched with great curiosity the May Day parade of the city laborers led by the socialists, and many more parades and mass rallies organized by the nationalists. Once he described at length the symbolic joint appearance of General Pilsudski, the Chief of State, and the Bishop of Warsaw at such a rally, and the tremendous enthusiasm of the huge crowd.

The Polish national anthem was played, and Mass celebrated: Pilsudski appeared very devout. It seemed most significant that the Church and the State were working so closely in harmony. . .When the Mass had been finished a Polish priest who is a member of the Diet stood upon the table, he being clothed in his surplice, and made a most eloquent address. All I understood was "Polski" but I could tell that he was eloquent and he convinced me absolutely although I really have not the faintest idea what he was preaching about. . .Then we witnessed the most impressive military parade I have ever had the good fortune to see. I have seen larger parades, I have seen more elaborate ones, but never have I seen one which was as interesting and as moving. There was no reviewing stand save for a cobbled sidewalk; there was no policeman to keep the crowd back. It was democracy itself. Pilsudski stood on the road and the members of the legations and ministries mingled with the people just behind him. After all the soldiers passed by, a company of marines were reviewed and then over ten thousand children marched by the Chief. . .Some of them were little girls of five or six years but the General saluted them all. This showed the democracy of the whole celebration — that the head of the Polish nation should stand out in the grilling sun for over an hour while the poor children of Warsaw marched by him. There was an oriental touch to the scene by many persons hanging out rugs and tapestries from their windows in honor of the day. We came through the ghetto and there saw hundreds of long bearded and long gowned Jews.

It was easier to understand and appreciate the social contrasts in Poland. The gulf between the landowning aristocracy on the one hand, and the peasants and workers on the other, appeared unbridgeable. The strange thing was that most differences seemed to be submerged in the sea of nationalistic passions. The intensity of the Poles' emotions fascinated Lane: love for the country (which did not even have defined frontiers), hatred for the Russians, and rejection of the Jews and other ethnic minorities. He was impressed by the austere and forbidding figure of Pilsudski, the embodiment of the national spirit, but was much more attracted by Paderewski, who was kindly and outgoing, and had "the soul of the artist." While Pilsudski was Poland incarnate, the prime minister — a friend of Woodrow Wilson and Colonel House — symbolized a bridge between Poland and America. Paderewski was worshiped by American Poles and it was largely because of him that large-scale American aid poured into the war-ravaged land. Although Lane was proud that his country showed such generosity, and was inclined to believe in the existence of certain "historic" ties between the two countries, he nevertheless remained a detached observer, preferring to stay at arm's length in dealing with these emotional Poles with their peculiar ways, their strange language, and their bellicosity.

Personal attitudes all too easily translate into political philosophy, and young Lane instinctively shrank from the prospect of the United States becoming closely entangled with strange and distant lands on the fringe of Europe where it had no real interests. Like the great majority of foreign service officers, he was a traditionalist in diplomacy and a believer in dealing with governments rather than nations. The newly founded nations in the east of Europe had to find their own place under the sun through trial and error, and their governments had to learn how to manage their own affairs without outside interference. Thus, much as Lane was disturbed by the treatment of minorities in Poland, he took strong exception when Wilson, under domestic pressure, sent a special mission to Warsaw to investigate reports about the alleged Jewish pogroms. To him, this was an impermissible "derogation of sovereignty" of the Polish Republic.

The principle of non-intervention in the internal affairs of other nations determined Lane's attitudes and judgments during the later years when he was associated with Latin American affairs, beginning with his first assignment to Mexico in 1925. Generally, he accepted the Monroe Doctrine but rejected the Roosevelt Corollary to it. Viewing the sad state of American relations with the Latin Americans, he was convinced that no improvement was possible without abandoning the interventionist practices of the past. He was sympathetic with the reformist and even revolutionary spirit which swept the Central American and Caribbean regions in the twenties; he earnestly labored for the improvement of United States relations with Mexico, inspired by a succession of ambassadors to Mexico City, especially his first chief there, Dwight W. Morrow, a farsighted and dedicated man of high moral character.

Yet at all times Lane's idealism was moderated by his strong sense of reality. Because of his intense interest in the people and conditions of the countries he was concerned with, he learned that there were limitations to what could be accomplished. This learning process was not painless, for by temperament Arthur Bliss Lane was impatient, if not impulsive. Nevertheless, he liked to think of himself as a hardheaded realist, and it was not by accident that during these years he developed a steady working relationship with Sumner Welles, who was to become a chief architect of the United States' Latin American policy.

This realism was, of course, relative, and at least in retrospect it appears that many State Department officials expected the transition to the non-intervention policy to be less painful than it actually was. Lane remained quite sensitive to the recurrent setbacks to American interests which accompanied the restructuring of Washington's attitudes toward the nations south of the Rio Grande. As he became better acquainted with Latin Americans, he discovered that they had many attractive characteristics. But he also judged them volatile, immature, and insufficiently versed in the art of self-government. Sharing the common paternalistic disposition of Latin American specialists in the Foreign Service, Lane was convinced that the enlightened Hoover and Roosevelt administrations knew better what was good for the Latin Americans than they themselves did. And although he realized the need for patience if the unfortunate experiences of the past were to be erased from everybody's memory, he also found it at times difficult to put up with what seemed like an awful lot of nonsense on the part of Latin politicos. Perhaps more than most of his colleagues, he needed a bright vision of the much happier Western Hemisphere he was helping to build to overcome his annoyances.

Arthur Bliss Lane's idealism stayed pretty much in the background of his daily life. He was not a preacher by nature, and he detested self-righteous sermonizing. Much as he was absorbed in his work, he fully enjoyed life. He liked good food and fine liquor, even though his superiors stayed prohibitionist to the core. He played tennis and golf, and, wherever possible, rode horses. Since his college years he had appreciated good company and salty anecdotes. While in Warsaw, he noted with delight that Prime Minister Paderewski "would on occasion tell almost unprintable jokes and would laugh heartily at them to the discomfiture of the ladies present at the table, and there was a mischievous twinkle in his eyes when he did so." Shocking the ladies in similar fashion became, in time, Lane's own stock in trade.

Lane's association with Latin American affairs, the most important area in the State Department's operations during that period, brought him to the attention of many top officials. He advanced faster than most of his contemporaries. At the age of thirty he already was first secretary in Mexico City, the key post in the Western Hemisphere. Two years later he became chief of the Division of Mexican Affairs. In 1930 he returned to Mexico, this time as counsellor of embassy and chargé d'affaires. Finally, in the summer of 1933, as President Roosevelt enunciated his "good neighbor" policy, Arthur Bliss Lane received the cherished assignment of Head of Mission. At the age of 39, he became the youngest career minister in the history of the American diplomatic service. His post—Nicaragua—had all the challenges an ambitious diplomat could desire. The future looked bright and promising.

II

Disengaging in Nicaragua

Managua in 1933 was a tough post for an American diplomat; one of the toughest in Latin America. Its prominence at the time of Lane's appointment was unquestionable: Nicaragua had just been launched on an independent path after two decades of American intervention and four years of intensive efforts to create a viable democratic government. The problems which Arthur Bliss Lane was to face in Nicaragua were compounded by a long record of instability, extreme violence, and widespread corruption which had plagued the country since its formation. Nicaragua had a constitution—the sixth one in force since independence—at the time of Lane's arrival, but the constitution seemed unable to ensure law and order for the citizens, most of whom were poor, illiterate, and unaware of their constitutional rights. This gloomy picture was a product of a long and unhappy history.

The two historical Nicaraguan parties, Liberal and Conservative, represented geographical divisions in the country to a much greater degree than social groupings or political philosophies. Both parties were tightly run by small cliques of politicos who exploited the regional and family allegiances of the impoverished and illiterate people. Each party had its own armed forces and, once having seized control of the government, perpetuated itself in power through extensive patronage, fraudulent elections, and outright terror. The party in power could be dislodged only through a revolution; periodic revolts were accompanied by bloody fighting, pillage, and destruction.

In the 1930s Nicaragua had a population of about 700,000 concentrated mainly along the Pacific coast. Its economy was in an embryonic state; its exportable goods consisted chiefly of bananas, coffee, sugar, and mahogany. A large section of the country, the north and the east, was sparsely populated, and there were no roads connecting various regions and population centers.

Nicaragua had attracted the interest of the United States since the mid-nineteeth century, because it occupied a strategic position between the two oceans and offered excellent possibilities for the construction of a canal linking them. As far back as 1852, after the discovery of gold in California, Cornelius Vanderbilt founded the Accessory Transit Company, which commenced passenger service between San Juan del Norte and the Pacific Ocean across Lake Nicaragua. A year later, one of the most colorful adventurers of his era, William Walker of Nashville, Tennessee, invaded Nicaragua with a gang of some fifty soldiers of fortune with the vague purpose of turning Central American countries into a new slave territory for the United States. He soon installed himself as president of Nicaragua but in the end luck turned against him and his spectacular career ended ingloriously in 1860, when he was caught by a British naval captain and executed.

Following Walker's death, under a succession of Conservative oligarchies, the country enjoyed considerable stability until the upset election victory in 1893 of President Jose Zelaya, a forceful and ambitious Liberal. Zelaya's meddling in the affairs of Honduras, Guatemala, and El Salvador spread disturbances over the whole region, affecting American interests. He was openly hostile to the *Yanquis* and attempted to counterbalance American influence in Nicaragua by granting generous concessions to the Europeans and the Japanese.

Zelaya's rule was despotic and corrupt, but even in those early days his bold challenge to the United States assured him enough popular support to expand his political base and successfully crush recurrent attempts by Conservatives to overthrow his regime. Although the Conservative revolutionary forces drew part of their inspiration—and considerable financial support—from American interests on the Mosquito Coast, the United States for a while maintained a watchful neutrality in this internal strife.

This attitude changed abruptly in 1909. After the Zelaya

government executed two American citizens employed by the revolutionists, Secretary of State Philander C. Knox severed diplomatic relations with Nicaragua and told Zelaya's envoy in Washington that Zelaya was "a blot on the history of Nicaragua" and that the revolution represented "the ideals and the will of a majority of the Nicaraguan people." Zelaya was forced to resign, and with some of his lieutenants went into exile, but "Zelayaism" remained an important political factor in the affairs of Nicaragua and became a rallying platform for diverse anti-Yanqui elements throughout Latin America.

With active American assistance, the Liberal armies were finally defeated, but peace did not come to Nicaragua. Passions ran high and bands of armed men continued pillaging towns and villages. The Conservative government of Adolfo Diaz was so weak that in 1912, when a new large-scale revolt broke out, the United States dispatched 2,700 marines to Nicaragua. The insurgents were quickly crushed.

The Marines Remain

It was a measure of the weakness of the contending Nicaraguan factions that the subsequent stationing—at Diaz' request—of one hundred United States Marines in Managua as a "legation guard" was sufficient to end further effective challenge to the government. In order to protect American interests, Nicaragua's finances were put under control of the Seligman Company and Brown Brothers' banking interests in New York. An American collector-general assumed the collection of customs and servicing the country's foreign debt.

These measures had limited impact on the internal politics of Nicaragua. The country was far from pacified and, contrary to the hopes of the State Department, the marines had to remain in Managua. Before long, the United States' commitment expanded further. Fearing European penetration into Central America, a few days after the First World War exploded in Europe the United States concluded a new treaty with Nicaragua which ended, for all practical purposes, Nicaragua's independence and placed it under a virtual American protectorate. By the Bryan-Chamorro Treaty, in exchange for a payment of $3,000,000, Nicaragua leased to the United States certain territories and conceded "sovereign authority" over a possible canal route.

The American intervention in Nicaragua provoked widespread indignation in Latin America and became a favorite target of all enemies of "Yanqui Imperialism." The country itself, however, gradually entered a period of relative political tranquillity and prosperity. The United States' paternalistic policies did not go much beyond the reorganization of Nicaraguan finances, which enabled the country—by 1924—to end its dependence on New York bankers and to pay off its European debts. But whatever credit the United States could claim for Nicaragua's financial solvency, it did not contribute to the Americans' popularity in the Latin world.

Sentiment against the Monroe Doctrine in all its interpretations greatly increased throughout Latin America during the First World War. Mainly as a result of the interventions of the Wilson administration, this sentiment was particularly strong in Mexico, ruled by a succession of leftist, bitterly anti-American regimes. Perhaps more importantly for subsequent developments, intervention became a factor in internal politics in the United States, where "non-interventionists" vociferously demanded the liquidation of American commitments in the Caribbean region and Central America. Concurrent with these pressures from outside, there was a growing awareness in the State Department in the post-Wilson years that from almost every point of view intervention was a losing proposition.

The overall Latin American policy of the State Department came to be based on three fundamental principles: the Monroe Doctrine, the strategic security of the United States, and respect for the independence and integrity of all nations in Latin America. Secretaries of State Root, Hughes, and particularly Stimson, enunciated the policy of non-intervention with increasing forcefulness.[1]

The new approach to Latin American affairs was imple-

---

1. The transition to the new look was far from smooth. The Clark Memorandum of 1928, for example, did not represent—as is usually assumed—a change in policy or a repudiation of the Roosevelt Corollary, although Undersecretary Clark apparently viewed it as an attempt to "purify" the Monroe Doctrine. For a number of reasons, President Hoover doubted the wisdom of even suggesting that the United States had repudiated the Corollary,

mented with growing consistency in various acts of foreign policy by each succeeding administration in Washington. The United States abstained from inspiring or fomenting revolutions against unfriendly regimes and imposed embargoes on shipments of arms to revolutionists in spite of the angry protests of American arms manufacturers and spokesmen for American business interests in Latin America.

Yet, until the Montevideo Conference of 1933 there were some notable departures from the new principles in the Central American and Caribbean regions where the desire to respect the independence and integrity of the nations clashed with the recognized need to insure the security of the Panama Canal. A series of bilateral, though admittedly unequal, treaties allowed the United States, under certain conditions, to intervene in the affairs of the Dominican Republic, Cuba, Haiti, Panama, and Nicaragua.

This ambivalence dominated the United States' attitude towards Central America throughout the twenties and was manifested during the Washington Conference of 1923 which produced a multilateral Treaty of Peace and Amity. Its main objectives were to preserve peace in Central America, to ensure the countries against intervention on the part of their neighbors, and to promote internal stability: one clause of the treaty obligated the signatories not to recognize any government which might come to power as a result of a revolution or a coup d'état.

The importance which the conferees attached to this clause raised certain doubts in the State Department. For many, it brought to mind Wilson's practice of using non-recognition as a lever against unfriendly regimes which had come to power through extra-constitutional means—a rather common phenomenon in Central America. But such misgivings had to be weighed against the need to insure stability in a region noted for constant rebellions supported and often fomented from

---

although his Secretary of State, Henry L. Stimson, the man most responsible for the United States' Latin American policy, refused to recognize the official nature of the Clark Memorandum, stating that "the present administration disclaims all responsibility for the opinions expressed therein." See Robert H. Ferrell's enlightening article, "Repudiation of a Repudiation," in *The Journal of American History*, Vol LI, No. 4 (March, 1965).

abroad. In the end, the United States—which itself was not a party to the treaty—endorsed this mutual reinsurance of the incumbents.

Shortly after the Washington Conference, the State Department announced its decision to withdraw the marines from Nicaragua after the election of 1924. In this election, the United States scrupulously avoided taking sides and limited its role to an impartial supervision of the voting. Although there was not much opposition at the polls, President-elect Solorzano felt so insecure that he pleaded with Washington to leave the marines in Managua. Secretary Kellogg ignored these pleas, and in August, 1925, the marines departed. The United States expressed hope that Nicaragua would become a fully independent nation.

The Second Intervention and the "Peace of Tipitapa"

American expectations did not take into account the volatile nature of Nicaraguan politics. The ruling Liberal-Conservative coalition survived the withdrawal of the marines by only a few months. General Emiliano Chamorro, a Conservative leader and an ex-president, staged a military coup and in January, 1926, Solorzano resigned and fled the country. Chamorro's success, however, was short-lived. All Central American states immediately invoked the terms of the Treaty of 1923 and refused to recognize his regime. Not without misgivings, the United States followed suit. The repercussions were immediate.

Encouraged by the American failure to support the pro-Yanqui general, the anti-Chamorro Liberals, led by Dr. Juan Sacasa, vice-president in the Solorzano government, launched a large-scale rebellion on the Mosquito Coast. Mexico, ever ready to back an anti-Yanqui cause and not a party to the Treaty of 1923, energetically supported the rebels. Inevitably, this support forced the State Department, leery of the expansion of Mexican influence, to denounce Sacasa's action without at the same time endorsing Chamorro. Left to his own devices, Chamorro could not contain the rebels. He resigned, and Adolfo Diaz, long an American favorite, took his place.

Since the Liberals continued their offensive, the United

States abandoned its brief exercise in non-intervention, lifted the embargo on arms in favor of Diaz, and again sent the marines to the shores of Nicaragua. By then, however, the revolt had spread, acquiring a clearly anti-Yanqui direction. Mexico recognized Juan Sacasa as President of Nicaragua. The Liberal armies led by General Jose Maria Moncada kept advancing, by-passing the few areas which the marines—now numbering several thousand—effectively controlled. Nicaragua submerged into one of the bloodiest civil wars in its history.

In April, 1927, having rejected Diaz's pleas for a protectorate, President Coolidge dispatched Colonel Henry L. Stimson, future secretary of state, to Nicaragua as his personal representative with instructions to find a compromise solution. Coolidge hoped that a way might be found to extricate the United States from this embarrassing situation and to placate public opinion in the Latin world where anti-Yanqui feelings had reached a high pitch. Stimson quickly established that both sides were hopelessly deadlocked in the struggle and welcomed his mediation. Although Liberal chieftains were far from unanimous in their sentiments, Moncada's firmness and statesmanship made possible an agreement which became known as "The Peace of Tipitapa." According to this agreement, the soldiers of both armies were to surrender their arms to the marines—at $10.00 a rifle, not an unattractive sum to impoverished Nicaraguans—in exchange for an American promise to organize truly free elections in 1928. The old national army, ridden with politics, was to be dissolved and a new constabulary force, La Guardia Nacional, was to be trained by the marines and officered, for the time being, by Americans. Until the elections, President Diaz was to remain in office.

Moncada's lieutenants accepted the peace—all except one. "General" Augusto Cesar Sandino, the most violently anti-Yanqui Liberal chieftain and an ultra-nationalist with pronounced leftist leanings (which he had acquired during his residence in Mexico), quietly slipped away with some three hundred of his men to the mountains of the Segovias. Moncada's efforts to induce Sandino to disarm were fruitless. Sandino denounced both the Liberals and the Conservatives as stooges of American imperialism and commenced guerilla operations in the sparsely populated regions adjacent to the

Honduran border. He continued these operations with intermittant success for the next four years.

It is beyond the scope of this study to attempt to establish whether Sandino was a "bandit," a "guerrilla," a "communist," or a "patriot."[2] Most likely, he combined all these and perhaps other elements in some proportion unknown to us. The core of Sandino's forces included some highly-motivated Nicaraguan nationalists along with all kinds of adventurers and some of the most sadistic butchers to be found in Central America. The majority of Sandino's forces consisted of illiterate peasants impressed into "service"against their will.

The Sandinistas' major targets were American enterprises in Nicaragua, but they never shrank from sacking and pillaging villages and towns where there were no Americans. They tortured and mutilated their victims and killed without mercy. Sandino's popularity among Nicaraguans was questionable, but in strictly military terms, his guerrilla tactics proved to be highly effective against the marines and the Guardia Nacional. Because of the success of his raids, Sandino became a legendary hero who was worshiped by anti-Yanqui nationalist extremists throughout Latin America.

Before long, Sandino was "discovered" in the United States, thanks chiefly to reports which started appearing in *The Nation* in 1928. Carleton Beals, a newspaperman who attached himself to Sandino's headquarters, succeeded in creating a highly attractive image of the Nicaraguan which appealed to a wide variety of "non-interventionists" from Senator Borah to the communist-led All-American Anti-Imperialist League which became an important source of Sandino's political and material support. The 6th Congress of the Comintern sent "the heroic army of National Liberation of General Sandino" its "fraternal greetings" and Sandinista delegates addressed a number of communist fronts and "anti-imperialist" rallies in Europe, Asia, and the Americas.

---

2. For a competent sympathetic treatment of Sandino see Joseph O. Baylen's "Sandino: Patriot or Bandit?" in *The Hispanic American Historical Review*, Vol. XXXI, No. 3 (August, 1951), and his "Sandino: Death and Aftermath," in *Mid-America*, Vol. XXXVI, 1954. Even more sympathetic—and much more detailed—is *The Sandino Affair* (Chicago: Quadrangle, 1967) by Neill Macauley, former officer of Fidel Castro's Rebel Army.

While Sandino was glorified elsewhere, the American military and civilian representatives in Nicaragua proceeded with determination to implement the terms of the Peace of Tipitapa. They organized the electoral machinery, and the presidential election of 1928 passed without incident thanks to the supervisory efforts of General Frank R. McCoy, the marines, and the Guardia. General Jose Moncada was elected President of Nicaragua. Even the Conservatives, who lost badly, praised the fairness of the elections.

The struggle against Sandino's bands continued with the Guardia gradually assuming the main burden of the operations: by April, 1932, the number of marines in Nicaragua had been reduced from its peak of about 5,000 to under 1,000. After the congressional elections of 1930, also supervised by the United States, the State Department, now headed by Stimson, informed Moncada that his government would have to be ready to assume sole responsibility for the maintenance of peace because the marines would be withdrawen from Nicaragua as specified at Tipitapa. The State Department repeated this warning in April, 1931, in spite of a savage Sandino attack on Cape Gracias a Diós in which many Nicaraguans and some Americans, all civilians, were massacred. On December 10, 1931, President Hoover told Congress that the last marine would be taken out of Nicaragua after the next presidential election.

It is difficult to say whether the American determination to end intervention was properly appreciated by Nicaraguan politicians of both parties. President Moncada, who had not developed strong support among the population, and who feared an intensification of Sandino's drive and general upheaval in the country, hoped that the marines would stay. But American military and civilian officials (who otherwise did not always see eye to eye) agreed that the only way to assure stability was to further strengthen the native Guardia Nacional, which was soon to be turned over to the Nicaraguan government. The Americans further recommended that both parties come to terms with Sandino.

The political situation, however, was aggravated by the dissension within the governing Liberal Party. Moncada, by far the strongest personality in the party, could not, according to the constitution, succeed himself. Nor could he select his successor. The nomination went to his major rival, Juan Sacasa, leader of the left wing of the party, less tainted by collaboration with the Americans. The Conservatives nominated Adolfo Diaz; Sandino, who did not respond to the informal overtures from Managua, nominated his aide, Horacio Pontecarrero, to head the Sandinista ticket.

The November, 1932, election was again supervised by the marines reinforced by the Guardia, and Admiral Clark H. Woodward, together with the Guardia chief, Lt. Colonel C.B. Matthews, USMC, made sure that the people cast their votes without intimidation and interference. The Liberals won by a large margin and Juan Sacasa became president-elect. The remaining detachments of the marine brigade started an orderly withdrawal.

It may be difficult to believe these days, but the overwhelming majority of the population did not rejoice. Most Nicaraguans had in no way resented the United States military presence. It guaranteed relative peace at a time when bitter memories of the 1925–1927 civil war were still fresh. It provided a degree of protection to the impoverished peasants who were no longer forced to serve in the Liberal or Conservative army. The marines were subject to a discipline unheard of in Nicaragua and behaved well. The few American businesses in the country, having been warned by the State Department that they should count on no protection of their interests by the United States, were adopting more benevolent practices, providing a good contrast to those of native entrepreneurs. The Nicaraguan government had in the marines a free police force. It also preferred to employ Americans to supervise the collection of customs, the main source of revenue, because this prevented a diverting of the funds into the private pockets of political appointees. The Claims Commission, in arbitrating foreign claims, leaned over backwards in an effort to protect Nicaraguan interests.

The more responsible Nicaraguan politicians, Liberals and Conservatives alike, had accepted the paternalistic policy of the United States and only a few die-hard Sandinista nationalists and left-wing intellectuals displayed signs of jubilation over the forthcoming departure of the marines. The people at large dreaded the possibility of a return to the rough-and-tumble political traditions of the past, while seasoned leaders preferred to operate under the protective wing of the United States which had proven its impartiality in dealing with both parties.

Confronted with the prospect of being on their own, not only the Conservatives (who had no chance to come to power at this time) but also the Liberals felt insecure in a country which lacked an established political structure and a tradition of orderly government. Foremost among the Liberals was Juan Sacasa, president-elect. This old foe of Yanqui imperialism and revolutionary of long standing frankly told the American Minister in Managua many times that the marines should stay in the country longer.[3]

Sacasa had ample reason to fear the future. Conditions of abject poverty and mass illiteracy remained. In the northern provinces, the armed bands of Augusto Sandino, aided by Mexico, still ravaged the countryside. Although the Guardia forces seemed to be keeping Sandino's operations in check, Sacasa had no way of predicting what would happen when he was left to cope with the situation on his own. Shortly before Sacasa's inauguration Sandino announced his desire to come to terms with him, provided that their alliance would be directed against those Liberals and Conservatives who had collaborated with the Yanquis, especially Moncada and his followers. This proposal Sacasa could not easily accept. Sandino loomed large in his jungles, but his potential value as an ally under peaceful conditions was problematical and his trustworthiness questionable. The price which Sandino demanded for his cooperation was high: Sacasa could ill afford to make enemies of the pro-American Liberals who might combine forces with the Conservatives. Besides, they still had the ear of the United States minister in Managua.

Therefore, acting within the limited bi-partisan mandate he had, Sacasa carried out negotiations with Sandino with caution and without fanfare, at first through intermediaries and later directly, in Managua. Finally, on February 2, 1933, a truce agreement was signed. In exchange for a promise to disarm, the

3. See Hanna to Hull, November 4, 1932, FR, 1932, V, 876–878.

Sandinistas received amnesty, the assurance of preferential treatment in employment, and a promise of an important political position for Sandino himself, together with the privilege of maintaining a personal guard of 100 men.

Sacasa apparently entered this agreement in good faith, acting in the interests of the country rather than his own: there is no proof that the agreement was accompanied by any kind of political understanding between the two men. Yet the implementation of its terms ran into difficulties. The four years of Sandino's rebellion had left too many scars in the country, and the opposition to a full integration of Sandino's bandits into Nicaraguan life remained strong.

In addition, Sandino himself, having settled with several hundred of his followers on an "agricultural project" on the Rio Coco, did not live up to his part of the agreement. His men remained armed and from time to time pillaged villages and small towns in the remote areas where the Guardia did not venture. Increasingly, Sandino's "army" emerged as a force rivaling the Guardia and a haven for all those who, for whatever reason, would not or could not stay in the areas controlled by the government. Essentially, however, President Sacasa's inability to surmount the opposition of Sandino or to effect some kind of political alliance with him arose from the fact that despite the popular mandate he had received in the election, he had little real power to rely on. His government did not have a clear majority in Congress. Perhaps more importantly, it did not have its own army composed of loyal members of the ruling party (and impressed peasants) as had other regimes prior to the American intervention. Instead, there was the Guardia Nacional over which Sacasa had little control.

The marine-trained Guardia, then some 2,300 strong, was the sole military force in the country. According to the American design it had almost complete autonomy from the government. It was carefully balanced politically, with officers and enlisted men alike representing both parties equally. Unfortunately for Sacasa, the Guardia had been built up during the presidency of his predecessor, General Moncada, and in its Liberal quota were included many of Moncada's protégés. Moreover, the newly-appointed Jefe Director, General Anastasio Somoza, was no great friend of the new president.

The Americans attached paramount significance to what they regarded as the "non-partisan" character of the Guardia, it being expected to replace the marines as the main stabilizing force in the country. In various degrees, many politicians agreed with this scheme. On November 5, 1932, on the eve of the Nicaraguan presidential election, the candidates of both parties for the offices of President and Vice-President signed an agreement at the American Legation in Managua promising to respect the "non-partisan" structure of the Guardia, not to create any other armed forces, and not to play politics with future appointments and dismissals.[4]

Although the president was considered commander-in-chief of the Guardia, his power over it was thus greatly restricted. Sacasa signed the agreement with grave misgivings, and only after Matthew H. Hanna, United States minister (who also signed it, as a witness), assured him that the United States would "morally guarantee" the agreement. Later Sacasa claimed that he understood this to mean that the United States would somehow enforce the Guardia's loyalty to the president.[5]

Once elected, Sacasa did his best to safeguard his personal interests. He filled the government with his friends (as well as with his strong-willed wife's numerous relatives). He organized a small presidential guard composed of devout Liberals of his faction, a development which was in violation of the November 5 agreement but which, for the time being, was accepted gracefully by all concerned. For the rest—and Sacasa was well aware of it—his future and the stability of his regime depended primarily on the influence and goodwill of the United States.

With the departure of the marines this influence, although still great, became much less tangible. Some Americans, familiar with Nicaraguan ways, were apprehensive. Others, especially in the State Department, were—or appeared—optimistic. The main thing, however, was that the United States' decision to disengage in Nicaragua was final and irrevocable.

On January 2, 1933, the State Department officially an-

---

4. See FR, 1932, V, 887–888.
5. See Sacasa, Chamorro, and Diaz to Hull, November 30, 1936, FR, 1936, V. 844–847.

nounced "the termination of the special relationship which has existed between the United States and Nicaragua." It pointed out that the Guardia "has developed into a well-disciplined and efficient organization with a high *espirit-de-corps*" and stressed that the direction of the Guardia was now fully in Nicaraguan hands. It declared that with the departure of the last marine, no American armed forces remained in Nicaragua "in any capacity whatsoever."

Thus the United States moved towards complete consistency in its new Latin American policy of non-intervention, making no exceptions for any country on whatever grounds. American citizens and private interests had ample warning (and evidence) that the United States would not intervene on their behalf by force of arms no matter how badly they might be mistreated by local governments. There were some minor vestiges of the intervention era left in Nicaragua, like a degree of control over the collection of customs,[6] but these were of little significance. All in all, the United States was determined to break away from the legacy of the "big stick" and "dollar diplomacy" even if it meant acceptance of infringements on its interests.

The Challenges of Arthur Bliss Lane

The mission of Arthur Bliss Lane, Envoy Extraordinary and Minister Plenipotentiary of President Franklin D. Roosevelt, was to implement the "good neighbor" policy of his government within the context of Nicaraguan realities. He arrived in Managua with his wife in the fall of 1933.

Managua, then a town of some 30,000 inhabitants with few paved streets and no industries, was slowly recovering from the catastrophic earthquake of 1931. The setting was picturesque but otherwise offered little to a man familiar with gracious living in major European capitals. The minister's residence, high on the hill overlooking Managua, had lovely grounds— Lane's predecessor, Hanna, was an amateur gardener—but few

---

6. This arrangement was made because the United States was responsible to the European bondholders for the loans given to Nicaragua. But the American officials were legally in the employ of the Nicaraguan government. The last of them left the country late in 1949.

conveniences. Because of the location, water barely dripped from the faucets and had to be accumulated during the night in the bathtub. The screens kept larger mosquitos away but giant cockroaches crawled all over the place. The tropical climate was hot and very humid; medical facilities were meager. Because of the absence of an American school, the Lanes left their young daughter behind.

Nicaragua was making headlines in the United States, but the American legation in Managua, erected after the earthquake, was a small single-storied building one third of which was leased to the Chinese legation. After the final transfer of responsibilities to the local government the legation was left with a staff of two officers and one clerk, while a couple of Nicaraguan employees performed minor chores.

To any but the most ambitious young diplomat, the Managua post would have appeared one of the least desirable in the whole foreign service of the United States. It had, however, two rewards. One was that an American minister in the Nicaraguan capital was by definition the most important member of the diplomatic corps and, in the opinion of many natives, perhaps still the most important man in the country. The second reward was that Nicaraguan affairs still loomed large on the State Department's horizon and the success — or failure — of the minister could make or break his career.

Lane's challenge was great. The legacy of the intervention era, the volatile nature of Nicaraguan politics, and the still uncertain path of the country's independence had to be dealt with in an entirely new spirit. His task was to launch Nicaragua as a fully sovereign nation and to liquidate the last vestiges of American paramountcy in Nicaraguan affairs, while at the same time assuring civil peace and the preservation of constitutional order. Lane had to prod the Nicaraguan government and the opposition to work in harmony, all the while avoiding any appearance of interfering in the internal affairs of the country.

The latter task was of supreme importance. Nationalistic-minded elements felt no special gratitude to the United States for its efforts, usually well meant, to insure peace, public order, and economic progress in the country. The Liberal government of Juan Sacasa needed American backing for the success of its administration, but old suspicions did not die easily, and there were people around who did not quite believe in the change of heart in Washington.

Nevertheless, all things considered, the position of Minister Lane appeared strong. There was no rival foreign power whose influence in Nicaragua even remotely approached that of the United States. The governments and public opinion of the sister Central American states watched the unfamiliar moves of the United States with various degrees of suspicion and mistrust but were generally sympathetic to the cause of Nicaraguan independence and to the Liberal government in Managua. Even that section of public opinion in Central America which was hostile to the United States had not emerged as a significant factor in Nicaraguan political life; its expressions were often moderated by the continuing American influence and various economic inducements which Washington, in spite of the economic depression in the United States, could offer.

Internally, there was still the problem of Sandino, the self-styled standard-bearer of the fight against Yanqui imperialism, whose bands conducted occasional raids against government-held towns and villages. But in spite of the earlier setbacks, communications between Sandino and Sacasa continued and the chances for their eventual reconciliation seemed good. Finally, the very fact that President Sacasa was a leader of the party identified with the nationalist cause implicitly helped Lane's task of promoting the full independence of Nicaragua and extricating the United States from the country's internal affairs.

In effect, Lane had an almost entirely clear field before him and could enjoy a high degree of freedom of action, freedom which few ambassadors have in the modern world. In addition, Lane seemed to be well equipped for his mission. He had in no way been associated with "dollar diplomacy" or American corporations with interests in Latin America. He had years of diplomatic experience behind him, a good command of Spanish, and familiarity with Central American affairs. He was young, intelligent, and energetic, and had a great capacity for communication with people of widely divergent views and interests. Along with President Roosevelt, Secretary Hull, and the Assistant Secretary of State for Latin American Affairs, Sumner Welles, he sincerely believed in the need for American disengagement in Nicaragua.

Perhaps he was a bit too anxious to succeed and attached too much importance to his mission. While it was true that Nicaragua in 1933 was a critical spot where the Latin American policy of the United States was being tested, it was only a spot, and there were other much more significant developments—in the Far East and in Europe—which increasingly attracted the attention of Washington policy-makers. This was something the American minister in Managua did not always take into account.

He could hardly be blamed for it, for in those days the State Department did very little to inform American envoys abroad (especially in such small places as Nicaragua) about the state of the world and its plans for dealing with it. On occasion, the ministers and ambassadors in neighboring countries exchanged information which they thought to be of common interest and visited each other. Otherwise, they had to rely on an inadequate supply of news in the local press, on whatever they could learn through private correspondence with their colleagues elsewhere, and on the State Department's infrequent communications.

The Guardia vs. the Government

Lane soon discovered that the stability of Nicaraguan political life was illusory and that the democratic forms of government introduced by the United States had not taken root. Instead of institutions he had to deal with personalities. As a traditionalist in diplomacy, Lane felt obliged to act loyal to the established government of President Sacasa. And since the threat to Sacasa's regime was serious, this sense of loyalty required of him a much deeper involvement in local affairs than the spirit of "non-intervention" seemed to permit. All the local problems were overshadowed by political instability; by the intricate maneuvering of various leaders and their cliques which greatly gained in volatility after the American protectorate of the country ceased. Of all the challenges it had to face, the Sacasa government was most preoccupied with that presented by the armed forces, the Guardia Nacional, and particularly by its Jefe Director, a young and ambitious general, Anastasio Somoza.

The talented son of a coffee planter, Somoza was a

well-educated and well-traveled man. He had lived for seven years in Philadelphia and during this period developed great admiration for the United States. He met there and married Salvadora de Bayle, a member of an aristocratic Nicaraguan family and a niece of Juan Sacasa. Upon his return to Nicaragua, Somoza tried a variety of jobs, none too successfully, until around 1926 he found his genuine vocation in politics. His family associations and his acute political sense directed him to join the Liberals. He loyally supported General Moncada, his relative, after the Tipitapa settlement, and in 1928, at the age of 32, after the first free elections, was rewarded with the post of Governor of Leon, a Liberal stronghold. He held several other important positions, including that of foreign minister in the Moncada government, and caught the eye of Matthew H. Hanna, United States minister. Moncada's appointment of Somoza as the Jefe Director—strongly endorsed by Hanna—was not warmly welcomed by the members of Sacasa's group who had reasons to question his loyalty and fear his ambition.

A colorful and engaging personality, Somoza quickly developed his personal following among the Nicaraguan military, the role of which, after the marines' withdrawal at the end of 1932, was rapidly increasing in importance. He drew his main political support from among Moncada Liberals but had many friends among the Conservatives also. Although Somoza displayed outward signs of loyalty to the president, he jealously guarded the Guardia's autonomy, which was also his autonomy. Before long, Somoza let it be known that he might one day become interested in the presidency. The gregarious general did not care to conceal his conviction that he could give Nicaragua better leadership than anyone else, and his friends in the Guardia readily agreed.

Once Lane had sized up the situation, he realized what President Sacasa had realized long ago, namely that the American idea of a "non-partisan" native military force was undergoing a characteristically Latin American twist and that the Guardia was evolving into an independent political force. Sacasa started exploring the possibilities of arresting the growing influence of the Guardia even before the last marine had left the country. Theoretically, this was an internal Nicaraguan

affair and could be handled within the established constitutional framework. In practice, any curtailment (or "reorganization," as it was euphemistically called) of the Guardia required forceful presidential leadership and the cooperation of
Congress. Neither was available. Sacasa was anything but
forceful, and although the Congress was two-thirds Liberal,
only a fraction of its members followed Sacasa's wishes.

Under such circumstances any reorganization of the Guardia
required American support. Washington's disclaimers notwithstanding, the United States, in Sacasa's view, remained responsible for the Guardia's behavior and, even if indirectly, for the
preservation of his government. In order to obtain American
support, Sacasa needed to convince the State Department that
the Guardia, instead of being the backbone of his regime, was
in fact menacing it. This proved to be an impossible task.

Immediately after his inauguration, when he found that the
chances for the passage of a law placing the military under his
control were nil, Sacasa began his efforts to obtain American
consent to the reorganization of the Guardia. He addressed his
inquiries to Hanna. The minister, who was himself deeply
committed to the "Guardia plan," merely referred them to the
State Department. In reply, Francis White, Assistant Secretary
for Latin American Affairs, in a personal letter to Hanna dated
January 9, 1933, instructed him to maintain an entirely
hands-off position. "The legation should scrupulously avoid
interference in this matter," wrote White, and "take the attitude that . . . observance or violation (of the November, 1932
agreement) is a question to be determined by the parties to the
agreement." White added that "the legation should make perfectly clear to them that the responsibility is entirely theirs and
is shared in no way by the legation."

Hanna made this clear to Sacasa, who obviously was neither
prepared to assume responsibility for such a move nor thought
it practically possible. There the matter rested for several
months until Hanna was replaced by Lane and Sacasa decided
to renew his efforts.

The American Minister vs. the State Department

In December, 1933, at the Pan-American Conference in

Montevideo, Sacasa's Minister for Foreign Affairs, Arguello, submitted to Secretary Hull a memorandum requesting the United States' consent to the reorganization of the Guardia on the grounds that the agreement of 1932 was signed by the leaders of both Nicaraguan parties at the American legation in Managua. Hull sent the memorandum to Washington for study and the State Department, on December 16, replied that although the American minister in Managua had witnessed the signature, "the United States was not a party to the agreement and Nicaragua incurred no obligation to consult us concerning any action contemplated under it or with reference to it."

Transmitting this exchange to Arthur Bliss Lane on December 28, Sumner Welles (who had replaced Francis White) emphasized that the Department could not "comment officially on the proposed reorganization of the Nicaraguan Guardia any more than it could on the reorganization of the military forces of any other independent, sovereign nation." Lane was permitted "orally and informally" to tell Sacasa and anyone else that in the Department's opinion "the continued maintenance of a Guardia Nacional organized substantially as at present is important to the future peace and welfare of Nicaragua." Welles stressed that the preservation of the "non-partisan principle" in the Guardia constituted "one of Nicaragua's strongest guarantees of peace."[7]

Thus the American desire not to see a Nicaraguan government trying to preserve law and order in a manner more compatible with Latin American traditions was reaffirmed. In the opinion of the Roosevelt administration, the existence of a "non-political" Guardia (and conversely, of a basically weak government) was necessary for assuring honest elections, for the protection of the minority party, and for keeping open the path for a peaceful change of government.

In Managua, Arthur Bliss Lane viewed the situation differently, chiefly because he had to deal with specific matters of immediate concern. To him, the predicament of the Nicaraguan president was quite real. In a long personal letter to Edwin C. Wilson, chief of the Latin American Division of the State Department, dated February 3, 1934, Lane brought up

---

7. Welles to Lane, December 28, 1933, FR, 1933, V, 850.

the point that the Guardia was not "non-partisan," but a bi-partisan and consequently highly political organization. "The Guardia plan," he wrote, was not "working out as the non-political organization which we hoped it would be," especially in view of the well-known ambitions of General Somoza. Lane also pointed out the inconsistency in Welles' letter of December 28 which instructed him to avoid taking any position on the reorganization of the Guardia "officially," while at the same time directing him to object to it "orally and informally." This was a delusion, Lane warned Wilson; in his judgment, "any expression of views, no matter how informally, is bound to be regarded as an important factor; and should such expression result in an unfortunate condition, the responsibility will be pinned on us, whether we agree or not as to our responsibility."

In order to elicit a reconsideration of the official view on the matter, a week later Lane wrote a personal letter to Welles. In it he developed three arguments in support of Sacasa's position. One was that the "heavy outlay of funds which the maintenance of the Guardia entails [is] at the expense of public health, education, and roads. When a country which has nothing to fear from its neighbors spends 60 percent of its budgeted income on the maintenance of its army, there cannot be much optimism for its economic and educational development." Another argument was that the setting up of a "permanent military caste . . . is practically defying the constitutionally constituted government." Finally, Lane pointed out that "the main argument now advanced for the maintenance of the Guardia at its present strength, is to afford the country protection against Sandino." Since there was a good chance for reconciliation between Sacasa and Sandino, and hence for an end of the civil conflict, Lane suggested that the Guardia question could soon be reconsidered.

In his personal letter of February 19, Welles replied cautiously. He agreed generally with Lane's views but at the same time said "that only time and ability on the part of the government to tackle the problem when favorable opportunitites present themselves can improve this situation. I do feel very strongly that no opinion should be expressed by our government at this juncture." Welles linked the possibility of the reduction in the Guardia to the general question of reduction of armaments which was expected to be taken up at the forthcoming conference of Central American states. And he did not mention Sandino.

The Problem of Sandino

Welles' letter was clear, but Lane remained unconvinced and utilized every opportunity to reiterate his views in his communications with Washington. In the meantime, he concentrated his attention on local developments which promised to strengthen Sacasa's government.

The first order of business was to facilitate a rapprochement between Sacasa and Augusto Sandino, who wished to abandon his extra-legal existence in the mountains of the north and take an active part in Nicaraguan politics. This rapprochement promised to kill several birds with one stone. Pacification of the country would add a feather to Sacasa's cap. Some kind of alliance of Sacasa's followers with the Sandinistas would create a more even balance of power in Nicaragua and help preserve its fledgling democratic institutions. The case for reducing, if not eliminating, the Guardia would be much stronger.

There were significant differences between Sacasa's and Lane's expectations. To Lane, Sandino was little more than a bandit; he was not prepared to forget Sandino's record of vicious anti-Yanqui agitation and of pillage and atrocities committed over the years. Lane hoped, not quite realistically, that after the settlement was reached, Sandino would go voluntarily into exile, instructing his followers to loyally support President Sacasa. Lane also expected that the Sandinistas would surrender their arms to the Guardia, an act which, in his opinion, would create a most favorable effect both in Nicaragua and Washington and would form a solid foundation for a more healthy state of political affairs.

Sacasa's exact expectations are not known, but it may be surmised that at least on one point—the disarming of Sandinistas—the president held a more realistic view than the United States minister in Managua. It was common knowledge that Sandino and Somoza heartily hated each other and that the forces they commanded preserved an uneasy truce only with difficulty. On many occasions the Jefe Director expressed preference for the physical extermination of Sandino's bands to their disarmament through negotiations and repeatedly voiced his concern about the political consequences of the Sandinistas' re-integration into the country's life. Sacasa, on the other hand, increasingly regarded the Sandinistas as the factor best suited to offset the growing power of the Guardia; in several instances, he alerted Sandino against possible Guardia moves and indicated his receptiveness to the idea of joining hands with the opposition forces. Nevertheless, the amnesty for Sandino's followers could not be effected without prior surrender by them of their arms. This act inescapably emerged as a key point of the expected agreement.

In spite of his differences with Sacasa, Lane wanted the negotiations to succeed and was prepared to do what he could to that end. Of course, he was under instructions to leave the resolution of all such knotty problems to the now sovereign government of Nicaragua. But he had also been given sufficient discretion to exercise his influence. For example, before he left Washington, President Roosevelt and Secretary Hull explicitly permitted him to have direct talks with Sandino if the latter asked for it. And he certainly felt free to express "orally and informally" his views to a large number of people of influence in Nicaraguan affairs.

It should be added that in pursuing his strategy, Lane successfully kept above his personal likes and dislikes. Although he considered the Guardia a menace, he liked its vivacious and enthusiastically pro-American Jefe Director who so anxiously sought his advice and at least appeared to be ready to follow it. By the same token, while striving to encourage Sacasa and strengthen his position, Lane could not warm up to his weak and rather colorless personality; and he did not try to conceal his distaste for Sandino. Like Cordell Hull and Sumner Welles, he was inclined to be guided by long-range considerations tailored to Nicaragua's specific conditions; in addition, he was a career diplomat who wanted to do his job and do it well.

Sandino Comes to Managua

General Augusto Cesar Sandino arrived in Managua on February 16, 1934, with a group of his followers. He was lodged with his aides at the house of Salvatierra, minister of agriculture in Sacasa's government, who was known as Sandino's supporter. The conferences at the Casa Presidential started immediately. Although the Sacasa-Sandino talks were supposed to be secret, the American legation had enough friends in Managua to be informed about the developments in sufficient detail.[8] One of the first things Lane learned was that Sandino indicated that he would not turn over his arms to the Guardia because of the "unconstitutionality" of that organization; and that Sacasa was not greatly upset by this announcement.

Although Lane deemed the disarming of Sandino's bands essential, he remained sufficiently flexible to see some positive value in Sandino's refusal to surrender his arms to the Guardia. Lane felt that this refusal might provide the needed leverage for making the Guardia "constitutional"—perhaps by the passage of the law drafted in 1932 by the then Jefe Director of the Guardia, U.S. Marine Colonel Matthews, and cleared by the State Department. This draft defined in detail the Guardia's organization and clearly subordinated it to the president. So far its passage had been effectively blocked by competing political groups with vested interests in the continuing weakness of the government.

Lane was concerned about Sandino's repeated anti-American statements to the press, such as the one he made to the effect that the United States "would like to get him out of the Rio Coco region in order that the land there might fall into American hands." Perhaps in order to prevent excessive optimism in Washington, Lane reported to the State Department that several leading members of Sacasa's government "referred in disparaging tones to Sandino's intellectual capacity" and his incoherence in the presentation of his views in the talks with Sacasa. Lane also transmitted the rumors circulating in central Nicaragua that Sandino's forces were about to resume their

---

8. Among Lane s confidential informers were such men as Sacasa's Foreign Minister Arguello and some of the president's close relatives. Perhaps his most valuable information came from Doña Maria, Nicaragua's First Lady, a much more powerful personality than her husband, and the hub of all complicated intrigues in Managua's government and politics.

"bandit activities" and might even launch an attack on one of the towns "for the purpose of looting." "Very little, if anything, has so far happened to justify such fears," added Lane cautiously, "but there obviously exists a feeling of tense uncertainty."[9]

A feeling of tense uncertainty was also spreading in Managua. Sandino's presence in the capital and the anticipation of his agreement with Sacasa caused great excitement. The past exploits of Sandino's bands had been accompanied by such brutalities that the military of all ranks bitterly resented any thought that these bandits might now become "acceptable." Sandino had a few political friends in the country, but his enemies, who strongly opposed any deal between him and President Sacasa, greatly outnumbered them. Behind the scenes, General Moncada, ex-president of Nicaragua, skillfully directed this opposition. General Anastasio Somoza, the Jefe Director of the Guardia, clearly emerged as its principal leader in Managua.

Somoza's freedom of action was still restricted. He had presidential ambitions, but he was not prepared to use force in order to dislodge Sacasa. He operated within the constitutional framework, reiterating his loyalty to Sacasa and restating that he would not take any action to embarrass the president. While his sincerity was questionable, he indubitably wanted to promote his image of a selfless public servant and a guardian of the constitutional order. His immediate target was not Sacasa but Sandino: the Guardia was strong enough to contain Sandino's bands, but only so long as they remained outlaws; once they were given amnesty and allowed to join the ranks of Sacasa's followers, they would be beyond Somoza's power.

The position taken by the American minister presented Somoza with a different problem. On the one hand, he could not bring himself to believe that the United States truly desired to see its most implacable enemies start playing a legitimate role in Nicaraguan politics to the obvious detriment of the American interest as he understood it. On the other hand, he found Lane totally unreceptive to any suggestion of "positive action" with regard to Sandino.

---

9. Lane to Hull, February 20, 1934, FR, 1934, V, 529.

Somoza had many times expressed his hostility to Sandino in Lane's presence, evidently hoping to detect a sign that the American diplomat shared his feelings. One week before Sandino's arrival in Managua, he invited Lane to a dinner at the Casino Militar and in the course of the conversation said that if Lane only gave him the word, he would "lock Sandino up." Lane answered that "such action would be most foolish," and admonished him not to do anything rash. To this Somoza replied: "I give you my word of honor that I will do nothing without first having your approval."[10]

The Murder

On February 17, 1934, the day after Sandino arrived in Managua, Lane went to the airport to see off Henry de Bayle, Somoza's brother-in-law, a nephew of Sacasa, and Nicaraguan chargé d'affaires in Washington. De Bayle asked Lane to use all his influence with Somoza to restrain him. Having met Somoza at the airport, Lane invited him to lunch, during which the General again asked Lane "to wink his eye" so that he could lock up Sandino. Lane refused to wink and made Somoza repeat his word of honor that he would do nothing without consulting him.

The Jefe Director was so friendly and so solicitous that Lane was tempted to believe him. Even if Somoza did not keep his word, reasoned the American minister, there was little he could do in the absence of the marines. The physical protection of Sandino and his group was in the hands of the government, which was aware of the potential danger. In addition, Lane was under instructions not to meddle in the internal affairs of the country. He had made his point as forcefully as he could to Somoza and hoped that the passionately pro-American Nicaraguan would take notice.

He did not. And perhaps he could not, for Somoza played for high stakes and had every reason to fear that the impending

---

10. See Lane's personal letter to Ambassador Josephus Daniels, March 4, 1934. The following events are reconstructed on the basis of this letter, Lane's four dispatches of February 22, and one of May 4, 1934 (FR, 1934, V, 529-533, 552-554), the State Department's file of unpublished documents, and recollections of Ambassador Paul C. Daniels, who was then senior secretary at the legation in Managua.

realignment of Nicaraguan politics would impair, perhaps irrevocably, his chances to become president. Minister Lane could only guess how far Somoza's ambitions would drive him. Not quite reassured by Somoza's word of honor, he watched the developments with considerable apprehension.[11]

On the morning of February 21, Lane received a telegram from General Moncada, that he was on his way for one of his rare visits to Managua and hoped to have lunch with the minister. Lane went to a scheduled appointment in the morning. Upon his return to the legation he was told that Somoza had telephoned, saying he had something "very important" to tell the minister. Lane returned the call.

Somoza sounded very excited. He told Lane that the Guardia had just learned that Sacasa had promised Sandino to "reorganize" the Guardia within six months, and that General Pontecarrero, former Sandinista candidate for president, had been chosen as chief of the central area of the country where the main forces of the Guardia were confronting those of Sandino. The news, according to Somoza, infuriated the Guardia and he had had a hard time controlling his men. Somoza asked Lane either "to do something about it" or permit him to "lock up" Sandino, which would settle everything once and for all.

Lane reminded Somoza about his promise to abstain from rash actions and told him he would call him back after he found out more about the developments.

For a large part of the afternoon, Lane was immobilized because of the protracted lunch with General Moncada, during which no politics were discussed. As soon as Moncada left, Lane went to see Dr. Calderón, a moderate Liberal, who had participated in the negotiations at the Casa Presidential. Calderón confirmed the planned appointment of Pontecarrero but insisted that Pontecarrero had been completely disillusioned with Sandino and that otherwise the choice was excellent because of Pontecarrero's ability and loyalty to Sacasa.

Lane then went to see Somoza at the Guardia headquarters

---

11. According to one account, after this meeting Somoza gathered his lieutenants in the Campo del Marte and blandly told them that Lane "assured me that the government in Washington supports and recommends the elimination of Augusto Cesar Sandino, because they consider him a disturber of the peace of the country." Macaulay, 253.

on the Campo del Marte. The General appeared even more nervous than he had sounded in the morning. Lane told him what he had learned from Calderón. Somoza replied that although he personally accepted Calderón's estimation of Pontecarrero, the Guardia "would be furious at the 'insult' and that things had reached a point where he could no longer control the Guardia." But as Lane left, Somoza again assured him that nothing would be done without first consulting him.

After a late dinner with a visiting Polish diplomat, Lane returned to the legation to finish the day's work. Soon after, at about 11:00 P.M., he suddenly heard a burst of machine gun fire. He tried to call Somoza, but the telephone connection had been cut. Suspecting that something serious was happening, Lane jumped into his car and drove into town.

As he approached the house of Minister of Agriculture Salvatierra, where Sandino had been staying, he saw across the street from the house a detachment of the Guardia, armed with machine guns and rifles; the smell of gunfire was still noticeable. A wounded man lay in front of Salvatierra's house crying, "*Soy civil!*" ("I am a civilian!").

Ignoring the rifles pointed at him, Lane shouted to the nearest soldier, asking him what had happened. An officer came up and told Lane that the guard had been fired on from the house and had returned the fire.

Lane drove back to the legation, summoned his aides, and telephoned the Casa Presidential. Sacasa's mother, who answered, asked him to come there at once. As Lane drove through the town, he noticed that Somoza's headquarters on the Campo del Marte were heavily protected by sandbags and machine guns and that all the gates were closed.

At the president's house he found Sacasa surrounded by all the members of his cabinet and many political friends. Sacasa told Lane that about 10:30 Sandino had left the Casa Presidential with his father, his brother Socrates, and his aides, "Generals" Estrada, Umanzor, and Salvatierra. Their car was stopped by the Guardia near the Campo del Marte and taken with the occupants to a nearby military prison. Salvatierra's house was attacked at the same time. Sacasa had just received the information that Sandino had been killed.

The president then told Lane that he was unable to reach

Somoza by telephone and asked the minister to go and fetch him. Lane agreed. It was well past midnight, but when Lane found the Jefe Director at his home, Somoza was still fully dressed. At first Somoza refused to go "because of the possibility that violence might be done to him," but as Lane insisted, he consented to accompany him to his car.

Confronted by Sacasa, Somoza professed complete ignorance of what had happened and said that he had been attending a concert all evening. He promised to investigate the affair forthwith. At that time, the news came that two men from Sandino's party—his father, Don Gregorio, and Minister of Agriculture Salvatierra—were still alive in the military prison. Somoza, who continued to play his role of an innocent and uninformed man, remarked that he would not guarantee their lives insofar as the Guardia was concerned. Sacasa again addressed Lane, asking him to get the men out of the prison.

The American minister painfully realized the significance of the momentous events which were taking place. He did not believe for a moment in Somoza's innocence and was furious with him for this violation of his "word of honor" in which he had put too much trust. On the other hand, Lane could not permit himself to be carried away by his feelings, for it was imperative to salvage whatever possible from the mess caused by the assassination of Sandino. So long as President Sacasa accepted Somoza's protestations of innocence at face value and abstained from drastic moves which could bring about his own downfall, not everything was lost. The alternative was another civil war, total chaos, and a blood bath.

At the same time, Lane rightfully expected that because the Guardia was widely assumed to be an American creation, Sandino's murder was bound to have most unpleasant repercussions for the United States. If now, along with Sandino's father, Salvatierra were also murdered, the situation would become even more grave. Since he was a cabinet minister, his murder would constitute an act of open revolt against the government on the part of the Guardia.

Swearing under his breath, Lane again got into his car. At the military prison he was met by several armed guards. Putting diplomatic language aside, he demanded that on orders of the president and the Jefe Director, Don Gregorio and Salvatierra be released immediately and brought to his car. After a tense moment, the men were brought out. Lane drove them to the legation, telephoned Sacasa, and at his request, sent the men to the Casa Presidential, still under the protection of the legation car.[12]

It was 5:00 A.M. when Lane finished writing his dispatch to the State Department, summing up the events of the day and relaying the information which had accumulated at the legation during the night. He reported that orders had been issued by Somoza to the Guardia "to concentrate on Wiwili with a view to bringing about the surrender of the arms of the Sandinistas and in case this were impossible, to exterminate them." He ended his long message by pointing out that Sacasa had evidently little control over Somoza, that Sandino's followers might resort to reprisals, and that public confidence in the government was at a low ebb.

Lane did not have much sleep that night. Early in the morning, on February 22, Sacasa summoned him again to his headquarters and asked him to take General Pontecarrero and Dr. Calderón to the airport and put them on the plane for San Salvador. Having done that, Lane went to see Somoza, who told him that the number of victims of the previous night had included Sandino's brother and two of his principal aides. Somoza did his best to convince Lane of his loyalty to Sacasa and his government and promised to issue an appropriate statement to the press to calm possible rumors to the contrary. Reporting this conversation to the State Department later in the day Lane added that "it is evident that the relations between the president and his associates, on the one hand, and Somoza, on the other, are severely strained. . . .Somoza assures me he will support the president and his government. Since the events of last night, however, I have less confidence in his assurances."

With the political situation so drastically changed and so many of his original premises no longer valid, Lane had to rethink his line of approach. The Sandinistas were being eliminated as a factor in Nicaragua and even the president himself

---

12. According to Sandino's father, his two sons and two of Sandino's "generals" were killed at the airfield on the outskirts of the city; the skirmish at Salvatierra's house resulted from the Guardia's attempt to arrest a key Sandino aide, "General" Ferretti. See the *New York Times*, February 23, 1934.

now told him, as Lane later wrote to Ambassador Daniels, that "if Sandino had returned to his area and had turned [over] his arms then the government would have proceeded against him with energy."

Civil war had apparently been avoided; although sporadic clashes continued in the north, *Sandinismo* without Sandino did not have the same appeal. Managua and other cities remained calm and, in Lane's estimate, the majority of the people felt that Sandino's disappearance from the scene was a blessing. Some, especially those who had suffered at the hands of Sandino's bandits, approved even the manner in which Sandino was killed. And the Guardia's operations against the remaining rebels proceeded successfully.

What disturbed Lane now was that the Guardia had clearly emerged as a major force in the country: it had challenged the president—and got away with it. Sacasa, aware of his weakness, was more preoccupied with his personal safety than with the need to assert his authority. He imposed press censorship. He also mentioned to Lane that it would be helpful to have an American war vessel sent to Carinto to demonstrate the United States' preoccupation with the crisis. The Casa Presidential was transformed into an armed camp, with trenches, machine guns, and a vastly increased presidential guard, to which only devout Liberals of Sacasa's faction were admitted. Although the danger of an armed clash, in Lane's view, had somewhat subsided, the situation remained very disturbing.

Lane had also visibly changed his opinion of General Somoza. He developed a kind of grudging admiration for Somoza's cunning intelligence and the driving ambition which made him capable of resolute, well-timed moves. But the former friendly informality between the two men all but disappeared, especially after Somoza, in a rather casual manner, admitted to Lane that Sandino's assassins had acted under orders. Having been so deceived by Somoza, Lane realized that his ability to influence the General and his Guardia was much more limited than he had assumed. He was more than ever determined to oppose Somoza, but he suspected that the American minister was no longer a decisive factor in Nicaraguan affairs.

Lane's freedom of action was restricted before long by a

development which he had feared and anticipated: in spite of all his heroic efforts on Sacasa's behalf following Sandino's murder, a rumor began to circulate in Managua and in other Central American capitals that Lane had had a hand in the assassination. By common anti-Yanqui logic, the Guardia would not possibly act without the knowledge and consent of the American minister.[13]

Lane tried not to appear personally affected by this rumor (he wrote to Josephus Daniels that "it is not very pleasant, but all in a day's work") although, in fact, he resented it bitterly. The subsequent outburst of anti-American sentiments among a large number of people whom he considered friendly to the United States greatly disturbed Lane.

He knew that the government did not believe the rumor. He also knew that President Sacasa needed his help more than ever. And Lane could not help but be upset when it appeared that Sacasa's circle was trying to take advantage of his discomfort and the defensive position into which he had been forced.

This aspect of the situation was, however, soon overshadowed by a much more ominous development: the mere suggestion that the United States conspired with the Guardia, in a peculiar Nicaraguan way, was actually strengthening Somoza's hand in his developing conflict with the government.

Somoza's ploy emerged only gradually. For the moment it looked as if the situation in Managua had improved. Somoza issued a statement to the press reaffirming his and the Guardia's loyalty to the president and promising "a minute investigation" of Sandino's assassination. He offered to place in his office one of Sacasa's brothers as a liaison officer and give him copies of all his messages to the Guardia commanders. And in dramatic fashion, the Jefe Director told Lane that if the president distrusted him he would resign immediately, together with all his officers and men.

Lane, however, remained apprehensive. He believed that this improvement was only temporary and that Somoza was

---

13. That kind of logic was not restricted to the Latin Americans. Macaulay in his book—published in 1967—says that although there is "no evidence of a formal 'deal' between Somoza and American officials for the murder of Sandino, Somoza was, in effect, a time bomb, planted in Managua by the Hoover administration, and Franklin Roosevelt allowed it to explode."

merely trying to repair the damage caused to his position by the affair of February 21. Lane rejected the idea of Somoza's resignation. He took an equally negative view of the suggestion that Sacasa should resign—a step which was seriously considered by the president. In Lane's opinion neither resignation could solve the basic institutional conflict between the Guardia and the government.

Preoccupied with the overall situation, Lane did not notice initially that the shrewd Jefe Director was trying to utilize the American minister for his schemes: the General associated himself with "United States' interests" in Nicaragua, creating the impression that the United States was behind him.

Once this tactic became evident Lane became alarmed. He was distressed to learn that the rumors about his complicity in Sandino's murder in many cases actually originated with the Guardia. Since he was helpless to do anything about it personally, he decided that Somoza needed a rebuke in the form of an official statement. Such a statement was, in his opinion, the only effective way for the United States to dissociate itself from the ambitious General.

There were only two ways, in Lane's judgment, to accomplish this. One way was for the State Department to demand severe punishment for those found guilty of Sandino's death. Lane's suggestion to that effect, however, was quickly turned down by the State Department on the grounds that it was a matter for the Nicaraguan government to deal with.[14]

Another move, conceived by Lane, was to issue an official statement reaffirming United States support for a legitimate government and stating American opposition to any would-be revolutionary regime which might come into power through an overthrow of such a government. Such a statement did not have to refer specifically to the Nicaraguan situation, but its timing and language could make the warning unmistakably clear both to Somoza and his opponents.

He tried this idea on Somoza the day following Sandino's

---

14. Sandino's assassins eventually escaped punishment. The Nicaraguan Chamber of Deputies granted amnesty to all of them since the investigation of documents presented to the Guardia showed that Sandino plotted to overthrow the government. "The consensus of the members was that the incident had been tragic but beneficial," reported the *New York Times* on August 25, 1934.

murder and quickly noted its effect on the General. When told that the legation might issue such a declaration, Somoza "strongly objected. . . .on the ground that the public would feel that it involved the Guardia. This naive admission of the connection between the Guardia and a possible unconstitutional government," wrote Lane in one of his dispatches to the State Department on February 22, "is I think an added reason for such a statement to be made; either in Washington or, by him, to the local press."

The State Department remained unreceptive. The thinking of the leading officials had changed considerably since the days of the Washington Conference of 1923, at which the principle of non-recognition had been decided upon as one way to ensure stability in the troubled Central American region. Some now regarded non-recognition of revolutionary regimes as a form of "negative intervention" and as an unfortunate residue of the Wilson era. Others felt that withholding recognition deprived the United States of the opportunity to exercise influence through normal diplomatic channels in the countries where such a revolution did take place.

Moreover, under the impact of the momentous developments in Europe and the Far East, the more liberal elements of the State Department and elsewhere had actually come to favor, as a matter of principle, a revolutionary change in Latin America. They preferred revolution to stability, because they believed that revolutions were the only way by which oppressive regimes could be dislodged, thus opening the road towards political evolution. They also reasoned that since more and more Latin American governments had come to believe in the sincerity of the non-interventionist policy, the chances for survival of the revolutionary regimes in the face of an open hostility by the United States had greatly increased. Hence, even from a purely pragmatic point of view it did not pay to resort to threats which were unlikely to impress anybody.

All these considerations produced a broad consensus in the State Department which ruled out the acceptance of Arthur Bliss Lane's proposal to use the outmoded tool of non-recognition against the ambitions of Anastasio Somoza. Although the principles of the Treaty of 1923 had not yet been repudiated officially, they were in the process of being quietly abandoned. Only one month before the crisis erupted in Managua, the United States recognized General Martinez' government in El Salvador, which had come to power two years earlier and which had denounced (along with Costa Rica) the Treaty of Peace and Amity of 1923.

Without enlightening the minister to Nicaragua about the general evolution of official thinking on this issue,[15] on February 23, Secretary Hull instructed Lane to "say orally to Somoza" that there had been no change in the Department's policy but forbade him to issue any public statements to that effect.

Lane immediately answered, restating his arguments, and pointing out the potential gravity of the situation and the need for forcing Somoza to subordinate himself to the president. A statement from the Department indicating its policy of non-recognition of non-constitutional governments, insisted Lane, "should serve not only to quiet the anti-American feeling but also to check any military movement against the government."[16]

Familiar with the informal policy-making machinery of the State Department, Lane appealed privately to Edwin C. Wilson, chief of the Latin American Division. Hoping that Wilson would better appreciate the urgency of the situation and be able to convince Hull of the wisdom of the statement he recommended, he reported to Wilson over the telephone on February 22 and 23. On the 24th, Wilson telephoned Lane. The conversation, as recorded at the legation in Managua, went as follows:

MR. WILSON: I wanted to tell you that I talked the situation over with the secretary and with Sumner Welles yesterday afternoon. We feel that in connection with making a statement, there is a larger issue involved with reference to the conference in Central America which is coming on, and that the principle of non-recognition will come up for consideration there. If we make a statement now it might be construed as an attempt on our part to influence the other Central American countries in favor of the continuation of the principle. We do not want to give that impres-

15. This thinking was not to crystallize for another two years. See the State Department's policy statement on its attitude towards the Treaty of 1923, in FR, 1936, V, 126-148.
16. Lane to Hull, February 23, 1934, FR 1934, V, 535-536.

sion. We wish to continue a complete "hands off" attitude in regard to that policy. We do not want to do anything which will give the impression or appearance of intervention in any way in these questions in Central America. However, we are in full sympathy with your point of view. There are two things which you may keep in mind. First, to make a statement to Somoza might serve to stabilize things and prevent a revolutionary movement in Nicaragua.

MR. LANE: I have already told Somoza. You can continue to tell him, but what good will that do as far as any effect upon him is concerned?

MR. WILSON: Statements that the United States government or you personally were implicated in the Sandino matter are not going to have any effect upon the responsible elements. Things like that are said by various elements in Latin America. It is not the first time, and they will be said again.

MR. LANE: The opinion seems to prevail that the United States is supporting Somoza in an attempt to bring about a coup d'état.

MR. WILSON: Sacasa does not share that opinion, does he? Certainly responsible people do not. De Bayle has been in and has told us that you were being of such help to them before Sandino was killed and that they all thought a great deal of you.

MR. LANE: I think that Somoza must feel encouraged by the fact that we have made no statement. I do not care about myself, but the feeling against us is strong because they think we support Somoza.

MR. WILSON: You can tell Somoza absolutely straight from the shoulder.

MR. LANE: I told him that. I have been telling him for over three weeks, but the fact that the Department does not say anything might lead him to believe that it is only my personal opinion.

MR. WILSON: Tell him that it is not. Tell him that it comes straight from the Secretary; that you have spoken to us up here; and that there is absolutely no change in our policy.

MR. LANE: What you want me to do, I shall do, but I want you to know and to tell the Secretary that I assume no responsibility for the consequences.

MR. WILSON: I told him that last night. I put forward your views as strongly as possible, from your point of view.

MR. LANE: I think that if nothing is done we will probably have anarchy here.

MR. WILSON: What do you base that on?

MR. LANE: There are two governments right here in the city, both of which are fully armed. I was in the presidential palace last night and the place is full of machine guns, with Somoza and his men a few hundred yards away. The president is not running the country at all. There is sure to be a show-down sooner or later. When it comes, where is your government? There is, in addition to Somoza, the Conservatives to consider. Our consular Agent Willey arrived this morning from Matagalpa and reports that up there everything is very anti-Sandinista. When there comes the question of a conflict or show-down between the government and Somoza, who knows what is going to be the outcome? Up to now it has been a question of Sandino, but now there is a bigger issue involved. It is between the government and the Guardia. What will happen? It is not for me to say what the policy shall be, but you are inviting a military dictatorship.

MR. WILSON: I do not know how we are inviting it in any way. Tell Somoza straight from the shoulder. We are not going to do anything to involve us in any interference or intervention in Central America. We are not going to issue a public statement which will serve to embroil us in any intervention. We are not seeking to influence the course of events.

MR. LANE: We are not influencing the course of events.

MR. WILSON: Statements are always misinterpreted and misconstrued. You can tell him just as definitely that the policy of this government has not been changed. A public statement, in my opinion, will not have more effect than a statement coming from you.

MR. LANE: In my own personal opinion I think it will. Disinterested people think that it will be the one good thing. Everyone is looking to the United States. I do not mean to interfere with their politics. It is a question of law and order. You have to assume the responsibility of American interests and the protection of them. I shall do what you want, but I absolutely assume no responsibility for what may happen.

MR. WILSON: Don't think for a moment that the question has not been fully considered. It was discussed at great length yesterday afternoon. We were reluctant to go against your wishes, but the secretary and Mr. Welles feel that there is a larger issue involved. We wish to continue to have your views. As far as not being able to discourage the one gentleman in question who is concerned, you may make the statement to him as you have repeatedly made it to him and that will discourage him. . . .In my opinion, the only solution is to try and get Somoza and Sacasa together . . . .

MR. LANE: In my cable No. 65, I expressed my views about the only way this question could be worked out. . . . In that telegram I discussed what might happen if there were some replacements. In case either of them were replaced, I suggested that it would not finally solve the question at issue between the government and the Guardia. In my opinion, in the absence of a more radical solution, the best method would be to work together harmoniously, and it was understood that I would lend my good efforts along this line. Further, that it is difficult to work harmoniously together when the constituted people feel that they do not have our support.

MR. WILSON: What reason do they have for feeling that way?

MR. LANE: Nothing has been definitely said. It is, however, a question of personalities: one weak and one strong. The strong one is on the wrong side.

MR. WILSON: I know. Certainly, there is no reason why the constituted authorities should feel that we have any sympathy against them. We are all for law and order. They realize that. We just cannot intervene and bring pressure to bear. We are in favor of law and order.

MR. LANE: I have a suspicion that Mexico has already done something.

MR. WILSON: We want you to know that we are with you one hundred percent and are most sympathetic with the things you have to deal with, but the secretary is very reluctant to go along with you entirely on this point. . . .

Lane was not easily discouraged, however. Having completed his conversation with Wilson, he sent its transcript to the Secretary of State together with a formal memorandum in which he restated his arguments in favor of the declaration he was attempting to have issued:

> . . . I have been informed from a variety of good sources that a report has been widely circulated to the effect that the legation conspired with Generals Moncada and Somoza to have Sandino killed; and that this report has given rise to bitter animosity toward the legation in many quarters. The fact that I had been with General Somoza on a few occasions during the days immediately preceding the murder seemed to lend credence to this view in the popular mind, particularly when coupled with our former attitude toward Sandino and the Guardia Nacional and the widespread impression that Somoza has enjoyed the sympathy of the United States ever since assuming charge of the Guardia. . .
>
> In view of the fact that the elimination of Sandino has not

simplified the political situation, except in that one respect, but rather has thrown into bold relief the split between the president of the republic and the Guardia Nacional, a situation which appears to have been slowly developing for some time past, the report referred to in the preceding paragraph is particularly unfortunate. It causes doubt to arise as to whether we are really desirous of seeing President Sacasa remain in the presidency. It leads some people to think that we might look with favor on the assumption of political power by the Guardia, tending perhaps toward a military dictatorship. The recent recognition of El Salvador, which has been interpreted in some quarters as a weakening of our policy of not recognizing revolutionary governments, has tended to confirm the view that a revolutionary movement by the Guardia would not be strenuously objected to by the United States.

However, it is my understanding that our policy has been in favor of the maintenance of constitutional governments and the avoidance of revolutions or coups d'état. If this is the case, it occurred to me that a frank announcement of this policy, which is not a new departure, would have a decided effect in clearing up the misapprehension which apparently exists at present. To be sure, there is an atmosphere of excitement tending to cause a distorted outlook in the Nicaraguan public, and with the passage of time no doubt saner views will prevail. But the moment is now a tense one for the very reason that excitement and uncertainty prevail, and in this sense constitutes an emergency. The whole affair may still quiet down, but considering the grave danger which still exists of a general conflagration within the country, with an unpredictable outcome, it is my belief that anything which might appropriately be done to diminish the uncertainty would have a quieting effect. . . Therefore I felt that if the Department, in reply to a question on the point, could state publicly that its policy has not changed and that it continues to follow the principle laid down in Article II of the 1923 Treaty of Peace and Amity which is still in force between Nicaragua, Honduras, and Guatemala, at least pending a possible revision or denouncement thereof, such a statement, reproduced locally, should have a very positive and desirable effect in clarifying our position with respect to recent events, should diminish the animosity which has so unjustly arisen in some quarters against the legation, and should perhaps go far in contributing to the reestablishment of normal conditions within the country. If made in some such way as that outlined above, it does not seem to me that the possible criticism of intervention in Central American affairs would be very serious, because we would merely be repeating what has often been said before, and without a direct reference to the present difficulty in Nicaragua. Of course, if the policy of the Department has changed, and if it were no longer intended to follow the principles of the 1923 treaty, then the foregoing would be inappropriate. . . .

Again, rather than informing Lane that the policy of the State Department was indeed undergoing a change, the Department chose to justify its position on general grounds. In his reply to Lane, Secretary Hull said that: (a) the principle of non-recognition was expected to be discussed at the forthcoming conference of Central American states; (b) Costa Rica and El Salvador were against the continuing of this principle; and (c) a public declaration, which Lane wanted, would probably be interpreted as an effort to put pressure on the conference.

Referring specifically to Nicaragua, Hull said that the United States had been accused for many years of trying to impose its own views on that country and that, therefore, "we desire not only to refrain from any interference, but also from any measure which might seem to give the appearance of such interference." If Somoza was unimpressed by private warnings, wrote Hull, it would be "difficult to see that a public statement would have much more force in dissuading him from a movement against the government." As to the possible effects of such a statement on the rumor linking Lane to Sandino's murder, Secretary Hull was equally doubtful. "The ignorant and irresponsible individuals who circulate such rumors," wrote Secretary Hull philosophically, "would, in our judgment, not only fail to understand the significance of a public statement on our part, but might conceivably misinterpret or twist its meaning in such a way as to cause further embarrassment."[17]

Lane, who was quite familiar with the Department's ways, understood the rebuke. He replied that if he had seemingly over-emphasized his own view, it was merely because he wished-ed the Department to realize fully the gravity of the situation, and that he would endeavor to accomplish in personal contacts that which he had hoped might have been done by an official statement.

---

17. Hull to Lane, February 26, 1934, FR, 1934, V, 539.

The American minister in Managua realized now that he had to be more careful. He had failed three times within a short period. His suggestion that the Guardia be "reorganized" had been turned down by the State Department. A political combination in which the Guardia would be counter-balanced by a Sacasa-Sandino alliance had been ruined by Somoza's bold stroke. And now the Secretary of State himself refused to support Lane with a move which, in Lane's judgment, would alone have arrested the expansion of the Guardia's influence.

A New Approach

Anyone less involved and less convinced of the soundness of his views would have probably taken a more detached position. But Lane had a single-track mind which would not allow him to give up. He did not accept Hull's implied position that Somoza's ascent would not necessarily represent a calamity either for Nicaragua or for the United States, and was determined to do everything in his power to prevent it even if the success of his actions hinged entirely on his capacity for influencing the personalities on the scene.

Lane could not do much to strengthen Sacasa's government, which was far from unanimous as to how to meet the situation. Some members of the cabinet, notably Foreign Minister Leonardo Arguello (who himself nourished presidential ambitions) complained to Lane about Sacasa's procrastinations and pressed for a showdown with Somoza. Others realized the government's weakness in its confrontation with the Guardia and did not want to take risks, hoping for a favorable turn of events. Sacasa, who had no illusions about who held the trump cards, counted heavily on Lane to help bring the military under the control of the government.

This was more than Lane could do, but he was resolved to try. After all, in the eyes of the Nicaraguans he still was the representative of the United States and his words commanded appropriate attention. His contacts reached into every important quarter; by applying the sheer force of his personality and his diplomatic skills he felt he could affect the course of events in no mean degree. The lack of support from Washington annoyed but did not discourage Lane. His task had become more difficult. But then, if he succeeded, his accomplishment would be so much greater. The first order of business was to establish a truce between the government and the Guardia.

Lane did not as yet consider Somoza a lost cause. He felt that the Jefe Director of the Guardia would be more likely to behave if the Sacasa circle restrained itself and stopped the attempts to humiliate Somoza. He also considered it important to remove Somoza from the influence of the latter's old chief, General Moncada, who appeared to be the main force behind the anti-Sacasa drive. Somoza, who was having his own difficulties with Moncada, shrewdly contributed to this line of thought when he "confessed" to Lane that Moncada's arrival in Managua on the fateful day of February 21 had not been accidental, and that the ex-president of Nicaragua had come solely "for the purpose of bringing the Sandino matter to a head."

The American minister saw his function mainly as that of mediator between the conflicting factions. By constantly talking to the antagonists, by bringing whatever pressure he could muster to bear upon them, he hoped to keep the situation under control. Some help came from the Managua diplomatic corps: the ministers of Mexico and El Salvador had received instructions to cooperate with Lane. The Mexican, however, did not want to have anything to do with Somoza and limited his stand to an unqualified support of the government. He favored a "reorganization" of the Guardia through a special law which Sacasa wanted to see enacted by Congress.

Lane refused to commit himself to the support of this law, not only because such action on his part would have violated the spirit of his instructions, but also because in his own judgment its passage would only have irritated Somoza without accomplishing its purpose. President Sacasa was powerless to enforce it and the whole situation could be expected to deteriorate further. Even as it was, the Jefe Director of the Guardia was complaining that in spite of his declarations of loyalty to the president, the latter's residence remained an armed camp, manned by the Presidential Guard, whose members were openly hostile to the Guardia. In the end, Sacasa avoided a showdown: instead of attempting to push the law through Congress, where it was threatened with defeat by the combined forces of the Conservatives and Moncadistas, he satisfied himself with the issuing of an executive order defining his relations with the

Guardia. This order represented a watered-down version of the bill and was thus acceptable to Somoza.

It was apparent that no compromises of this sort significantly affected either the relations between Sacasa and Somoza or the actual distribution of political power in Nicaragua. All the president's efforts to bring the Guardia under his control had been unsuccessful; the trend was clearly against him. On May 3, 1934, Lane received further evidence of the growing confidence of the anti-government forces. On that day, with Sacasa's approval, he had a long conversation with General Moncada, who came to Managua on one of his infrequent visits.

Moncada wished to know what the American policy with respect to the Guardia was, and particularly, how the United States viewed possible changes in the Guardia's status as established by the bi-partisan agreement of November, 1932. The General was so specific in his questions that Lane could answer him only by restating the Department's official position. He assured Moncada that "the Guardia is a matter entirely for Nicaragua to decide; that Nicaragua as a sovereign nation must decide her internal problems; but that our silence should not be interpreted either as approval or disapproval." Moncada said that he entirely approved of the American policy of non-intervention, and informed Lane that both he and General Chamorro's Conservatives intended to fight in Congress the known intent of Sacasa to have the forthcoming elections supervised by a president of the Board of Elections appointed by him rather than one elected by Congress.

Lane replied that the elections were again a purely Nicaraguan matter, and that the United States would not take any part therein "either directly or indirectly, and should use no influence in any way in connection therewith." Moncada remarked that although neither he nor Chamorro wanted a conflict with Sacasa, they intended to press for free and impartially supervised elections, and that he was fully satisfied with Lane's assurances.[18]

The American minister appreciated the grave significance of Moncada's visit. The opposition, although far from united, was preparing to give battle to the government on two crucial and

18. Lane to Hull, May 4, 1934, FR, 1934, V, 552-554.

closely related issues: the Guardia's autonomy and control over
the elections. If the government, as seemed likely, lost this
battle, the constitutional regime would probably be replaced
by some form of military dictatorship, thus nullifying the good
work of the United States in Nicaragua.

"Hands-Off" by the "Good Neighbor"?

This prospect deeply troubled Lane. His resolution to fight
the ominous trend had not diminished, and he became increasingly convinced that the United States had abandoned
Nicaragua to its own devices too early.

At this point, asked Lane, was the official "hands-off" policy
of the United States really compatible with the "good neighbor" approach? Shouldn't a good neighbor do somewhat more
to avert disaster in his neighbor's home? These questions were
directly related to Lane's role in Managua, to the limitations
imposed upon him by the State Department, and to his ability
to fulfill his mission. Lane raised these questions in several
official dispatches to Washington and in a personal letter to
Sumner Welles who, he believed, had the final say in Latin
American matters. On April 12, 1934, the Assistant Secretary of
State answered Lane in a private letter:

> I fully realize how difficult and perplexing the situation is with
> which you are now confronted. There is, of course, no doubt that
> your personal influence on behalf of a peaceful solution of the
> civil-military problems will be peculiarly effective, as has already
> been demonstrated. In my judgment, the kind of personal in-
> fluence which an American minister in a Central American post
> can have when he has obtained the confidence of the officials with
> whom he has to deal and the people in general in the country
> where he is stationed is almost invariably of the utmost value. I
> feel that you have those qualifications to a very marked degree.
> Officially, of course, I think we all agree that we ought to continue
> to follow the same line we have been following up to the present
> time, and that is, a complete reversal of the policy which was so
> often followed in the past of constant hectoring and meddling in a
> public manner. Our "hands-off" attitude in the Central American
> Conference has been productive, in my judgment, of good re-
> sults. . . .

Welles added that the way to demonstrate the American desire to cooperate in a constructive manner, without dictating policies involving Central American relationships, would be through assistance in the construction of the Pan-American Highway—Welles' pet idea for some time—and through a trade agreement with Nicaragua which would offer it some real benefits.

Lane favored economic aid to Nicaragua. The roads in the country were in frightful condition, leaving whole regions virtually isolated. The Pan-American Highway could not really solve the country's transportation difficulties—trade had been conducted almost exclusively through sea ports—and in the absence of commercial relations between Central American states, the highway's economic significance would be limited. But its construction seemed to Lane a step in the right direction.

He equally favored the trade agreement which had been under negotiation for some time; Nicaragua could, in Lane's opinion, be helped if granted an importation quota on cane sugar and rum, a measure which influential American domestic interests opposed. But neither the highway nor the sugar quota could possibly help to solve Lane's predicament in dealing with Nicaraguan politics, and here Welles offered no help.

Lane returned to the "hands-off—good neighbor" theme in the dispatch of May 4th in which he reported Moncada's visit to the legation. Naturally, the United States should not interfere in Nicaraguan internal affairs, wrote Lane. "Should we feel, however, that a word from us might serve to maintain the peace of the country and consequently avoid bloodshed and disorder, we should not refrain from assuming the responsibility of the 'good neighbor' by expressing our views." And Lane formally requested the Department's opinion on the issue.

On May 15, keeping up his private correspondence with Welles, he wrote to the Assistant Secretary:

> ... I am entirely in sympathy with you as to the matter of policy in Central America and I agree with you that the "hands-off" attitude in the Central American Conference has had a salutary effect as our "hands-off" policy will undoubtedly have in general. As I wrote the Department officially the other day, it is sometimes difficult to reconcile the "good neighbor" and "hands-off" pol-

icies. In Nicaragua I have been able to convince myself satisfactorily that the two policies can be justifiably reconciled. I think
this can be done by not meddling in the internal affairs of Nicaragua, but by being ready to use our good offices or extend calming advice should it appear to us that a crisis, imperiling the
peace of the country, is impending. . . . I endeavored from the start
to create the impression that the old order had changed and that
instead of having a special position here, the American minister
has the same relations with the government of Nicaragua as has
the American minister in any other country. The people here have
become so accustomed to our intervention and to the special
position in which my predecessors were placed as a result of the
intervention, that it is difficult, I think, for them to realize that I
am sincere in my desire not to be regarded in a special light. . . .

This was perhaps excessively modest and not quite candid,
for Arthur Bliss Lane did occupy a very special position in
Managua, a fact he was sure Welles recognized. Indeed, if it
were not for this position, his opportunity to extend calming
advice (with a chance that it would be taken) would have been
severely limited. He requested for himself more discretion in
deciding when to offer his advice. Aware of the implications,
and probably not without hesitation, Welles officially granted
this request on May 22. Simultaneously, he wrote Lane a personal letter. In it, he happily informed the minister that the
appropriation of $5,000,000 for the Pan-American Highway had
been included in the Public Works Administration Bill then
before the congressional committees. Commenting on the point
of vital interest to Lane, Welles added:

As to the general policy and as to the role in general which an
American minister must play in Nicaragua, I am decidedly in
accord with the views expressed in your letter under acknowledg-
ment and as expressed in some of your official dispatches. The
line between official meddling in Nicaraguan affairs and the informal and helpful efforts of an American minister to be of assistance behind the scenes is not always an easy one to draw and
depends necessarily upon the tact and discretion of the man on
the job. For obvious reasons, the post of American minister in
Nicaragua is the most difficult of any of our Central American
legations and I feel very strongly that in a very trying situation you
have carried through most successfully and with great advantage
to the interests of this government.

"A Very Trying Situation"

The "very trying situation" to which Sumner Welles referred was the one which had arisen after a San Jose, Costa Rica, newspaper published on April 12, 1934, an interview with a Colonel Ferretti. In it, the former aide of Sandino, who had escaped being murdered with his chief in Nicaragua, to become a leader of Nicaraguan expatriates in Costa Rica, declared that "the American minister is the true chief of the Guardia Nacional and, with Moncada, the principal person responsible for the cowardly assassination of my unforgettable chief." Ferretti offered no information to support his allegations, but nobody looked for any. The effect of this salvo was that the rumor which theretofore had been no more than gossip circulating among Nicaraguans (particularly among the Sandinistas living in the other Central American countries) broke into the press. Ferretti's charge immediately spread as "news" throughout Latin America and was repeated in the United States. Many Yanqui-baiting editors eagerly exploited this occasion to vent their political sentiments.

Informed about the Ferretti interview by the American minister in Costa Rica, Secretary Hull replied that "the Department of course does not intend to dignify such malicious and absurd stories by issuing any denial or taking notice of them."[19] The government in Managua promptly branded Ferretti's charge as "absolutely false and absurd" and reminded the public that Minister Lane had saved the lives of Sandino's father and Salvatierra at great personal risk. This statement, however, attracted little attention in the press. To his chagrin, Lane found out that his position was becoming increasingly embarrassing.

The immediate significance of this development was not only in the apparent boost it gave to anti-Yanqui agitation in Central America but also in the hardening of the opinion that the United States was supporting the Nicaraguan Guardia Nacional in the latter's conflict with the government. The situation was further aggravated when Somoza, in a speech at a banquet in his honor on June 17 at Granada, publicly accepted

---

19. Hull to Sack, May 21, 1934, FR, 1934, V, 554.

responsibility for Sandino's murder and indicated that Lane was backing him in his political ambitions.[20]

The American minister in Managua was on the spot. At his forceful request, the State Department reconsidered its position and permitted him to issue a public statement — cleared with President Sacasa — refuting the "unfounded and malicious rumors" that Lane had approved and instigated "certain acts committed in Nicaragua in February." Having referred to Roosevelt's "good neighbor" policy, the statement asserted that "neither the government of the United States nor its representative in Nicaragua have interfered directly or indirectly in the political affairs of the Republic of Nicaragua." Local papers carried the statement on June 26. It was unlikely that many people, in Managua or elsewhere, changed their minds as a result of this declaration.

Normally not easily discouraged, Arthur Bliss Lane was gravely upset. He asked the Department to give him protracted leave, extended by a period of consultations in Washington. He wrote Welles that his absence from Managua during the congressional elections in November might be beneficial in quelling the suspicions which had arisen lately. Welles was sympathetic and readily agreed. Toward the end of August Lane left Nicaragua not to return until the following February.

Passive Resistance to Somoza's Ascent

During the autumn of 1934 and the following winter, Anastasio Somoza continued to consolidate his position. Although the Sacasa government seemingly functioned as before, its popular base shrank perceptibly. It had not been challenged openly, and the Guardia, strengthening its image as the main source of stability in the country, was as disciplined as ever. The Jefe Director did not appear to be in a hurry to move against Sacasa; he understood that the United States was still behind the constitutional government and did not wish to alienate the power

---

20. Somoza's complicity in the murder had been widely assumed anyway. Yet, Sandino's mother may not have believed in it when only ten days before she delcared that "she would wholeheartedly support General Anastasio Somoza . . . if he becomes a candidate for the presidency" and although she herself could not vote, her remaining three sons would back Somoza. See *The New York Times*, June 7, 1934.

for which he had so much respect and admiration. Nevertheless, Somoza did everything he could to expand his influence both in Nicaragua and in neighboring countries and to prepare the ground for his future triumph. He and his lieutenants traveled widely, delivering speeches all over the country and strengthening and establishing political contacts to be utilized at a later date.

Arthur Bliss Lane, who during his stay in the United States had spent some time in Washington in talks with high officials, returned to Managua with a better understanding of the overall Latin American policy of the State Department. The policy makers now seriously took into account the opposition in Central American capitals to all forms of intervention. They specifically ruled out any forceful move aimed at arresting the ascent of the Guardia, including an official reaffirmation of the principle of non-recognition of revolutionary governments, the cornerstone of the Treaty of Peace and Amity. The treaty itself was rapidly losing force; of its six signatories, only Nicaragua, Guatemala, and Honduras had not yet denounced it, and the latter two, although friendly to the Sacasa government, strongly opposed intervention.

The position of Mexico, deeply involved in Central American developments, was closely watched by the State Department. In spite of its proclaimed opposition to intervention, the Mexican government appeared ready to make an exception, or at least a compromise, in the case of Nicaragua. It held the United States morally responsible for the Guardia's behavior, if not for Sandino's murder. In order to evoke some anti-Guardia action, it officially maintained that Somoza's ascent to the presidency, by whatever means, would be a tremendous blow to American prestige. More than any other country, Mexico appeared willing to do something in order to eliminate Somoza from the Nicaraguan political scene.[21]

Upon his return to Managua, Arthur Bliss Lane carefully

---

21. Reyes Spindola, Mexican chargé d'affaires in Managua, was more active in taking part in Nicaraguan politics than any other diplomatic representative. He made numerous public speeches and freely associated with the more radical groups which held Sandino as their hero. Spindola was the only member of the Managua diplomatic corps who attempted to embarrass the United States through the exploitation of Lane's alleged complicity in Sandino's murder. See Lane to Welles, February 8, 1936, in Yale's collection.

avoided taking any position on the issue of Somoza's presidency. Whenever pressed by friends and enemies of the General, he would merely say that this was strictly a Nicaraguan question. If asked whether a Somoza government would be recognized by the United States in view of Somoza's constitutional ineligibility for the office, Lane would merely say that the United States could not express any opinion in advance on a hypothetical situation. But he was a stubborn man, and in his correspondence with the State Department, while paying homage to the official non-interventionist policy, Lane continued to express his skepticism about Somoza. He explained at length that Somoza was ineligible for the presidency according to the Nicaraguan constitution because of his position as a military chief and because he was related through marriage to President Sacasa. He questioned the validity of the amendment to the constitution, then pressed for by Somoza's allies in the Nicaraguan Congress, which could remove these obstacles to the Jefe Director's ambitions. Time and again, Lane pointed out that Somoza was also barred from the presidency by the provisions of the Treaty of 1923, and, if elected, would be denied recognition by Guatemala and Honduras. He reported Somoza's opinion that he could live without this recognition the way Martinez had for a while in El Salvador, but he did not fail to mention that recognition or non-recognition by the United States would be of crucial importance to Somoza.[22]

The American minister in Managua no longer asked for a modification of the Department's policy, (although his dispatches in no small degree reflected his unhappiness with the restrictions imposed upon him), but he reported the developments in Nicaragua in such a way as to make his superiors at least question the wisdom of the course they had embarked upon. And he gravely warned the Department of the consequences of doing nothing. These warnings made little impact on the people dealing with Latin American affairs in Washington, who refused to become involved in the legal aspects of Somoza's eligibility for the presidency. One official, in a memorandum of April 2, 1935, commented that "we want to avoid having to express an opinion regarding the validity of the amendment to the Constitution. . .the prudent thing at this time

22. Lane to Hull, March 15, 1935, FR, 1935, IV, 846.

is to say as little on that subject as possible and preferably nothing."

Sumner Welles went a step further. He officially notified Lane, for his "strictly confidential information," that the United States did not regard the Treaty of 1923 as a valid ground for blocking Somoza's ascent either, and that the State Department intended to be quite flexible in interpreting the Treaty's non-recognition clause.[23] This position, although it hardly surprised Lane, effectively deprived him of the last real leverage he could use in Managua. Its implication seemed to be that the United States was quite willing to see Somoza elected president of Nicaragua. Yet Lane was determined to do nothing which could directly or indirectly enhance the Jefe Director's fortunes.

One minor episode helps to illustrate Lane's attitude. Upon his return to Managua, he learned that the legation had received a letter from Matthew H. Hanna, minister to Guatemala and Lane's predecessor in Nicaragua. In it, there was a sealed envelope which Hanna requested the chargé d'affaires to deliver personally to General Moncada. Lane also learned that a Mr. De Besa, a representative of the Hearst newspaper chain, had appeared in Managua with letters of introduction from Hanna to local dignitaries but had failed to first present himself at the legation. De Besa reportedly had assured Somoza that Hearst was very much interested not only in constructing a canal across Nicaragua but also in seeing Somoza elected to the presidency. Finally, Lane learned that Hanna himself, in the letter to Moncada, had expressed a desire to visit Managua, presumably for a reunion with his old Nicaraguan friend.

This news infuriated Lane. In a "personal and strictly confidential" letter to Wilson of March 5, 1935, he forcefully objected to Hanna's activities, and especially to his proposed trip to Nicaragua. Lane reminded Wilson about Hanna's amicable relations with Monacada and Somoza, "both of whom at the present time are openly hostile to the constituted government." Hanna's arrival, Lane contended, "might easily have a very unfortunate effect on our policy in Nicaragua," especially since Hanna's name is "associated here with the intervention." Referring to one of Hanna's dispatches, Lane acidly added that "it

23. Welles to Lane, April 5, 1935, FR, 1935, IV, 847.

may be difficult, if not impossible, for Mr. Hanna to realize that
the intervention or interventionist policy no longer obtains
here." After having reported that Hanna, in Guatemala City,
had freely expressed his opinion as to who might be the most
qualified man for the presidency in Nicaragua, Lane concluded:

> Mr. Hanna's action is, in my opinion, an intrusion in Nicaraguan
> politics, such as I, here, would under no circumstances attempt. I
> do not know what you can do about this matter and I am sorry to
> have to put such an embarrassing situation in your lap. Because,
> however, of the increasingly tense situation which exists as a
> result of the unfortunately strained relations between the presi-
> dent and Somoza, and the possibility that violent action may be
> taken on the part of Somoza, it is more essential that care be taken
> by American officials, not only here but elsewhere, to avoid creat-
> ing the impression that we are carrying on liaisons of a clandestine
> character with elements not friendly to the government.
>
> If I may be so bold as to make a suggestion, I submit that it
> might be advisable to send a circular instruction, regarding the
> necessity of American diplomatic and consular officers of refrain-
> ing from (1) corresponding with political leaders outside of their
> own country unless such correspondence is transmitted by open
> means either through the Department or through our mission in
> the respective country in which the official is located, and (2)
> expressing any opinions regarding the fitness or unfitness of candi-
> dates for political offices in Latin America.
>
> These two points seem so obvious, and are so fully covered in
> Instructions to Diplomatic Officers, as to constitute almost an in-
> sult to the intelligence, discretion, and good manners of our repre-
> sentatives abroad. . . .

Not fully counting on Wilson to take appropriate action,
Lane wrote to Hanna directly, using for an opening the latter's
invitation to visit him in Guatemala which had been received
by the Lanes about the same time. In a "Dear Matt" letter of
March 19, Lane wrote that "we should hesitate to accept your
hospitality unless we were in a position to reciprocate." Then
he proceeded to explain why he could not reciprocate. Moncada and Somoza, "your old friends here," wrote Lane, "appear
to be most anxious that you should come to Nicaragua. Ordinar-
ily this would be no reason for your desisting, in fact, it would
merely give you another proof of the affection in which

you. . .are held in Managua." Since, however, both Moncada and Somoza had been waging a bitter political campaign against the president of Nicaragua, and since "the rumor is more than prevalent that because of the intervention, the United States must have some say as to the next president here," Hanna's presence in Managua, said Lane, might provoke demonstrations "which would be embarrassing not only for you and President Sacasa, but for our government as well." Because of this situation, he concluded, he felt that he should defer his invitation to Hanna "until such time as the political situation has cooled off."

This was one of the few skirmishes which Lane won. In a letter dated March 21, 1935, a friend from the Latin American Division confidentially notified Lane that Hanna "had been enjoined not to touch Nicaragua" on his planned trip.[24]

The April Crisis

By the end of the spring, Lane sensed that he was fighting a losing battle. Somoza was determined to become president and there was nothing that could stop him. In these circumstances, the American minister decided to utilize his influence for a more limited purpose, namely for the prevention of an armed clash between the forces of the antagonists. Specifically, Lane attempted to impress upon Somoza that in the pursuit of his ambition he should not resort to any violence. On one occasion, Somoza cheerfully assured the minister that he had no such intentions and gave him a promise not to take any violent action against President Sacasa; the general earnestly added that "I broke my word to you once, but I will never break my word to you again." Reporting this conversation to the State Department, Lane commented that Somoza said, "without any apparent intent of being humorous," that he would not use violence unless it were for the purpose of defending himself. "In view of the physical strength of the Guardia as compared to the Presidential Guard," remarked Lane, "the use of the term

24. The enjoiner was contained in an official telegram from Assistant Secretary of State Wilbur J. Carr to Hanna the day before. "You are specifically instructed," wrote Carr, "not to visit or travel through Nicaragua in view of the possibility of misinterpretation of a visit in that country at this time even if you were merely to pass by airplane."

'defense' would be laughable were it not illustrative of what may be in the minds of the military element."[25]

This was correct, but only up to a point. As events soon proved, Lane underestimated the capacity of the Sacasa group for mischief. On April 19, Abelardo Cuadra, an officer in the Guardia linked with Sacasa's circle, attempted to kill General Somoza. The attempt did not succeed: Cuadra was seized, and two days later a Guardia court-martial sentenced him to be shot. Cuadra's connections with Sacasa's circle were not brought up during the trial: Somoza was not yet prepared for a complete break with the government.

For this reason or another, and probably under the prodding of his willful wife Doña Maria, Sacasa decided to take a stand and show that he was still the president. He refused to confirm Cuadra's sentence and told Lane, who hurried to see him at his summer residence, that "the execution of Cuadra would be unconstitutional and would be an act of open rebellion on the part of Somoza." Since the Jefe Director was determined to have Cuadra shot—he showed Lane a petition signed by many officers demanding that the sentence be carried out—another crisis appeared inevitable.

The president had evidently braced himself for the show-down. His secluded summer residence on the lakefront had been equipped for siege and was guarded by over fifty heavily armed men. Cannon were pointing out toward the lake, the only direction from which an attack could be successfully carried out. The Guardia appeared excited, and the talk in Managua was that a clash could occur at any time.

Again, "in the interest of peace," the exasperated Lane offered Sacasa his good offices to act as an intermediary. Militarily, the president's position was hopeless. Sacasa, who himself was having second thoughts, eagerly accepted the offer and asked Lane to intercede again. Upon his return to Managua, Lane invited Somoza to visit him. During a prolonged and sometimes heated talk, Lane employed all his persuasiveness in order to change Somoza's mind, make him defer to Sacasa's wishes, and spare Cuadra's life. In the end the American minister succeeded and Cuadra's sentence was commuted, but in

25. Lane to Hull, April 16, 1935, FR, 1935, IV, 849.

his report to the Department describing this episode, Lane said that although he had complied with the president's request "as an evidence of good will," he felt that "this legation should not be used any further to pull his chestnuts out of the fire."[26]

Disillusionment

Arthur Bliss Lane's impatience with President Sacasa reflected the growing sense of frustration which he had experienced since his return to Nicaragua. The Sacasa regime, which initially appeared to Lane almost as an embodiment of democratic virtue, was not only weak but also ridden with nepotism and corruption. The American minister had to court not only the president but his relatives as well, especially his all-powerful wife. "One condition here—the graft—is sickening," wrote Lane in his April 16, 1935, letter to Sumner Welles, "especially when one considers it in conjunction with the appalling general poverty and lack of even the most elemental comforts." Writing to Welles again on June 8, he returned to the subject of corruption and of the common practice among the members of the government of transferring funds abroad. "Although the president receives a salary of $200.00 a month, he has been regularly allotted dollar exchange at the rate of $1,500.00 per month," complained Lane. There were other instances, involving illegal roulette concessions and extortions from American businessmen, in which close relatives of Sacasa and his wife played a major role. All in all, Lane sounded less sure that such a regime was worth salvaging.

This disgust with corruption might have been more of a rationalization of Lane's inability to strengthen the constitutional government than a cause for abandoning the efforts to that end. Although Lane still exercised a measure of influence over Somoza, each time the Jefe Director followed his advice this influence seemed to shrink. Somoza made his concessions in such an obliging personal way that Lane found it difficult to ask him for a favor the next time.

It was true that the American minister had succeeded in averting a number of confrontations between the government

---

26. Lane to Hull, April 25, 1935, FR, 1935, IV, 853. Cf. Lane's dispatch of April 26, 1935, *ibid.*, 858.

and the Guardia at least some of which were laden with the danger of bloodshed. But to Lane, these successes did not appear significant. He felt he was expending the influence of the United States on relatively minor matters without accomplishing what he himself considered of paramount importance: the arresting of the Guardia's power in Nicaragua. By this measure, Lane's mission seemed to him a failure.

Arthur Bliss Lane was beginning to sense the limits of what he could do as the representative of the United States in this small and impoverished land. He could perhaps delay the inevitable; he could resolve, usually through great exertion and by applying all his skill, minor local conflicts; he could, up to a point, help to keep passions from getting out of hand. But he could neither reverse the prevailing trend nor significantly arrest it. No amount of praise received by Lane from his superiors in the State Department for his performance could compensate him for his own deepening feeling of inability to be in command of the situation. He decided he had had enough of Nicaragua.

In a personal letter to Sumner Welles of April 16, 1935, Lane, having again expressed his disgust with the local situation, hinted that he would not mind being transferred to another post. Welles answered on April 23, displaying full understanding. He wrote that a vacancy was expected to open soon in Riga, and that both he and Under-Secretary Phillips agreed that Lane was "the most desirable man" to fill it. He could give no assurances, but saw "no reason to anticipate any unforeseen obstacles" to the transfer "in view of the admirable service you rendered the government in Managua and of the special reasons which would make your transfer to a European post desirable."

This was a bitter pill, for "the special reasons" were, of course, the repercussions of Sandino's murder, which put Lane in an unfavorable light against the background of the Latin American policy of the United States. Too sensitive not to realize that he had become a diplomatic liability, Lane redoubled his efforts to accomplish his transfer from Managua. To one of his influential friends, James C. Dunn, Assistant to the Secretary of State, he confessed that he would even be happy to be appointed minister to Albania, a post which, he had heard, was about to become vacant. On his behalf, Mrs. Lane—who traveled to the United States in the summer—visited Dunn to urge him to accelerate her husband's transfer.

Nothing, however, could be done soon. Lane knew that his departure was far off and feared that many unpleasant things were likely to happen in Nicaragua in the meantime. It was of small consolation to him that in the summer of 1935 Nicaragua did not loom nearly as important in the foreign policy of the United States as it had when he first arrived in Managua, and that therefore his failure would attract less attention. It was still important to him. After all, this was his first independent assignment, and he wanted to make his record as bright as he possibly could.

Lane's conscience was clear. He was certain that the recurrent crises in Nicaragua had not been caused by his errors in judgment, his own false moves, or poor understanding on his part of the overall purpose of his mission. He felt as strongly as ever that the principal source of all the difficulties in Nicaragua was the Guardia, this child of the intervention era which had evolved as a second government in the country in a process he had been unable to prevent. He resented what seemed to him to be hypocritical references to non-intervention which had constantly appeared in the State Department's communications at a time when he himself was forced to intervene in recurring crises. He knew that other Latin American governments freely meddled in Nicaragua's affairs,[27] and he regretted his own efforts were rendered ineffective because the Department failed to give him sufficient authority and backing.

Anyone less involved and less intent upon making his mission a success would have taken a more indifferent attitude in Lane's place, and concentrated on satisfying the implicit expectations of the Department by scrupulously abiding by the principle of non-intervention, the principle to which only a few years ago he himself had subscribed so wholeheartedly. But in

---

27. On June 14, 1935, for instance, Lane informed the Department that "the Salvadoran Minister here . . . was recalled to report to President Martinez . . . his activities in connection with the offer which he is reported to have made to President Sacasa of $300,000 to finance movement against Somoza and of arms and ammunition in case of disturbance."

the specific situation of Nicaragua, as it had developed by the summer of 1935, everything looked different. He could not sit back and calmly witness the disintegration of the constitutional government of a country which had been a ward of the United States. Moreover, by now Lane knew only too well that not only some of his counterparts in other Central American capitals but also a number of very important men in the Department gave to the lofty principle of non-intervention little more than lip service. To him, what *he* had tried to do, was fully justifiable because he had had as his goal a democratic and independent Nicaragua, while his superiors merely wanted to wash their hands of the whole mess, piously hiding behind a meaningless generality out of considerations which had little to do with Nicaragua. He candidly expressed his feelings in a letter which he wrote on July 27, 1935, to Willard L. Beaulac, Wilson's deputy in the Latin American Division, an old friend who had good-humoredly counseled him that conditions in Nicaragua were "not worth worrying about":

> ... I only wish that my predecessors (ministers, secretaries, military, and others) had not worried so much about the situation here then and had not created the major headache for their successors: the Guardia Nacional. You may recall that in San Salvador in 1934 you inquired of me whether I was completely serious as to my fear that the G.N. had brought about the establishment of a military caste. I may have been hesitant on the matter then due to my presence before an authority on the subject. After another year of living in proximity to that Nicaraguan-"North" American hybrid, I can say with rude sincerity that it is the biggest stumbling block to the progress of Nicaragua (the financial greed of the government group missing out by a matter of mere inches, but taking second prize by a handsome margin). In the first place, it is totally incongruous that half or more of the revenue of this country should be applied to the perpetuation of the clan of "the arms, the sword, the shield," particularly when no military danger from the exterior seems evident; secondly, can there be anything more ridiculous than the Guardia Nacional guaranteeing the "free" election for the presidency of one of its number; thirdly, the formation of a separate government (which has already asserted itself as a pseudo-fascist and obviously militaristic entity), is ridiculously inconsistent with our laudably pacifistic policy. Obviously, (I use this term advisedly, because even to my mediocre intellect the idea came before I set foot in Nicaragua) the people who created

the G.N. had no adequate understanding of the psychology of the people here. Otherwise, they would not have bequeathed Nicaragua with an instrument to blast constitutional procedure off the map. Did it never occur to the eminent statesmen who created the G.N. that personal ambition lurks in the human breast, *even* in Nicaragua? In my opinion it has been one of the sorriest examples on our part of our inability to understand that we should not meddle in other people's affairs. When the foolishness of the policy of hectoring Latin American countries is understood by *all* of our representatives in these countries, then perhaps we may expect a more beneficent feeling towards us. What is the use of my explaining to people here that I am not trying to control their destinies, when two of my colleagues in Central America (and I am not speaking of the Antilles now)[28] appear continually to be endeavoring to make their influence felt in internal affairs? Presumably the Department thinks that I likewise have the inclination to meddle in internal affairs: as witness some of the following *bon mots* from the Oracle: "while it is of course for Nicaragua to decide what steps it will take in the matter, etc.," and "while of course we can't tell Nicaragua what it should do, etc., etc." The need for a sense of humor in the situation is apparent if one considers the foregoing quotations in the light of the following:

"Your departure in such event might be referred to by interested persons as an indication that you intended to leave them free to carry out their designs."

You probably think, in the terms of intervention, that the American minister here should be in the country during all elections . . and be a father-confessor to Joe the Monk, Emiliano and the other less important denizens of the goldfish bowl. Bluntly, I disagree with you. The sooner we can get these people (and perhaps, others) to realize that we have no special or exalted position here, the better it will be for Nicaragua and other Central American countries, *and for us as well,* which I assume is the real *desideratum.* We should get away from the idea that the American legation in Managua is the "neutral" meeting place for the contending factions. (I put the term "neutral" in quotation marks because a reading of some of the Department's and this legation's ancient memoranda on the subject indicates that certain officers have a hazy, if not totally incorrect, impression as to what legal implications the term "neutrality" has.) . . .

I am glad that you find my reports interesting. I have not been

---

28. A transparent reference to Sumner Welles' own forceful policies in Cuba. "The Oracle" whom Lane quotes in the next sentence is Mr. Welles.

sending in all the rumors, gossip, and political chichat, because in
my opinion it is essentially (at least from our point of view) unimportant. When you and I are able to sit in front of the fire some
evening we can discuss the situation *ad libitum* (I hope not *ad
nauseum*) and have a good laugh in doing so. . . .

The Fall Crisis

A good laugh was far away. Towards the end of the summer,
the legation started receiving reports that the government was
preparing a major move against the Guardia. According to
Lane's information, the members of the cabinet, apparently
without Sacasa's knowledge, had decided to oust Somoza from
the post of Jefe Director. This information was confirmed to
Lane on September 26 by none other than Doña Maria Sacasa,
who herself was deeply involved in the plot.

The meeting at the legation was apparently a stormy one;
"her hatred of Somoza makes it difficult for her to assume a
calm attitude," Lane reported to the Department. As the First
Lady of Nicaragua unfolded the plan, presumably decided
upon by the cabinet, Lane could hardly believe his ears. The
plan was to ask for Somoza's resignation. If the Jefe Director
agreed, he would be rewarded by an important post abroad; if
he refused, force would be used against him. Doña Maria told
Lane that several local commanders of the Guardia were involved in the plot, and that El Salvador and Honduras had
promised material support in airplanes and munitions. And she
requested Lane's cooperation in this operation.

Lane had already learned from other sources that heavy
packages labeled "medicines" and addressed to Doña Maria
had been coming from a Sacasa agent in San Salvador for some
time. One such package had been recently inspected by Salvadoran customs officials who discovered that it contained not
medicines but ammunition. Now he had the explanation.

Lane immediately recognized the gravity of the situation. He
replied to Doña Maria that in his view an attempt to do away
with Somoza would probably bring civil war and destruction to
Nicaragua. The only way out of the situation, said Lane, was to
concentrate efforts on bringing about understanding between
Sacasa and Somoza. When told this was impossible, Lane reminded the First Lady that intervention was a thing of the past,

and that "this legation cannot assume functions of the government."

Doña Maria left, threatening that "we will then depend on our neighbors," and that airplanes from Honduras would bomb the Campo de Marte, Somoza's headquarters, while other forces, including dissenting Guardia units, would quickly finish the job on the ground. Lane recorded his impression that "she is fully determined to proceed with her plans regardless of the consequences," even without her husband's consent; according to her, Sacasa had been kept in the dark by the conspirators because of his "special character."

Concluding his follow-up report to the Department about this visit, Lane wrote, with a touch of sarcasm, that although in his view the request for the removal of Somoza would "very probably create a national crisis with resultant disorders," he would assume that the sovereign Nicaraguan government "should be allowed to take such steps as it considers advisable to meet the situation."[29]

This allusion to the non-intervention policy was lost on the Department. Its hands-off attitude notwithstanding, it was not prepared to allow the Nicaraguan government "to take such steps as it considers advisable," especially the steps involving the bombing of Managua by Nicaragua's neighbors. Secretary Hull reacted immediately. "This government as the traditional friend of Nicaragua," he telegraphed Lane, "earnestly hopes that nothing will occur to disturb the peace of Nicaragua. It would be a matter of profound regret to all friends of Nicaragua if any action were taken which would bring about intervention on the part of other Central American countries, thus risking the dangers of a general Central American war." And the Secretary authorized Lane to convey these views to the persons concerned.[30]

The next few days passed with mounting tension. Lane spoke as forcefully as he could to the plotters and to President Sacasa himself, who turned out to be not so innocent of the plot after all. Lane showed them Hull's telegram and stated that the United States viewed the whole affair with the utmost gravity. He talked to Somoza, who was already aware of the move

29. Lane to Hull, September 26, 1935, FR, 1935, IV, 872-873.
30. Hull to Lane, September 27, 1935, *ibid.*, IV, 874.

against him and who declared that he would resign "tomorrow," but that in such a case he "would not be responsible for what will happen." Somoza reiterated his loyalty to the president but said that the president "must not allow any disloyal action against him."[31]

In the end, the plot collapsed. President Sacasa realized that the scheme had no chance to succeed without at least the tacit approval of the United States. That this approval was not forthcoming he knew not only from Lane, but also from his brother Frederico, whom he had sent to Washington to explain the situation and ask for assistance in his predicament. Frederico Sacasa visited Beaulac, Wilson, and Sumner Welles, all of whom categorically refused not only to support any move of the government against the Guardia but even to give informal "advice" as to the possible course of action for the Nicaraguan government. In vain, Frederico Sacasa insisted that the United States marines had been withdrawn prematurely and that the United States was responsible for the Guardia's behavior. Welles answered that the United States had formally and finally withdrawn from Nicaraguan affairs in January, 1933, and that henceforth "its relations with Nicaragua were in no wise different from those with any other country with which we have friendly diplomatic relations." In conclusion, Welles expressed his sincere hope that Nicaragua would be able to work out her own problems in a satisfactory manner.[32] This was clear and final.

The Last Crisis

It was evident to experienced observers, both in Managua and in Washington, that the days of Sacasa's regime were numbered. The only question that remained was whether it would be overthrown by force or disintegrate in some other fashion. There was no dearth of predictions of a coup in the near future, and minister Lane dutifully passed them along to the Department, more in order to protect himself than in the hope of eliciting some action along the lines he favored.

---

31. Lane to Hull, September 28, 1935, *ibid.*, 876.
32. See the State Department memoranda of October 1 and 16, *ibid.*, 877-879, 883-886.

Most of these predictions proved wrong, mainly because the prophets underestimated Somoza's desire to attain his goal in the most legitimate manner possible and without alienating the United States. Lane, who understood Somoza probably better than any other American, did not discount the possibility of the Guardia revolt. But until the very end of his stay in Managua, he was inclined to feel that his influence over the Jefe Director would be sufficient to dissuade him from resorting to violence, provided he understood that the United States firmly supported the constitutional government.

Somoza, who undoubtedly was one of the shrewdest politicians in Central America, had probably come to suspect that this support was not as firm as Lane tried to make it appear. Although Somoza had no way of knowing the contents of the dispatches sent to Lane, the very absence of any official American statement which could be interpreted as directed against his aspirations, or as aimed at the curtailment of the Guardia was in itself suggestive.

Nevertheless, to the Jefe Director Lane was the representative of the United States in Nicaragua whom he could not afford to alienate. In addition, knowing that in his mediation efforts Lane treated him fairly, Somoza felt obligated to proceed with his plans in such a way as to avoid the risk of incurring Lane's displeasure.

Lane correctly appraised this caution on the part of the Jefe Director and took it into account in devising his own tactics. He knew that his own game was lost; he was anxious to leave Nicaragua as soon as possible. All he wanted now was to delay adverse developments; to postpone the showdown until after he himself had left the country.

At this late date, Lane could view the situation with greater detachment. He still believed that the Guardia was the greatest menace to the constitutional structure of the country so recently launched on the trying path to independence. Yet he was aware that it was not solely to be blamed for the troubles. So far, the crises he had dealt with had been initiated by the Sacasa circle: by its far-fetched scheme to form an alliance with Sandino; by its attempts to curtail the Guardia's power without developing first the adequate means to achieve this goal; by its petty intriguing which had constantly irritated Somoza; by its foolish attempt to assassinate the Jefe Director; and by its latest plot which had threatened to extend the theretofore internal conflict beyond Nicaraguan borders. All of these plans had fallen through, but they had created an atmosphere of mutual suspicion and hostility between the antagonists for which Somoza could be held only partially responsible. The main thing was, however, that no peaceful solution was in sight.

For the time being, the Guardia remained ostensibly loyal to the government and performed its duties in a relatively "non-partisan" manner. It supervised the municipal elections in November, 1935, so impartially that even President Sacasa declared its performance had been above reproach. There were new rumors that a coup d'état would take place early in December, but they proved to be without foundation. Nevertheless, tension was in the air and was increasing rapidly.

Lane had not changed his opinion that the cardinal issue was institutional, involving the conflicting sovereignties of the government and the Guardia. The clash of personalities was important but, in his view, of lesser significance. Somewhat paradoxically, on a personal plane, Lane increasingly sympathized with Somoza. Although the latter had gone very far in his bid for the presidency, he was still willing—or professed to be willing—to entertain the possibility of remaining in his Guardia post for the duration of the next administration, provided that the United States underwrote this arrangement. This was out of the question, as Lane well knew, but the very readiness of Somoza to compromise appeared in favorable contrast to Sacasa's unpredictable fits of intransigence.

At this stage of the game Lane had essentially lost interest in solving Nicaragua's problems. On December 26, 1935, President Roosevelt finally approved his appointment as minister to Estonia, Latvia, and Lithuania. Lane was elated and lost no time in making the necessary personal arrangements for the move.

The news of Lane's impending transfer greatly upset President Sacasa, who had come to value the American minister's loyalty and feared that Lane's successor would be of much less help to his government. In a desperate effort to forestall this change of envoys, Sacasa instructed his chargé d'affaires in

Washington, De Bayle, to visit Sumner Welles to plead that Lane's transfer be rescinded or that he at least be allowed to remain in Nicaragua until after the presidential elections of 1936.

As Welles wrote Lane on January 9, 1936, he replied to De Bayle by "stating that I deeply appreciated in the name of this government the very glowing comments made concerning our minister in Managua, and that I was glad to have confirmed in this very appreciative manner the opinion I myself formed as to the very fine work which you have done." Nevertheless, Welles told De Bayle, "the exigencies of the Service would make it impossible" for Lane not to go to his new post in the immediate future.

Lane was very pleased, not so much by Welles' flattering words as by the now distinct prospect that his frustrations would soon be over. He was ready to leave Nicaragua with the next sailing early in February but did not want to appear too anxious. By now he neither wanted nor expected to accomplish anything more. Suspecting that his successor, Boaz W. Long, would probably take a very different approach to the situation in Nicaragua, he wished to do nothing which would tie Long's hands.

What disturbed Lane was that a new crisis was developing in Managua and that his very departure might become a factor in it. In fact, Somoza, whose attitude had become "quite dangerous," visited Lane on January 21 and advised him—as "his good friend"—to leave as soon as possible. On the 22nd, Lane called Welles on the telephone and suggested that he probably should stay until the next sailing in March because, he said, he hated to leave his successor "with a mess to begin with." Welles, who viewed the situation from an entirely different vantage point and manifestly cared much less, rather reluctantly answered that Lane "could try" and stay in Managua for an extra month.

The crisis which worried Lane was caused this time by Somoza's forces, which had begun intensive agitation in favor of a constitutional convention. Its purpose would be to amend the constitution in such a way as to allow the Jefe Director to become a legitimate candidate for the presidency. Although

Lane had come around to the State Department's view that under the circumstances this would probably be the best way out, he knew that this option was not open.

The alteration of the constitution required Sacasa's approval, and the president had publicly and categorically declared that his approval would not be forthcoming. Lane ascribed the new assurance of the Sacasa group to influences from abroad, and particularly, to the intrigues of Reyes Spindola, Mexican chargé d'affaires. As Lane wrote Welles on February 8, Spindola had told Sacasa's advisers that "Mexico would never recognize Somoza, should he reach the presidency, because of his complicity in the assassination of Sandino, and that the United States would never recognize him."

Sacasa's intransigence on the constitutional issue threatened to provoke a blow-up because Somoza had reached a point of no return in his campaign for the presidency. But, as had happened many times before, Sacasa realized the weakness of his position and asked Lane to mediate. Again, grinding his teeth, Lane plunged into a series of negotiations. For a moment it looked as if he would succeed in his peacemaking: Somoza expressed willingness to abandon his campaign if his personal security and his position in the Guardia would be guaranteed. Taking Somoza's concession as a sign of weakness, the government categorically refused to guarantee anything. The deadlock appeared final.

On February 11, 1936, rioting broke out in Managua. It started with a chauffeurs' strike in protest against a shortage of gasoline but quickly turned into a riot when a British subject, Carlos Wheelock, killed a chauffeur, who was in the crowd attempting to stop all traffic in Managua. The ever-scheming members of Sacasa's circle immediately attempted to exploit the riot for the purpose of discrediting the Guardia. President Sacasa ordered Somoza to ask the crowd to disperse and to open fire if it refused to obey. The Jefe Director personally appealed to the rioting mob but did not instruct his lieutenants to open fire when the mob failed to disperse. Before long, the rioters started clamoring for the resignation of a number of high officials, including Sacasa himself. As the excitement spread to other cities, radical elements joined in, agitating against foreign interests. The Guardia ominously stayed on the sidelines.

This looked like the beginning of a revolution. Lane, who

was scheduled to depart in three weeks, went into conferences with Sacasa and Somoza with great reluctance. From the Jefe Director he extracted a promise to restrain the mob and not to use the riot as a pretext for an assault against the constituted authorities. Next, Lane made strong representations to the president and convoked the diplomatic corps to inform his colleagues of the steps taken and to obtain their approval. In his talks with Lane, President Sacasa accused Somoza of fomenting these disorders in order to embarrass the government in the eyes of other nations and to discredit it domestically. This charge was unfounded, although Somoza probably was in no hurry to extricate Sacasa from such a humiliating position.

For the American minister, the disturbances in Managua offered an opportunity to demonstrate to the Department that all this talk about non-interference in the internal affairs of Nicaragua was so much nonsense. On February 14, he telephoned the new chief of the Latin American Division, Laurence Duggan, to report on his activities. Relaying his conversation with the president's brother, Lane sarcastically remarked that he had told Frederico Sacasa that he "did not wish to interfere in matters of internal administration" but that "as dean of the diplomatic corps and minister of the United States" he had insisted that order be maintained. If the government did not want to "reorganize" the administration in the Managua district by firing the officials who were distasteful to the rioters, Lane told Federico Sacasa, that was its business. But in such a case, it still was obligated to prevent chaos. Lane requested Sacasa to relay this demand to his brother "at once."

Next, Lane told Duggan, he went to see the president and told him that although, of course, he "did not want to interfere in the internal affairs of the country," as dean of the diplomatic corps and American minister he "insisted that order be maintained for the protection of the lives and property of Americans and other foreigners." And, again, without wishing to meddle in Nicaraguan affairs, Lane told Sacasa that he felt Somoza should not be ordered to fire on the crowd.

The reaction of Duggan, one of the more outspoken non-interventionists in the State Department,[33] is not on record. On February 27, Sumner Welles telegraphed Lane

33. See Duggan *The Americas: The Search for Hemispheric Priority* (New York: Henry Holt, 1949).

commending him "for the prompt and effective steps you took as American minister and dean of the diplomatic corps to obtain protection of the lives and property of Americans and other foreigners."

That was probably all that really mattered, for it was evident that the government of President Sacasa had entered its last crisis.

During the last few weeks of his stay in Managua, Lane concentrated on one piece of unfinished business, working feverishly in an effort to conclude the negotiations on the reciprocal trade agreement with Nicaragua, negotiations which had been dragging on for two years. By putting maximum pressure on Washington and on the Nicaraguan delegation, he finally succeeded, and the agreement was signed at the legation on March 11, 1936. The next day Arthur Bliss Lane left Managua, never to go back.

Postcript

Helpless to cope with the growing disorders, the Nicaraguan president and vice-president resigned from their respective offices early in June, were given a substantial sum of money to repair their health, and departed to Costa Rica. This departure ended several weeks of frantic activity when, having lost most of his original support in the country, Sacasa desperately pleaded for help from abroad. Although many governments were sympathetic, only El Salvador was willing to intervene.

During these last weeks of Sacasa's struggle, all eyes were focused on Washington: the United States' position was decisive. Several Latin American governments made representations to the State Department in order to forestall another intervention in Nicaragua. These requests turned out to be wholly unnecessary, for the United States had no intention of intervening to rescue the Sacasa government, or for any other purpose. Faced with a choice between an attempt—probably futile—to salvage the constitutional government in a small Central American country and raising again the spectre of intervention so much resented throughout the Western Hemisphere, the State Department did not hesitate for a moment. To make his position absolutely clear, Secretary Hull even refused to join several other governments in an appeal to Somoza to stop the attack on the Sacasa forces at the *Fortin* of Leon, their last redoubt. In response to Long's appeals, Hull permitted the new American minister to inform both Sacasa and Somoza that "the Government of the United States confidently anticipates that the local authorities of Nicaragua will give adequate protection to the life and property of United States citizens." But, wrote Hull, this was as far as the United States was prepared to go at that juncture.[34]

While the government was undergoing its last convulsions, and Sacasa was sending his pathetic appeals for help,[35] Secretary Hull released on June 5 an official statement explaining the American position. He acknowledged the suggestions he had received "from various sources" to cooperate with other American governments in extending good offices to the warring factions in Nicaragua in order to effect a peaceful solution of the conflict. He stated that the United States' participation in such a joint effort depended entirely "upon the willingness of all political factions in Nicaragua to invite the good offices of other friendly American nations." But unless such an invitation were unanimously extended, said Hull, "the United States would take no initiative in the matter and would under no circumstances even consider whether or not it would exercise its good offices" even in association with other American states.[36]

The reaction to this statement—which was perhaps the final American break with the interventionist past—was almost invariably favorable in the Latin American capitals. Much as the United States was blamed for the advent of Somoza in Nicaragua, nobody wished to see the marines reappearing in that unfortunate land. Especially important to Hull was a near-unanimous support of his position in the American press: the country was turning decidedly and consistently isolationist.

After Sacasa's departure, an interim government under Carlos Brenes Jarquin, M.D., was installed in Managua in accordance with the constitution. The question of recognition did

---

34. Hull to Long, May 31, 1936, FR, 1936, V, 829-830.
35. See Sacasa's memorandum of May 29, 1936, *ibid.*, 825-827.
36. *Ibid.*, 836-837.

not arise; the State Department merely acknowledged the change. The new government quickly removed constitutional obstacles to Somoza's candidacy for the presidency. A "nationalist" bi-partisan coalition was formed to nominate Somoza, and the election campaign started, leaving no doubt as to who would be the winner. The only threat was from the outside. Bitter criticism of Somoza and expressions of implacable hostility reached a high pitch throughout most of Central America and especially in Mexico, which was then governed by the leftist regime of Lazaro Cardenas. But this threat could be dismissed: nonintervention, for the moment, was a two-way street.

On the eve of his election, Somoza proposed to the other states of Central America the formation of a defensive alliance against communism, and the Nicaraguan government, in anticipation of Somoza's victory, inquired in Washington "what would be the attitude of the United States of America in case, as a consequence of this anti-communistic campaign, Nicaragua should be attacked by some large nation on the continent either directly or by supporting some revolutionary movement with arms or tangible forces."[37]

The State Department replied with the expression of hope that "the hypothetical contingency . . . will never arise" and that if there would be "differences which might lead to such a contingency an endeavor should be made to arrive at a satisfactory adjustment by friendly negotiation between the parties concerned." The American minister was instructed, in delivering the Department's reply, to add orally that in embarking on such an anti-communistic venture the Nicaraguan government should "fully realize the gravity of the step under consideration."

---

37. *Ibid.*, 852. Before making this proposal, Somoza visited Guy W. Ray, American chargé d'affaires in Managua, and complained bitterly about communistic propaganda and labor agitation directed from the Mexican legation which in his judgment posed a threat to Nicaragua. Somoza also talked about the necessity of establishing Central American solidarity, and about his desire to recognize the government of Francisco Franco in Spain without waiting for the fall of Madrid. Ray apparently was inclined to be sympathetic: only the day before, his British colleague in Managua told him that the new Mexican chargé d'affaires, Baumbach, had openly admitted that he was a communist and that he indeed had instructions from his government to spread communistic and anti-American propaganda in Nicaragua.

In the December elections, General Anastasio Somoza defeated his "constitutionalist" opponent, Leonardo Arguello, by gaining 110,000 votes against Arguello's 1,200. There were charges of voting irregularities, but although the Guardia was doubtless partial in supervising this election, there hardly could be any question that the overwhelming majority of the electorate favored the Jefe Director.

As Somoza was about to begin his long rule, the American minister in Managua "respectfully suggested" to the State Department that President Roosevelt send a telegram of congratulation to President-elect Somoza. The Department, which had had its share of embarrassment in connection with the Nicaraguan developments, and which was blamed for Somoza's ascent by every Yanqui-baiting editor in Latin America, advised minister Long that such telegrams "are not customary."[38] It limited itself to appointing Long to represent the President of the United States at the inaugural ceremonies in Managua.

Arthur Bliss Lane, in far away Riga, could only be thankful that this honor had not been bestowed upon him.

The rule of Anastasio Somoza lasted twenty years. Internally, it was marked by political stability, extensive road and school construction, and substantial economic growth. Somoza's personal popularity among the Nicaraguans remained high.

Externally, Somoza succeeded in making his influence felt throughout Central America. Although he became a whipping boy for most of the Latin American press, he established friendly relations with many governments. Mexico and Costa Rica were notable exceptions. The latter, after the revolution of 1948 which brought to power the leftist regime of Jose Figueres, became a base of operation for a variety of anti-Somoza groups, sporadically plotting to get rid of the Nicaraguan president. Armed clashes along the border between the two countries were common and kept Pan-American relations continuously in a state of strain.

Throughout his life Somoza preserved his attachment to the United States. He created the best possible climate for foreign investment in Nicaragua. He loyally supported the United States in all international conferences. Before, during, and after the Second World War, his envoys constantly sought advice in

---

38. Hull to Long, December 19, 1936, *ibid.*, 849

Washington, and the occasions were extremely rare when this advice was not followed.

Yet Somoza's loyalty remained unrewarded. American public opinion was not sufficiently gratified by the State Department's consistency in upholding the principle of non-intervention, and demands for sanctions against Somoza were not infrequent. Because Somoza had dashed the hopes for an American-style democracy in Nicaragua, and perhaps because he was viewed as an outgrowth of the intervention era, a certain section of the American public never forgave him his victory over Sacasa.

Such attitudes were reflected in the State Department. Although many officials were relieved when the crisis was over, nobody was exactly happy. The feeling of embarrassment which began in 1936 proved to be lasting. Somoza's efforts to please the United States were taken for granted, but his own requests, no matter how legitimate, were usually turned down. Economic aid to Nicaragua was negligible.

On September 21, 1956, Anastasio Somoza was mortally wounded in Leon by an assassin. A week later, attended by American physicians flown in from the United States on the orders of President Eisenhower, he died in a Panama hospital. On October 1, the *Washington Post* commented: "Anastasio Somoza was personally admirable to those who could tolerate his self-serving, anti-democratic regime. Some could not, including his assassin, whose foul deed cannot be excused. Now that this bullet has ended President Somoza's life, however, Nicaraguans can seize the opportunity to liberalize their political machinery." A certain liberalization did actually take place. But because of the fact that the government of Nicaragua continued to be dominated by the Somoza "dynasty," these changes were little appreciated abroad.

III

A Brush with Russian Affairs

The assignment to the Baltic states was a most welcome change to Arthur Bliss Lane; this transfer was also a relief to Sumner Welles and other high-ranking officials in the State Department who, having adjusted their thinking to the inevitability of a military regime in Nicaragua, had come to the conclusion that Lane had outlived his usefulness in Managua. Nobody in the Department was willing to admit the failure of the American experiment in democracy in Central America. Lane's departure took place without any fanfare, and his official personal record remained unblemished. For his part, the American minister put up a good show. In a January 1936 letter to J.V.A. MacMurray, his predecessor in Riga, he wrote that in the Department's view "the critical nature of the European situation makes it imperative for me to leave at the earliest possible moment," adding in parenthesis that "were it not for my having had some experience with Departmental methods and motives I might otherwise feel I were going to Europe as Laval, Eden, Hitler, and Mussolini all wrapped in one."

No such urgency of course existed, and Lane did not depart for his new post from New York until June. On his way he stopped for a few days in Paris and for more than a week in Berlin to renew his personal contacts with colleagues in the foreign service and to get his own impression of "the European situation."

Such lack of haste in getting to Riga reflected the aloof attitude of the United States government towards not only the Baltic states but Europe as a whole. Mindful of the powerful isolationist sentiment in the country, President Roosevelt adhered strictly to a policy of non-involvement in European affairs. Lane, with his well developed political sense, was prepared to follow this policy faithfully even if it meant playing a largely ceremonial role. One year after his arrival in Riga, he commented in a letter to James C. Dunn—without a shade of bitterness—that "the Eastern European area (with the possible exception of Russia) is in itself perhaps the least important of all areas in the world with which the United States has to deal."

This unimportance of the area was reflected in the limited scope of the legation's activities. There were few Americans living in Estonia, Latvia, and Lithuania whose interests needed protection. There was no tourist traffic. Commercial relations, never of any significance, had ceased altogether after the Johnson Act of 1934 had made countries in default of their debts to America ineligible for American credit. This included all of Eastern Europe except Finland.

Nor did Lane's mission include any tasks of a political nature. While the Baltic states were being gradually absorbed into the German economic sphere, their foreign policies continued to be based on neutrality and collective security through the League of Nations. Public sentiment was pro-British and pro-French, spurred by the latent threat to the security of the region from two powerful neighbors. Of the two, the Soviet Union (and the communist subversion which it directed) was the more feared, despite a German minority problem aggravated during those years by the revisionist propaganda pouring out of the Third Reich. The United States had no position on either communism or German irridentism, but even if it had, there would have been no practical way to make American desires felt.

International relations aside, the internal affairs of the Baltic states provided little food for Lane's curiosity. After a period of unhappy experimentation in parliamentary democracy, Lithuania had passed under the benevolent rule of Antanas Smetona following an army coup d'état in December, 1926. A more prolonged internal struggle in Estonia ended by the spring of 1934 with the establishment of the rule of Konstantin Päts; and Karlis Ulmanis disposed of the remnants of democracy in Latvia in April, 1936. The peoples seemed to have accepted these changes, and to an outsider, the political tranquility in the Baltic countries meant that there were no political developments worth watching.

This suited Arthur Bliss Lane well. For a while, the ghosts of Nicaragua haunted him (his colleagues from Central America kept him posted on the bloody struggle which broke out after his departure) and he instinctively shied away from anything dramatic. He was again a traditional diplomat who steered away from all contacts outside official and diplomatic circles. He knew none of the local languages and liked to repeat President Wilson's joke dating back to the Versailles days, that "Saint Peter would undoubtedly forbid him entry at the pearly gates because of his having resurrected three dead languages."

In spite of the undemanding life, there were certain things to be done. Lane had to acquaint himself with the complex European situation, increasingly agitated by the crises over Ethiopia, the Spanish Civil War, and the German challenge to the Versailles system. He also needed to re-establish personal and professional contacts with members of the foreign service elsewhere, contacts which are such an integral part of the career diplomat's life and which Lane had neglected in the Managua turmoil. A great deal of his time was taken up by protocol; by the necessity to attend official functions and meet local dignitaries and diplomats in Tallin, Riga, and Kaunas; by administrative and personnel matters in all three legations; as well as by minor problems such as finding suitable cooks, maids, or chauffeurs, or stocking up his wine cellar. It was a busy and not entirely unpleasant life, but it clearly lacked the significance and color which were typical of the ambassadorial experience in Latin America.

The Russian Section

During most of the interwar period the majority of the American diplomatic missions in Europe amounted to little more than "listening posts" where information — usually second-hand — and diplomatic gossip were gathered and transmitted to Washington for the Department's desk officers to sort out and file away. Staffs were small and consisted for the most part of career foreign service officers who were periodically rotated without having much chance to develop intimate knowledge of a country's traditions, culture, and history. A gradual accumulation of professional experience and an expanding personal acquaintance within the diplomatic world were considered quite adequate grounds for a successful career. The State Department concerned itself primarily with the Western Hemisphere and the Far East; the success or failure of a mission in other parts of the world depended on an ambassador's ability not to create difficulties. Systematic exploration and study of local and regional problems had not yet come into vogue.

The legation in Riga, Latvia, in this respect differed from all other American missions abroad. In addition to the regular diplomatic and consular staff, it contained the so-called Russian section which had been established there in the early twenties on the initiative of Robert F. Kelley, chief of the Department's Division of Eastern European Affairs. The task of the section was to carry on a continuous study of developments in the neighboring Soviet Union, whose revolutionary regime presented a mystery and possibly a threat to the established social order in other countries of the world. The research in the Russian section was based on Soviet publications (easily obtainable in Riga) and on other sources of information which from time to time became available to the legation. Among these sources were travelers to Russia, many of whom passed through the Baltic states and were willing to submit themselves to intensive "debriefing." It was the Department's first attempt to accumulate knowledge of a foreign country in a systematic and scholarly fashion, and it was so successful that, on Kelley's insistence, the Russian section—although with somewhat diminished functions—was retained even after the establishment of the embassy in Moscow in February 1934 opened a possibility for conducting observations within the Soviet Union.

The uniqueness of this undertaking almost inevitably led to its somewhat privileged and autonomous status within the legation, a status further enhanced by the fact that the official who headed the Russian section at the time of Lane's arrival, Felix Cole, was simultaneously counselor of the legation and the man directly in charge of both political and economic reporting and of big and small administration matters. The Russian section was staffed by several young and talented specialists in Soviet affairs, aided by a group of locally-hired experts. Its monthly reports were transmitted to Kelley under the signature of the minister who, not being an expert on Russia and communist affairs himself, usually did not venture to modify or contradict the findings of these reports.

This was an unorthodox situation, clearly deviating from one of the basic principles of the foreign service which, in that uncomplicated era, required that the head of mission had to be at all times in full control of all aspects of its activities. Lane's predecessor, J.V.A. MacMurray, felt quite unhappy about it but accepted the status which he had inherited from his predecessors. Lane, however, found this state of affairs intolerable. A proud bearer of the espirit de corps of the foreign service, up in the tradition of the diplomatic service in Latin America, he could not put up with the notion that some members of his staff were somehow exempt from his authority. To Arthur Bliss Lane, it was only the minister himself who represented the president of the United States in a given country; the mission's personnel were there to aid him in the performance of his duties and for no other purpose. The minister was not unlike the captain of a ship in open seas; his word, in all matters, was supposed to be final.

It was not therefore surprising that barely a month after Lane's arrival in Riga he undertook to affirm his authority over the Russian section. The fact that it was the most important function at the legation in the eyes of the Department was of no consequence. On the contrary, this was an additional reason to cut it down to size and perhaps even to eliminate altogether "this tail that wags the dog," as he referred to it in one of his early reports. In addition, Lane was provoked by the air of superiority which the Russian experts sometimes displayed in dealing with laymen. The legation over which he presided was not to be regarded as an appendage to any alien operation carried out under the same roof.

Having observed the situation, Lane wrote on July 23, 1936, to Wilbur J. Carr, Assistant Secretary of State for Administration, a long "personal and confidential" letter in which he demanded far-reaching changes in the legation. He found the Russian section "unwieldy" and "greatly overstaffed," not justifying the expense which it entailed to the government. He charged its members with ignoring their "primary duty . . . that of maintaining friendly relations with the Latvian government and of getting to know Latvia and the Latvian people." He complained about the lack of discipline in connection with office hours, expressing the feeling that perhaps it was impossible for persons "with a Ph.D. complex" to be good office workers. In the end he recommended the acceleration of the scheduled transfer of Felix Cole to another post and his replacement, not with another Russian specialist from Kelley's office (as had already been decided in Washington), but with a career foreign service officer "with an entirely objective point of view with respect to Russia and this part of the world."

Upon reflection, Lane decided that his recommendations had little chance for success unless approved by the chief of the Division of Eastern European Affairs. Therefore, two days later he wrote a letter to Kelley, assuring him that "with proper reorganization . . . the Russian section can turn out the same amount of work with a decreased personnel instead of, as at present, demoralizing the office as a whole by complete disregard of office hours and office orders." And he again requested Cole's replacement with a senior foreign service officer with an "objective point of view . . . who would not put exaggerated emphasis on Russian affairs in endeavoring to evaluate events and conditions."

Kelley, who had been struggling to expand the Department's knowledge of the country which, until 1933, had been officially regarded as an incarnation of evil and a threat to peace, was not only unimpressed by Lane's arguments but became alarmed by the prospect of destruction of the operation to the development of which he had devoted so much of his personal attention over the years. As it was, many a New Dealer regarded it with a fishy eye. At the moment, however, his influence in the Department was sufficient to prevent Lane's suggestions from being considered on higher levels. The minister's messages were left without reply.

The implied rebuke did not discourage Minister Lane. On the contrary, the more he read the reports of the Russian section, the more sure he was that its reform, if not its elimination, had been long overdue: he was now convinced that his Russian experts were far from being objective in their work and that, rather than enlightening the Department, they tended to perpetuate its imbedded negative attitude toward the Soviet Union.

In his experiences in Latin America Arthur Bliss Lane had regarded the communists with suspicion mixed with detestation. They were enemies of the United States who complicated the task of carrying out the good neighbor policy. But in his perception of Russia, Lane was much more detached. He did not share President Roosevelt's generous attitude toward the Soviet Union and his feeling that "the Bolshevik rule, for all its shortcomings, was an experiment designed for the improvement of the common man's lot."[1] The bloody purge then underway in Russia, and the whole repressive political system established there by the Bolsheviks, repelled him.

On the other hand, unlike Kelley (and the first American ambassador to Moscow, William C. Bullitt) he did not feel that there was much profit in insisting that the Soviet government fulfill its commitments undertaken at the time of the establishment of diplomatic relations and be held accountable for those activities of the Comintern which violated the spirit of the Roosevelt-Litvinov agreement.[2] Furthermore, unlike Bullitt, Lane saw certain harmony between the American and Soviet immediate goals which, at that time, he envisaged as the preservation of peace in Europe and the Far East, and the expansion of trade. For this reason, he could not see the Russian Bolsheviks in the same light as their Latin comrades. As to the global schemes of communism, if they were what his experts thought they were, they were none of his direct concern.

Perhaps decisive for his attitude was his appraisal of the broad European picture of the period. Like so many Americans who had not followed the developments in Europe in their continuity, Lane was shocked to discover the extent of the menace to peace represented by the rising spectre of German nationalism. He was neither "interventionist" nor isolationist"; he shared the desire of the great majority of his fellow countrymen (and of President Roosevelt) not to become enmeshed in European affairs. His realization that non-intervention precluded effective American steps on behalf of peace, however, did not deter him from condemnation of those European leaders who failed to do their best for this noble cause.

1. Wm. L. Langer and S. Everett Gleason, *The Challenge to Isolation* (New York: Harper, 1952), p. 126.
2. On this, see Beatrice Farnsworth, *William C. Bullitt and the Soviet Union* (Bloomington: Indiana University Press, 1967), chapter VII.

With a tendency, characteristic of onlookers, to detach themselves from puzzling and annoying complexities of a situation, Lane believed that in the Europe of 1936, embroiled in ideological conflicts and nationalistic claims and counterclaims and threatened by the aggressive policies of Italy and Germany, the Soviet Union was a pillar of peace. This belief was further strengthed by Lane's emotional inability—so widespread in the age of relativism—to regard several devils opposing each other as equally evil. Such recognition would have made it difficult, if not altogether impossible, to reduce the complicated picture to a more manageable equation allowing for clear-cut attitudes and obvious policy decisions. Lane's aversion to German nationalism dated back to the First World War. The Huns were evil. But to him, evil had to be total and exclusive at the same time, and since the evil was embodied in the Axis, it followed that the Soviets, who appeared to be opposed to Hitler, had to be wooed rather than repelled. Aware of his countrymen's predisposition for moralizing, he knew that the unappetizing realities of the Soviet regime had to be minimized in order to make it more palatable to the American public and the government.

Not having to deal with the Soviets directly, Lane could not properly appreciate the frustrations of the State Department officials who since 1934 had been wrangling with the problem of how to handle the recalcitrant Soviet government. Even the most patient ones had been embittered by the crudity and arrogance of Soviet officials both in Washington and Moscow; by the end of 1935 the breakdown in communications between the two governments was complete. After Ambassador Bullitt was transferred, at his own emphatic request, to Paris, the small embassy staff in Moscow was left in the hands of Loy W. Henderson, acting as chargé d'affaires, functioning merely as yet another ineffectual "listening post."

It was perhaps a measure of Arthur Bliss Lane's self-confidence that he decided he could contribute to the improvement of Soviet-American relations from his post in Riga merely by changing the composition of the Russian section and the tenor of its reports. In a long message to Assistant Secretary of State R. Walton Moore, written on September 7, 1936, Lane suggested that the reporting of the Russian section "may in the future assume both political and international importance and cause the Department considerable embarrassment unless corrective steps are taken." Lane pointed out that although he could not be expected "to have more than a smattering of knowledge" regarding the content of the reports, he could see that all but one or two of the section's officers had a definitely anti-Soviet attitude." And he continued:

> It is entirely understandable that officers who have served extensively in Russia or on Russian work for many years, thereby forming very definite opinions with regard to Russia, should find it difficult, if not impossible, to treat the subject matter objectively. In fact, I have found that the drafting officers here, as a result of over-specialization on Russian affairs, have come to think in terms of Russia as a separate entity rather than in terms of Russia's relationship to Europe and the rest of the world.

In order to eliminate the consequences of such over-specialization, Lane again recommended putting the Russian section under a senior foreign service officer who "should not have specialized in this area but should bring a fresh point of view on matters dealing with Russia and with the other countries of the East European region." And Lane expressed doubt that the expected replacement of Cole by Earl L. Parker, Kelley's assistant, would help build up "a Russian section which could not be criticized on the ground that it is fundamentally anti-Soviet in its attitude." "I think it is fully as important," wrote Lane, "that it be free from such a charge . . . as to avoid the imputation of being communistic in its leanings." In conclusion, Lane suggested that foreign service officers specializing in the Eastern European area be periodically reassigned to other posts so that "they will have an opportunity to familiarize themselves with the problems which confront the average officer, i.e., problems of administration, protection work, cultivation of American commercial interests, and general diplomatic and consular duties which are now rarely performed by these Russian specialists." The trouble with these specialists, Lane felt, was that they acquired an academic attitude ("akin to that of a student preparing a doctoral thesis") which made it impossible for them to perform the "substantial duties with which the service as a whole has to deal."

The Assistant Secretary, not himself a specialist in European affairs, could not disregard Lane's eloquent presentations. He suspected that the minister's well-known tenacity would keep the issue open. Besides, Lane's views sufficiently conformed to the accepted concepts of the foreign service to evoke favorable response within the Department in spite of Kelley's determined opposition to any changes in the status of the Russian section at Riga or, in some cases, because of it. Therefore, although Moore let Kelley proceed with the appointment of Parker as chief of the Russian section, he at the same time ordered a formal investigation of Lane's complaints. J. Klahr Huddle, inspector of the Department, visited Riga in April 1937, listened to Lane, studied the situation, and recommended that the role of the Russian section be limited to research and translation; that it was to be enjoined from interpreting its findings, and even from employing adjectives or expressions "which might give a report an interpretive character." To satisfy the minister further, Huddle agreed that the Russian specialists should work harder, make their reports shorter and their hours longer. Even though Inspector Huddle's conclusions were not exactly what Lane wanted, they appeared a reasonable compromise, and he grudgingly consented to consider the issue closed.

The political aspect of the problem, however, continued to trouble Minister Lane and, in November, accompanied by his wife and daughter, he went for two weeks to Moscow in order to form personal impressions about the state of affairs in the Soviet capital. Loy W. Henderson, who was in charge of the embassy, arranged a series of meetings with communist officials and with American newsmen stationed in Moscow. The contents of Lane's conversations we do not know, but upon his return to Riga he wrote another long message to Moore. Recalling his experiences in Mexico and the wisdom and skill of Ambassador Morrow, Lane related how American relations with Mexico had, in a few years, undergone a most spectacular transition "from virtual hostility to the normal status which one expects should exist between the two nations." Lane suggested that an analogous situation existed in American relations with the Soviet Union. "There is a government here," wrote Lane, "which does things both internally and externally that do not meet with our approval. Their system of government is abhorrent to the American concept of liberty." Yet the interests of the United States required that correct, if not friendly, relations be established. This task, felt Lane, should be assigned to a new ambassador, since Henderson—although a diplomat of outstanding capacity and talent—did not wish to change ("even a particle") the policy which had been pursued by Bullitt "since his disillusionment of 1935."

To this, Moore, on December 2, skeptically replied that "knowing what has occurred since recognition was accorded the Soviet government, I now make the hopeless prediction that the new ambassador's experience there will resemble Bullitt's."

It should be noted that, far removed as he was from the American scene, Arthur Bliss Lane's overall approach to the Soviet problem was much closer to the dominant direction of American politics than was that of the State Department. The elections of 1936 indicated a noticeable swing to the left. The Spanish civil war was very much in the news, with the sympathies of the public overwhelmingly anti-fascist. Pro-Soviet sentiment was as fashionable as it was vocal, and those who dared to voice criticism of one or another aspect of Soviet policy were readily branded reactionaries if not pro-fascists. An influential group in the capital, centered around Mrs. Roosevelt and Justice Frankfurter, maintained close relationships with a number of leading advocates of a Soviet-American rapprochement and listened attentively to the interminable complaints of Soviet Ambassador Konstantin Oumansky about the unfriendly attitude of the State Department. President Roosevelt himself soon came around to the opinion that something must be done to improve the situation. As a successor to Bullitt he chose Joseph E. Davies, a devotee of peace (and a generous contributor to the Democratic party) who could be relied upon to inaugurate a new era in American relations with Moscow. Sumner Welles, and later, Cordell Hull, were prevailed upon to initiate organizational and personnel changes within the State Department which would facilitate the rapprochement with Moscow. In a drastic reorganization carried out with remarkable swiftness early in June 1937, the Division of Eastern European Affairs was abolished, its personnel dispersed, and its large reference library, which had been collected by Kelley, liquidated.

The significance of these changes did not escape the attention of Arthur Bliss Lane, who decided that the moment was propitious to reopen the issue of the Russian section. In an eloquent letter to Dunn, then chief of the Division of European Affairs, Lane restated his old arguments against having in Riga "a small body of so-called experts who in their reports have . . . copied the style of an academician preparing a Ph.D. thesis." In a second letter, written the same day and addressed to Moore, Lane expressed hope that the Russian section would be brought under greater discipline. He also advised against assigning Robert F. Kelley—who had lost his job in the reorganization—to Moscow "because of Kelley's known background with respect to the Soviet Union . . . particularly at this time when it is doubtful whether anybody who is not willing to accommodate himself to the abnormal point of view of Soviet officials would be able to accomplish anything." Kelley's position in Moscow, believed Lane, would be further aggravated by his religion: from his experiences in Mexico Lane knew that revolutionary regimes tend to assume "a very hostile attitude toward the Roman Catholic church." Along with so many of his liberal contemporaries, Lane considered the Roman Catholic church a main repository of resistance to revolutionary change, and certainly the most determined adversary of international communism. Whether because of his religion or because of his politics, Kelley did not get the Moscow assignment, but was sent off to Turkey instead.

No Dilution of Authority

In retrospect, it is difficult to say whether Arthur Bliss Lane truly believed in the feasibility of a radical improvement in Soviet-American relations or only wished to believe there were simple and rational answers to the increasingly complicated and ominous international situation. One year in Riga had doubtless augmented his knowledge of the Soviet Union: he read with great care the voluminous reports of his Russian section and, much as he might have resented their slant, he could not dismiss the factual information contained in them.

His dislike for the communists unquestionably strengthened towards the end of this period. Although he still regarded the Soviet Union as an international counterforce to Nazi Germany, Lane's uncompromisingly moralistic approach to human affairs precluded any rationalization of the butchery which the NKVD, on Stalin's orders, was perpetrating in Russia. He still felt that the Soviets should be utilized for the good cause but now believed that to whitewash the communists in the eyes of decent people the world over, and to present them as fighters for freedom and against despotism, would be going too far. It was at least in part due to his growing skepticism that Lane took an immediate and strong dislike to the new ambassador to Moscow, Joseph E. Davies, who, in the name of peace, was prepared to give a bill of health to Satan himself, and who — as Lane knew — was remarkably ignorant in European affairs. This dislike quickly intensified when Davies assumed the role of personal representative of the president, on a special fact-finding mission to Eastern Europe.

It was part of the unwritten code of the American foreign service that each envoy, no matter how junior or inexperienced, was the sole spokesman for the United States in the country of his accreditation, directly responsible to the president and the secretary of state. His political and economic reporting carried automatic authority. He could privately seek advice from his colleagues elsewhere if he chose to (few ever did) but he would resent any uninvited interference from a peer, least of all from an outsider to the foreign service. Thus when rich and politically influential but thoroughly tactless Davies appeared on the scene, Lane's reaction was predictable.

The first encounter took place in Helsinki, where Lane went to meet the ambassador, then paying an unsolicited visit to the Finnish capital. At a reception at the foreign ministry, Lane could hardly restrain himself while listening to Davies' peroration on the subject of the low caliber of American career diplomats who, according to him, were normally ignored by the president. When Davies remarked that he intended to visit the other Baltic countries in order to form his own impressions, Lane could only mutter "of course, you should." But he did not fail to report this episode to Sumner Welles. On the same day, August 6, 1937, in a letter to his old friend, Ferdinand L. Mayer, counselor at the embassy in Berlin, he wrote:

Next week Ambassador Davies is coming to Riga to inspect the legation and then proceed to Memel to make a report on the Memel situation. At least, I assume he is going to do so as he told me the president is anxious to have his view regarding conditions in the Baltic states. I believe the ambassador has made a very careful study of Russian affairs, he having been in a very advantageous position to do so objectively from the deck of the "Sea Cloud" [Davies' private yacht]. His total time spent in Moscow now amounts to almost six weeks and I believe he has been in the chancery twice.

Ambassador Davies' immense wealth, his role in the Democratic Party, and his well-known connections with the White House left Arthur Bliss Lane quite unimpressed. He had no use for Davies' opinions and was in no mood to put up with his presence any more than was required by the absolute minimal rules of courtesy. He instructed his chargé d'affaires in Tallin to advise the Estonian government that it was desirable to avoid "any formality in connection with the proposed visit" and announced that he himself would be unable to greet Mr. Davies in Estonia due to previous engagements. Lane arranged Davies' meeting with the Latvian foreign minister in Riga but declined to attend it personally. Simultaneously, he instructed the chargé d'affaires in Kaunas to "make sure that the Lithuanian foreign office sends nobody to meet Davies in Klaipeda—you are enough."

If Davies noticed that his reception in the Baltic states by a junior career minister fell somewhat short of being cordial, he did not betray it in his messages to Roosevelt, remarkably devoid of penetrating thoughts and lucid observations.[3] Being

3. Samples of Davies' reporting can be seen in his book *Mission to Moscow* (New York: Simon & Schuster, 1941). He stayed in Moscow for about a year, getting increasingly bored, disgusted with the food and general conditions in the Soviet capital. He coveted the post at the Court of St. James but the British would not accept him because of his previous divorces. Berlin was his second choice but the appointment was vetoed by Secretary Hull who did not want to have there a strongly opinionated and unpredictable politician, not subject to effective State Department control. In the end, Roosevelt assigned him to Belgium and Luxemburg, an unimportant but attractive "listening post." Davies came into prominence later, during World War II and the era of friendship with the Soviets, when he became Roosevelt's principal adviser on Soviet affairs. The transfer of Davies to Brussels left the embassy in Moscow to another chargé de affaires, Alexander C. Kirk, a career diplomat, until the arrival the following year of Laurence A. Steinhardt, a political appointee but a man of outstanding intelligence.

a practicing politician he possessed a rather thick skin and probably did not sense this reserve on the part of the American minister; he regarded all career diplomats as expendable anyway and unworthy of his personal attention. On his part, Lane was not concerned with what Davies might think of him. He feared no repercussions. His membership in the foreign service meant to him that he could exercise his own judgment, free of all external influences, not unlike a judge on the bench appointed or elected for life.

There was another reason why Lane could afford a degree of imprudence in dealing with the influential ambassador. Shortly before Davies' inspection tour, Sumner Welles informed Lane of his forthcoming reassignment to Yugoslavia, with the actual departure scheduled later in the fall. The reasons for Lane's transfer—for which Lane didn't ask—are not clear. On the one hand, it appeared to be a promotion: Yugoslavia was rated a more important country than the three Baltic states put together. On the other hand, several of his friends suspected that the transfer was a punishment for some indiscretion on Lane's part, perhaps even for his campaign against Kelley. Although out of favor politically, Kelley had many influential friends in the foreign service, a brotherhood which put loyalty to the institution above everything else. At any rate, Allan Dawson, consul general in Hamburg and Lane's friend, wrote him on August 31, 1937, that "not knowing whether you are pleased or not at your move to Belgrade I don't know whether to offer my congratulations or condolences. It ought to be interesting as a listening post but I can't quite see how it will keep your restless soul busy enough. There were stories extant in Paris as to your having been euchred from Riga but they can wait until we see you."

Lane, who always appreciated a good joke except when it was directed at him, did not enlighten Dawson as to the causes for this reassignment but answered that he looked forward to going to Belgrade since "this part of the world is quiet by comparison." Having arranged for an extensive leave to be spent in the more attractive parts of Europe and having gone through the tiresome round of farewell audiences in the three capitals prescribed by protocol, Arthur Bliss Lane departed from Riga on September 15, 1937.

IV

A Pyrrhic Victory in Yugoslavia

Yugoslavia in the Mid-Thirties

The kingdom of Yugoslavia, in which Arthur Bliss Lane arrived in October 1937, was a country of enormous complexity, populated by a conglomeration of nationalities without common history, language, or religion. The dominant Serbian group, above seven million strong, accounted for less than half of the total population; yet the official state religion was Serbian Orthodox. The second and third largest groups were, respectively, the Croats and Slovenes, both Roman Catholic. The Croats had a separate thousand-year-old history. They spoke the same language as the Serbs but used the Latin rather than the Cyrillic alphabet. Slovenian was a different language, but the Slovenes had never had any experience in self-government. The Moslem population of the kingdom included Bosnians and Albanians, although some Bosnians were Serbian Orthodox and some Albanians Roman Catholic or Greek Orthodox. In addition there were large German and Hungarian minorities inherited from the Hapsburg empire, mostly Roman Catholic, and a Rumanian minority, mostly Orthodox. The Montenegrins, whose independent kingdom was abolished at the end of the First World War, were akin to the Serbs in language and religion but accustomed to their own, distinctly different, way of life. The Macedonians, who were added to Serbia after the Balkan wars, were ethnically close to the Bulgarians, although Belgrade assumed that they were indigenous Serbs.

This geopolitical monstrosity, known until 1929 as the Kingdom of the Serbs, Croats, and Slovenes, emerged after the First World War in the era when the size of a country was considered the chief measure of its strength. Its appearance on the map was supported by the French, less by the British, still less by the United States, and was opposed by Italy, which had its own designs for Yugoslavia's western regions. "The Yugoslav Idea" as conceived by Messrs. Wickham Steed and R. W. Seton-Watson, with the powerful sponsorship of Lord Northcliffe's newspaper empire, promoted by South Slav politicians in exile, was envisaged as a federal union under the Serbian dynasty of Karageorgievich, with a broad local autonomy and democratic form of government. The federal idea, however, ran into a determined opposition from the pan-Serbs who regarded the new acquisition solely as a reward for Serbia's sacrifices in the war. Although future conflicts within Yugoslavia could easily be foreseen, the Allied and Associated Powers went ahead, overruling in the process most of the territorial claims of Italy, which then seized—in the Gabriele D'Annunzio escapade—part of the new state by force. Belgrade did not recognize this seizure until January 1924.

Among the many frictions within the multinational state the most vexing one was between the central government and the Croats. The latter had no liking or respect for the Serbs and resented bitterly the formation of a strongly centralized administration in Belgrade. They rejected the argument that the country could not be held together without such centralization, and for most of the interwar period boycotted the government. After a few futile attempts to realign Yugoslavia's politics on other than a national-regional basis, King Alexander resorted to a personal dictatorship, subjecting Croatia (and Dalmatia) to a virtual military occupation, run directly from Belgrade. The deadlock remained even after the king introduced a new constitution in 1931: although the most fanatical nationalists, the Ustaše, fled into exile, there was only one political organization in Croatia—the Croatian Peasant Party of Vladko Macek—and it refused to cooperate with Belgrade. The murder of King Alexander in Marseilles by an Ustaše terrorist in October 1934 only aggravated the situation. The Yugoslav melting pot refused to melt, and the links holding the unhappy peoples of the kingdom together weakened further.

At the time of Arthur Bliss Lane's arrival in Belgrade the country was ruled by a coalition government headed by Milan Stojadinović, probably the shrewdest Serbian politician alive, who managed to form a working majority in the parliament out of several political parties and cliques. The real authority, however, was in the hands of the regent, Prince Paul, the late King Alexander's cousin. Related by marriage to most of Europe's ruling dynasties, an aristocrat and an Anglophile who spoke English at home with his wife, Princess Olga, a cousin of the King of the Hellenes and a sister of the Duchess of Kent, Prince Paul had little taste for Balkan politics. An accomplished connoisseur of the fine arts and a musician, he stood above the government, attempting no reforms aimed at the inefficiency and corruption of the administration. His disapproval of pan-Serbian chauvinism cost him the disaffection of the Serb-dominated army which had been passionately loyal to the late king. Without trying to cure Yugoslavia's numerous politcal and economic ills, he concentrated on a twofold task: to achieve internal peace in his unruly country and to assure its external security so that he could deliver it intact to the young King Peter II. Prince Paul's ability to rise above political quarrels and intrigues seemed to make up for his lack of forcefulness. Although he left government affairs pretty much to Stojadinović and his cabinet, he retained ultimate authority in the affairs of state, not hesitating to assert it in critical moments. The disgruntled Serb politicians did not challenge him, in part because the traditional patriotism of the Serbs required an unswerving loyalty to the crown, and partly because the regency was the only recognized instrument of Yugoslavia's unity.

Externally, Yugoslavia faced grave problems. Four of its seven neighbors—Hungary, Bulgaria, Albania, and, particularly, Italy—coveted parts of its territory. Italy had vast ambitions in the Balkans in general and was determined to offset France's influence in Central and Southeastern Europe. Attempts at restoration of the Hapsburgs in Austria and Hungary, which appealed to the Roman Catholic non-Serbs of the kingdom, represented another threat. Because alien minorities were numerous and discontented, the hostile neighbors could—and did—encourage irredentist sentiments within the country. For its security, Yugoslavia depended on membership in the League of Nations, on its alliance with France, on the Little Entente (with Czechoslovakia and Rumania) designed to check Hungarian revisionism, and on the Balkan Entente (with Rumania, Turkey, and Greece) directed against Bulgarian and Italian ambitions.

This system of alliances provided Yugoslavia with a sense of security, until Mussolini's attack on Ethiopia revealed the weakness of the League of Nations and Hitler's reoccupation of the Rhineland, that of Great Britain and France. At this point, the whole international orientation of Yugoslavia had to be reassessed. Stojadinović mistrusted the *Front Populaire* government in France which favored the restoration of the Hapsburgs in Austria and sought accommodation with Moscow, the capital of world communism. More importantly, the alliance with France, intended as an insurance against Italian aggression, appeared inadequate in view of the formation of the Axis. As Germany asserted its role in Europe, Berlin, rather than far-away Paris, came to be viewed as the best protector of Yugoslavia against Mussolini's encroachments.

Hitler exploited this situation well by offering Stojadinović his support in dealings with Italy, along with important commercial concessions, in exchange for the loosening of Yugoslavia's ties with France. He kept his word by advising Mussolini to come to terms with Belgrade. Mussolini, who was weakened by the Ethiopian war and involvement in the Spanish civil war, and who expected the imminent seizure of Austria by Germany, was also inclined to straighten out Italy's relations with Yugoslavia. In tough negotiations in Rome, the Yugoslav delegation secured considerable benefits, one of them being the cessation of the Italian support to the Ustaše movement. The agreement was formalized in the Pact of Friendship, signed in March 1937. Its further benefits for Yugoslavia included a considerable lessening of tension with another unfriendly neighbor, Hungary; a treaty normalizing relations with Bulgaria was concluded even earlier, thanks again to Hitler's intervention with the Sofia government.

As seen from Belgrade, these developments were highly beneficial. By eliminating external threats, Yugoslavia seemed to have gained much needed time. The understanding with Italy, in addition to other advantages, was expected to offset the effects of the growing involvement of Yugoslavia in the German economic sphere. The two dictators, in spite of their alliance, were in active competition with each other, and a policy based on playing one mighty neighbor against another (which always has had an irresistible attraction for weak nations) appeared as the most sensible one.

The complicated diplomatic maneuvers which marked the new course in Yugoslavia's foreign policy were ably executed by Stojadinović with Prince Paul's blessing. They evoked indignation in France and Czechoslovakia, where they were interpreted as Yugoslavia's drift toward the Axis. But in view of the internal weakness of France and of Czechoslovakia's vanishing hopes for Soviet support against Germany, such sentiments could be disregarded in Belgrade. Of greater importance was the domestic reaction. Most Croats (and Slovenes) bitterly resented the rapprochement with Italy, which held part of the "historical" Croatian lands and mistreated its Slovene minority, while many influential Serbs remained resolutely Francophile.

Prince Paul was aware of the unpopularity of his course but to him, Yugoslavia's options appeared limited. He saw that the Western powers themselves had been actively seeking closer relations with Italy. They could not offer any help for Yugoslavia's catastrophically depressed economy at a time when Germany was willing to buy the lion's share of Yugoslavia's exports. Prince Paul also believed that the issue of democracies vs. dictatorships, so burning elsewhere, had limited meaning in the Yugoslav kingdom, where only communists and intellectuals were excited over the Spanish civil war and the Nazi-fascist ascendancy in general. Given the extreme diversity of conflicting cross-currents in the country, he could not satisfy any one group without alienating others. As he saw it, non-involvement in European conflicts was crucial if he were to hope to gain enough time to allow the Yugoslavs to evolve into one nation. All other considerations appeared to him decidedly secondary.

"Listening Post" in Belgrade

The United States legation in Yugoslavia was not expected to follow the intricacies of the country's internal politics: in 1937, those were of no concern to anybody in the State Department. Almost the same could be said about Yugoslavia's foreign policies, which were in no way, directly or indirectly, related to the recognizable objectives of the United States. There were no officials in the Division of European Affairs who knew or cared enough about the Balkans to appreciate the nuances of shifting trends in the interrelationships among the countries of the region. Reports from the field, some lucid, but for the most part superficial, were dutifully filed away by the appropriate desk officers who rarely attempted to attract the attention of senior officials to information the significance of which they themselves were unable to evaluate. Months, and sometimes years passed without a single Department message to the legation in Belgrade requesting specific information related to a particular episode or a comprehensive analysis of the situation as a whole.

Even if such requests had been forthcoming, the legation would hardly have been able to satisfy the Department's curiosity. The staff consisted of one minister, one secretary-of-embassy, and a part-time military attaché who "covered" several Balkan countries simultaneously. There was one American clerk-stenographer and three or four locally-hired interpreters and receptionists. In addition, three officers ran the consulate in Belgrade and two ran the consulate in Zagreb, Croatia's capital. This staff, however, was sufficient to attend to American interests in Yugoslavia which, in 1937, did not amount to much. During that year the United States imported six million dollars worth of Yugoslav goods, mainly crude copper and opium, and sold to Yugoslav importers cotton and other commodities worth about the same amount. To expand trade between the two countries was impossible, much as the Yugoslavs wished it: the country was in default in its payments of its war debts ($62 million) and thus was barred from obtaining credit in America; its own currency reserves were microscopic.

As the annual consular report of March 28, 1938, indicated, there were some 350 naturalized Americans of Yugoslav descent living in the country, but they rarely contacted the legation. There were no American religious missions, hospitals, schools, or colleges in Yugoslavia, and not a single American ship had dropped anchor in a Yugoslav harbor in the course of the year. The two-way correspondence with the State Department dealt with opium crops, the issuance of passports to Yugoslavs claiming American citizenship, and visas granted to occasional businessmen desirous of visiting the United States. Beyond that there was only the task of political reporting which was the responsibility of the minister himself; it consisted mainly of summaries of his talks with government officials and members of the diplomatic corps as well as extracts from the local press. More often than not, the minister's reports were superficial: even if he were an expert on Yugoslav economics and politics—which was not the case—he had to keep in mind the level of expertise in the State Department and predigest his information accordingly.

Arthur Bliss Lane had no intention of setting the world afire. Belgrade was to him just another post in his career where he expected to perform his duties competently and to the satisfaction of the State Department without venturing into undue initiatives. He transmitted his information as he obtained it without attempting to reflect upon it or to evaluate it. Although he knew that his reports did not stir up much interest in Washington, he still recorded everything which appeared significant in the local context. He probably believed that his reporting was objective, although anyone leafing through his dispatches in later years could see that he often colored them with his own opinions. Such coloration was not noticeable at the time, however, because those who read Lane's dispatches usually shared the minister's general outlook.

Lane was a man of strong convictions. Much as he strove for objectivity, it was all but inevitable that his reports from Belgrade reflected the great ideological debate which was then developing in the United States. He accepted his country's continuing isolationism and his government's firm desire not to become involved in messy situations abroad. An incurable moralist of the old school, he also felt a compelling need to pass judgment on the acts of other governments. The "international lawlessness" displayed by Italy in Ethiopia and the Axis intervention in the Spanish civil war, for example, were to be condemned. Since the Axis powers were "evil," truly "good" nations were expected to oppose them. If they did not, then something was wrong with their governments or rulers. Thus, on January 25, 1938, Lane informed the Department that "Yugoslavia is veering more and more towards the Rome-Berlin Axis," attributing this unwholesome course to "the hatred which Prince Paul has for the Soviet government." In Lane's uncharitable judgment, Prince Paul was also drawn to Italy "by sentimental ties as well as by the possibility of his succeeding to large properties in Florence and Rome belonging to his aunt,

Princess Abemelik, née Princess Demidoff." Lane saw Prime Minister Stojadinović as a political opportunist "who is out to feather his own nest"; since he saw no virtue in opportunism, he automatically assumed that Stojadinović was "highly unpopular" in Yugoslavia.

Lane made other assumptions not rooted in reality. For instance, in evaluating the public mood he tended to equate "the Yugoslav people" with the Serbs. He recognized the existence of the Slovenes' and Croats' "complaints against the Serbs because of Serbian insistence on controlling their affairs from Belgrade," but, like so many other observers, he greatly underestimated the degree of the Croats' bitterness. During his first year in Belgrade, Lane sincerely believed that "the Yugoslavs"—not merely the Serbs—had genuine affection for France and Czechoslovakia as well as dislike for Germany. At the same time he overestimated the capacity of the public to influence the government. He learned that communism was regarded as a serious issue in Yugoslavia, but felt that it was "fomented for political reasons" and was in fact of negligible importance.[1] In the Austrian crisis of March 1938, which ended in its absorption by Germany, "the Yugoslav people" seemed to Lane to be wholly on the side of Austria, although there was little evidence to support this assumption.

In most of the American "listening posts" in Europe, a newly appointed envoy had to go through a period of breaking in, the length of which depended on his intellectual curiosity and his capacity for understanding unfamiliar environments and detecting basic trends beneath the known and the obvious. His "briefings" in the State Department—on those occasions when they took place—consisted mainly of his leafing through a pile of old cables and of a few conferences with senior officials. During these conferences, the minister-designate would have explained to him the interests of the United States (if any) in the country of designation and would be admonished not to become involved in situations which could result in embarrass-

---

1. Lane to Welles, March 9, 1938. In this he was perhaps technically correct: the actual membership in the communist organizations at that time barely exceeded 10,000. But the police records listed as communists perhaps 10 to 15 times that number, including all leftist elements under this listing. See Ivan Avakumovic, *History of the Communist Party of Yugoslavia* (The Aberdeen University Press, 1964), Vol. I, 185-86.

ment for the United States or in an unwelcome extension of its commitments. Beyond that, he had no sources of advance knowledge; serious scholarly books—if they existed at all—were not customarily present on his night table. Having arrived at his post, he could rarely borrow of his predecessor's knowledge because the predecessor had usually been gone for some time, and the chargé d'affaires was of little help because he himself had not personally been involved in the gathering of information. Hence, by and large, the minister was left to his own devices, starting from scratch and relying for his learning on the expansion of personal contacts and other local sources of information. This appeared quite adequate for the needs of the time.

This routine was all too familiar to Arthur Bliss Lane. He had a fair idea that the United States had no particular policy in regard to Yugoslavia. He was satisfied that his new post was more significant than the previous one; at least things were happening here. This largest Balkan country was of definite interest to several great European powers; the local diplomatic corps was more numerous and the caliber of the diplomats higher than in Riga. On the local diplomatic ladder, Lane ranked below most of his counterparts: the ministers of France, Great Britain, Italy, Germany, Czechoslovakia, Rumania, even Poland, Greece, and Bulgaria played a much larger role in the Yugoslav capital, and this perhaps was not easy to accept for Lane, who had been used to being in the spotlight during his Latin American experience. Nevertheless, he was readily listened to; everybody was aware that, although inactive in European affairs, the United States was after all a major world power. Besides, Lane soon acquired considerable prominence due to the very personal relationship he established with the regent, Prince Paul.

Lane was a sociable man. He was an engaging conversationalist, and had an unlimited supply of jokes which he told with great skill on appropriate occasions. He had a lively interest in, and a keen understanding of, human nature. Prince Paul soon discovered that he had quite a lot in common with the American minister. Both of them loved Italy; Mrs. Lane could discuss endlessly her native Florence's great artistic treasures. Both Prince Paul and Lane appreciated fine food and rare wines, and before long they instituted rotating stag dinners, once every two months, in which they were joined by Baron Pierre Coche, counselor of the French legation. Each man could invite one guest, and the hosts proudly displayed the accomplishments of their respective chefs and prized specimens from their wine cellars. These were strictly informal social affairs during which no serious matters were discussed, but they led to a mutual understanding and liking between the ruler of Yugoslavia and the American envoy, facilitated by the fact—very much appreciated by Prince Paul—that Lane was one of the very few diplomats in the capital who did not attempt to influence the Yugoslav government's policies one way or another.

Yugoslavia Opts for Neutrality

The crisis of 1938—the Anschluss of Austria and the dismemberment of Czechoslovakia at Munich—stimulated further reorientation of Yugoslavia's foreign policies. The Stojadinović government regarded these events as manifestations of the progressive weakening of the Western democracies and the strengthening of the Axis. Along with the other Balkan governments, the Yugoslavs felt that the preservation of European equilibruim was the responsibility of the great powers and that the Balkan states could only try to adjust to the changing international situation. The emergence of Germany as one of Yugoslavia's neighbors had sharply reduced the opportunity for France and Great Britain to exercise effective influence in Belgrade. Having failed to stand up to Hitler themselves, they could hardly expect their weak Balkan allies to act as bulwarks against further German ambitions.

When the crisis over Czechoslovakia reached its peak, Yugoslavia's only concern was not to become involved, under the terms of the Little Entente, in a military conflict. The Yugoslav government's attitude, as summarized by Lane in a message to the Secretary of State on September 22, was that "if the Czechs are wise they will not only cede to Germany the Sudeten region but to Hungary and Poland those areas populated by the Magyars and Poles, and thus free themselves from all extraneous hostile elements, consolidate their position politically and economically, and thus attain greater international stat-

ure." Aware of Roosevelt's preoccupation with peace, Lane
reported to him personally the gist of an interview with Prince
Paul, stressing that because of the latter's "genuine pacifism
he will take steps not only to prevent Yugoslavia being involved in the war, but also to prevent other countries from
being involved." Since in the summer of 1938, from the official
American point of view, the main threat to peace was posed by
France and its allies, rather than by Hitler who appeared to be
merely trying to throw off the shackles of Versailles and to
unify the German people, Lane saw further assurances of Yugoslavia's neutrality in Stojadinović's "political opportunism."
Lane was convinced that the prime minister, "who does not
desire to lose the present excellent relations which he has with
Germany, should likewise contribute to the inaction of Yugoslavia." On the whole, Lane was optimistic regarding the
maintenance of peace. "I base this optimism," wrote Lane,
"principally on my belief that none of the great Western powers desires war and that in case of Germany, while every
measure short of war may be taken to achieve results, Hitler
will not risk his position, which would be the case should
Germany become involved in hostilities." This opinion, added
Lane, was confirmed by a German general with whom he had
had a conversation recently.

Lane's perception of Yugoslavia's position was flawless. The
government's determination not to become involved in the
conflict was well reasoned. Unknown to Lane, it was addition-
ally strengthened by the irritation of Stojadinović with France
and Czechoslavakia's meddling in Yugoslavia's internal politics
by giving financial support and moral encouragement to Serbian groups in opposition to the government, proof of which
the Germans obligingly furnished to Belgrade.[2]

The Munich crisis aroused great indignation in the United
States; the denunciations of Hitler and his regime were loud
and bitter. But only a few Americans suggested that the United
States do something practical about it. President Roosevelt for
a few days toyed with the idea of offering to arbitrate the
German-Czechoslovak dispute but then dropped it for fear of

---

2. J.B. Hoptner, *Yugoslavia in Crisis, 1934-1941* (New York: Columbia University Press, 1962), 111 ff.

undesirable domestic effects. On September 26 he appealed to Hitler, Beneš, Chamberlain, and Daladier, urging them to resolve their differences through peaceful negotiations. The next day the State Department sent a circular telegram to American envoys abroad instructing them to call "without delay" on the minister of foreign affairs and "express the opinion of this government that the situation in Europe is so critical, and the consequences of war would be so disastrous, that no step should be overlooked or omitted that might possibly contribute to the maintenance of peace." The envoys were told to ask the governments to which they were accredited to send "at once" appropriate appeals to Hitler, Beneš, Chamberlain, and Daladier. The State Department hoped that "the cumulative effect of such an expression of opinion might possibly, even at this late date, influence the course of events and contribute to the preservation of peace in Europe."

This optimistic view was reflected in the October 3, 1938, radio address by Sumner Welles in which he expressed con-.viction that the Munich settlement presented the best opportunity during the past two decades to establish a new world order based upon justice and upon law. But in London, Winston Churchill sharply attacked Chamberlain's policy of appeasement. In his speech in the House of Commons on October 5 he declared: "It must now be accepted that all the countries of Central and Eastern Europe will make the best terms they can with the triumphant Nazi power. The system of alliances on which France has relied for her safety has been swept away, and I can see no means by which it can be reconstituted."

Nobody in Belgrade disagreed. The officials sighed with relief when the Czechoslovak crisis ended without activating the Little Entente. The death of this alliance merely meant the end of one undesirable and burdensome commitment to Yugoslavia. The need for an even greater accommodation with the Axis became self-evident.

Almost imperceptibly, the decline of the political influence of France and Great Britian in European affairs affected the position of the American legation in Belgrade. On October 10, 1938, President Roosevelt wrote to Lane saying that he followed developments in southeastern Europe with close attention. "It seems to me," he wrote, "that Belgrade is now a key post in the European situation, as the expansion of Germany may very well come into conflict with Italian interests in Yugoslavia. Certainly the Yugoslav government will have to pursue a cautious foreign policy that will tax its ingenuity to the utmost."

Although Lane felt that this assessment of the impending German-Italian clash was perhaps excessively hopeful, he was flattered. The president's letter indicated that he was remembered in Washington. At the first opportunity, he conveyed to Prince Paul Roosevelt's appreciation of his sincerity in promoting peace and the warnings of stormy days ahead. To the beleaguered prince, who had been criticized in the West for his policy and who was extremely uneasy over the prospect of being abandoned by old friends because of it, this was a welcome gesture.

Yugoslavia in Search of Neutrality

In December 1938 Arthur Bliss Lane went on a prolonged visit to the United States. He spent some time in Washington, exchanging views with State Department officials, trying to take stock of the country's mood, and concluded that America was more than ever determined to follow a policy of non-intervention in European affairs. His parting instructions were to do whatever he could to foster the preservation of peace in the Balkans. This task appeared easy: the Yugoslav government had been determined to pursue a neutral course in its foreign policy anyway. Other developments, however, soon threatened the stability of Yugoslavia. When Lane returned to his post early in February 1939, he discovered that a brewing crisis in the government, which had been known but to a few initiated men, had suddenly come to a head.

Prince Paul had for some time watched with apprehension the growing boldness of Prime Minister Stojadinović who had been trying to cast himself in the role of a Yugoslav Führer through the expansion of his personal following, organized along the all too familiar line of the fascists. Capitalizing on his successful dealings with Italy and Germany, he had been getting increasingly close to both governments, cultivating particularly warm relations with Mussolini's foreign minister, Count Galeazzo Ciano, and not always keeping Prince Paul informed about the contents of his informal negotiations. Prince Paul, who had his private sources of information, learned that Stojadinović had secretly endorsed Italian plans for the annexation of Albania (in exchange for a cut in the spoils) and had promised to take Yugoslavia out of the League of Nations and join the Axis in the Anti-Comintern Pact. In addition, and perhaps more importantly, he concluded that Stojadinović was incapable of finding a solution to the perennial Serb-Croat conflict, a solution which, particularly after the Anschluss, he regarded as crucial for the country. Having reached a decision to get rid of his prime minister but realizing the dangers involved in a major governmental shake-up, Prince Paul proceeded to form a plot in which several key members of the cabinet took part. Soon after the election of December, 1938, which showed a heavy gain for the United Opposition, the plotting ministers forced a cabinet crisis by resigning en masse. Prince Paul then dismissed Stojadinović and asked Dragiša Cvetković, former minister of social policy who was known for his good relations with the Croatian leadership, to form a government. The Führer-to-be found himself without a job.[3]

The downfall of Stojadinović caused alarm in Berlin and Rome. Italy resumed support of the Ustaše separatists, and in April, 1939, proceeded with the occupation of Albania. Yugoslavia, however, did not abandon its precarious course. Cincar-Marković, the new foreign minister, visited Rome and promised Ciano not to align Yugoslavia with any combination of the anti-Axis states. At the same time, in an attempt to counterbalance the cooling of relations with Italy, Prince Paul went on a state visit to Berlin. Hitler, who turned the occasion into a spectacular demonstration of solidarity between the two countries, confronted Prince Paul with a request to join the Anti-Comintern Pact and to leave the League of Nations. This was much more than Prince Paul was prepared to do, and he avoided any commitments. His visit to England in July 1939 further aroused Hitler's displeasure. In August, shortly before

---

3. For a while, Stojadinović continued to hope that a favorable turn of events would return him to power. His intrigues, however, led to his arrest in April, 1940, and to his eventual banishment in March, 1941.

the conclusion of the Nazi-Soviet Pact, Ribbentrop expressed hope to Ciano "that Italy will wish to take advantage of the Polish affair to settle its account with Yugoslavia in Croatia and Dalmatia."[4]

In the summer of 1939 the Yugoslav government still tried to counter-balance its growing involvement with the Axis by retaining its ties with the West. It shipped its gold reserve to England and the United States for safekeeping. It made a determined effort to rearm the Yugoslav army with the help of the British and the Americans. But the British held hopes — which Prince Paul considered utterly unrealistic — of splitting the Axis by wooing Italy, the country which represented for Yugoslavia a far greater danger than Germany, and did not want to become involved with Yugoslavia. Since Yugoslav efforts to establish commercial links with the United States were equally fruitless, Belgrade was forced to turn for arms to Berlin, mortgaging a large part of Yugoslavia's output of strategic minerals in exchange for some modern weapons and aircraft.[5]

Yet if he had ever hoped to secure Yugoslavia's independence through building up a stronger and more up-to-date army, Prince Paul had not put his heart into it. He realized that any such effort, to be successful, needed not only much greater resources than the country possessed but also required a complete re-education and reorganization of the officer corps, a program which would require long years of guaranteed peace and much more forceful leadership than he could provide. In London he melancholically told Lord Halifax that in the forthcoming war Yugoslavia would be able to withstand the pressure of the Axis only if the British defeated Italy quickly and decisively. In any case, the prince regent informed the British, the only sensible policy for Yugoslavia would be

---

4. *Ciano's Diplomatic Papers* (London, 1948), 298. This offer — later withdrawn — was probably made to make the prospect of a European war more palatable to Mussolini. But the horrified Duce ordered a thorough review of Italy's military stature, which revealed that the Italian army was totally unprepared to wage war of any kind. See Macartney & Palmer. *Independent Eastern Europe*, 405-408, and F.W. Deakin, *The Brutal Friendship* (New York: Harper, 1962), pp. 11-13. Cf. GFP, D, VII, 42.

5. GFP, D, VI, 860-862. This secret agreement was implemented with some delay, and Yugoslavia received, on credit terms, the much-needed equipment. Cf. FR, 1939, 875 ff.

that of neutrality: its backwardness and, above all, its great internal tensions, stood in the way of its becoming a dynamic and vigorous nation.

The domestic situation in Yugoslavia seemed to take an important turn for the better in August when Prime Minister Cvetković, after several months of laborious negotiations, reached a comprehensive agreement with Maček, leader of the Croatian Peasant Party. By the terms of the *Sporazum*, Croatia was recreated as an autonomous province of the kingdom with a greater degree of self-rule than the Croats had known for a long time. For the first time in twenty years a feeling of trust appeared to have been established between Zagreb and Belgrade; Maček, with several of his colleagues, finally entered the Yugoslav government.

Amidst the growing tension in Europe, it was more and more difficult for Arthur Bliss Lane to retain optimism. After Munich, he became convinced that war was inevitable and that Poland would be the next victim of Hitler's aggression. Moreover, he feared that in one way or another Yugoslavia would also be involved, so much so that he several times brought to the Department's attention the need to work out contingency plans for the evacuation of Americans living in Yugoslavia.[6]

The War

The Nazi-Soviet Pact that shook the world late in August 1939 did not surprise Lane. He had always discounted the generally assumed ideological irreconcilability of the two totalitarian regimes. When, back in 1936, he was first advised of the possibility of a Nazi-Soviet rapprochement,[7] he gave the idea

6. A lively and informative description of the Belgrade scene after Munich is contained in chapters 8 and 9 of C.L. Sulzberger's volume, *A Long Row of Candles* (New York: Macmillan, 1969). As U.P. and *New York Times* correspondent, Sulzberger first visited Yugoslavia in 1938, fell in love with the Balkans, and stayed there until the Germans had conquered the peninsula.

7. Ferdinand L. Mayer, then chargé d'affaires in Berlin, wrote Lane on August 8, 1936, that he had received information coming from "an excellent source" that "there was something stirring toward an improvement in German-Soviet relations" both in Moscow and in Berlin. "Whether this is with the approbation of Hitler," wrote Mayer, "is not known, although my informant feels that he must be aware of it, as the people could hardly have gone so far as he feels they have gone without Hitler's knowledge." Mayer was not alone in recording this rumor. On Aug. 14, 1936, Prentice B. Gilbert,

serious attention. In a personal letter to Dunn, then special assistant to Secretary Hull, he wrote on September 5:

> In discussing the alternative to the visible trend in European affairs, the fantastic one of a German rapprochement with Russia must not be left out. You will remember that I have indicated from time to time the strong traditional background of German-Russian friendship and the complementary character of the economies of the two countries. "Everything is so foolish in Europe," as Hugh Gibson used to say, that I would not be greatly shocked if one of these days we find Hitler executing a remarkable *volte-face* and making arrangements with the Soviet. . . . Lending a certain indirect support to this crazy idea is the difficulty we have in judging this latest purge by Stalin. If the latter wants to maintain communism in all its brightness, why should he snuff out the very Founders of the Order in this degrading fashion? Is it perhaps rather to clear away the props of communist ideology for a radically different "conservative" policy?

Characteristically, Lane hesitated to condemn the Soviets for executing the deal with Hitler. This hesitation was quite common among liberal-minded men of the West who tended to blame Anglo-French "appeasers" of Hitler for driving Stalin into Hitler's arms. Lane also felt that even after having assumed a position of friendly neutrality toward Germany, Russia remained a factor of relative stability in Europe. While it did not serve any more as a deterrent to Hitler's aggressive plans and while its anti-fascist image became somewhat tarnished, it still retained a posture of detachment and independence not to be totally discounted. Thus Lane, on August 23, 1939, unhappily reported to the Department that Prince Paul was "upset by the Nazi-Soviet Pact which is not surprising in view of his professed hatred for Soviets because of his close ties with England." Almost a month later, on September 21, he again

---

American Consul in Geneva, obtained a copy of a report "from a German source associated with high governmental circles in Berlin" that efforts were being made to diminish the tension between Germany and Russia and that "the beginning of official communications is imminent." In Soviet circles in Berlin, added Gilbert, "the utmost discretion is shown," as manifested by the transfer to the Soviet embassy in Stockholm of all intelligence operations against the Baltic states. That the negotiations were in fact taking place has been confirmed since by the available German documents and the testimony of some high-ranking Soviet defectors.

reminded Secretary Hull that Prince Paul disliked the Soviet regime "through his relationship to the imperial Russian family" and that Yugoslavia had never recognized the Soviet government "largely due to Prince Paul's personal influence." Lane granted that Prince Paul was "a confirmed pacifist" who "realized that the future of the Yugoslav state depended on maintaining friendly relations with all its neighbors"—which included Germany—and probably was right in believing that a collective security pact with Russia, "a nation thousands of miles away," could not serve any useful purpose. But until the very end of his stay in Belgrade, Lane was reluctant to abandon the idea that a more far-sighted diplomacy of the democracies would have required them to take the Soviet Union as a positive element in the European equilibrium more seriously.

Viewing the internal Yugoslav situation, Lane was not greatly impressed by the *Sporazum* between the central government and the Croats. From his experience in Latin America, he was familiar with politicians' tendency to gloss over irreconcilable conflicts between contending factions. In particular, he did not see how the *Sporazum* could improve Yugoslavia's external position. To the Department he reported on September 17 that "regardless of the national political unity, the present coalition Serb-Croatian government will, because of divergent interests, undoubtedly be greatly handicapped in formulating a definite and consistent foreign policy, in functioning efficiently and in agreeing on a logical military policy in the event of foreign attack." He concurred with the conclusion of his military attaché, Colonel Louis L. Fortier, that such a policy would mean abandoning Croatia and trying to defend Serbia, something that Lane rated as politically unfeasible. And he expressed a feeling that Yugoslavia's best hope was that Hitler would not invade so long as it kept supplying Germany with its agricultural and mineral products.

Although the defeat of Poland was followed in Europe by a brief period of intensive diplomatic activity, diplomacy seemed to be fading under the impact of cruder means in dealing with international problems. Following the partition of Poland, the Soviets established military bases in the Baltic states, and on November 30, 1939, launched an attack against Finland. The "Winter War," which President Roosevelt called a "dreadful rape of Finland," provoked even more intense indignation in America than Hitler's attack on Poland. The administration imposed a "moral embargo" on exports to the Soviet Union, and many high-ranking officials, including Sumner Welles, favored severing diplomatic relations with Moscow.[8] Although Roosevelt ruled out such a drastic step, Soviet-American relations came very close to the breaking point.

At his post in Belgrade, Arthur Bliss Lane grimly watched signs of the impending German paramountcy in Europe. As for so many other politicians and diplomats who had hoped and predicted that the war would be avoided, the spreading conflagration was for him a proof that his judgment had been faulty. Hitler proved to be much more aggressive than he had looked a mere two years earlier; the dedication to peace of England and France had failed the test of the German attack on Poland; and the Soviet Union had turned out to be less of a pillar of peace than Lane had believed. The European tragedy could not be blamed on the United States, which stood for peace. Nevertheless, Lane could not get rid of a feeling that perhaps his government, through its hands-off attitude, had somehow contributed to the catastrophe. Never quite able to disassociate himself personally from his official function, Lane was becoming increasingly unhappy in Belgrade.

The situation was aggravated by the fact that in spite of the United States' continuing neutrality, the American legation in Belgrade was generally associated with the British, the French, or the Polish, and placed in the camp of the losers. The membership was soon expanded by the inclusion of the Danes, the Norwegians, the Dutch, and the Belgians. The atmosphere became particularly depressing after the collapse of France. From then on, Lane's reports to the Department contained very few references to general political developments in Europe. For a while he turned his attention to the internal affairs of Yugoslavia, an area which had never inspired him and which presented a similarly cheerless picture. But since the minister's duty was to report, he passed along information collected by

---

8. For details, see William L. Langer and S. Everett Gleason, *The Challenge to Isolation*, Chapter IX. This feeling did not translate itself into aid to Finland because the administration, having embarked on an intensive search for peace, was determined to uphold the spirit of the Neutrality Acts.

his staff, including translations from Yugoslav publications.
News was uniformly bad. John J. Meily, Lane's able consul in
Zagreb, kept reporting that anti-Serb agitation among the
Croats was sharply on the increase, eroding the position of the
moderates who followed Vladko Maček. There were recurrent
clashes between warring factions at Zagreb University. The
Croatian communists confused the picture further by joining
forces with the nationalist extremists, and large-scale disturbances erupted at Belgrade University, long a hotbed of leftist
agitation but now also the scene of activities of *Zbor*, a Serbian
ultra-nationalist, anti-Catholic, and pro-German militant youth
organization.

Facing growing discontent on all sides, the Yugoslav government floundered more than ever. In June, hoping to obtain
some room for maneuver vis-à-vis the Axis, it finally established diplomatic relations with the Soviet Union. But the
Soviets continued to live up to the spirit of their pact of friendship with Germany, while in Yugoslavia the appearance of a
large Soviet legation served as a shot in the arm both for the
communists and the pan-Serbian nationalists, who now felt
more free to rock the ship of the Yugoslav state.

The mood in official circles in Belgrade also offered little
ground for optimism. With the fall of France, Prince Paul took
an increasingly fatalistic view of his country's future. He assumed—correctly—that it was not in Germany's interest to
create a front in the Balkans and that Hitler would neither
invade Yugoslavia nor allow Italy to make trouble.[9] But this
was a short-range expectation. Things were too much in flux in
Europe to rule out the possibility that the defeat of Great

---

9. On July 7, 1940, Ciano told Hitler that Mussolini tended "to liquidate the
Yugoslav question" in about a month. Hitler replied that nothing of the kind
should be undertaken at least until England had been defeated, since Italy's
attack on Yugoslavia would set the whole Balkans ablaze, probably provoking Soviet intervention and a Hungarian attack on Rumania, which would
interrupt the steady flow of much needed oil to Germany. See GFP, D, X,
153–154, and *Ciano's Diplomatic Papers*, 377–378. Mussolini, who was not
discouraged easily, insisted on an invasion of Yugoslavia for some time
before retreating in the face of a most forceful and unambiguous Hitler veto.
See *Ciano's Diary* (London, 1947), entry for August 17, 1940. Fretting over
his dependence on Hitler (and envying Hitler's successes), the Duce
finally—again against Berlin's advice—launched a war of his own by attacking Greece on October 27, 1940.

Britain or Hitler's failure to restrain Mussolini could spell Yugoslavia's doom. In order to avoid, or at least to delay, such a turn of events, Prince Paul was prepared to further adjust to the Axis, paying this distasteful price for the salvation of the kingdom.

Arthur Bliss Lane sensed this unheroic disposition of the regent and disapproved. While he understood Yugoslavia's predicament, he could not take a charitable or sympathetic view of its problems any longer. He was too emotionally involved in the drama of the situation to be magnanimous. Prince Paul's many problems were not of his or the United States' making and anyway, there was nothing he could do about them. What troubled Lane more was that for the first time in his career he could not, even in his own mind, decide what course taken by the local government would be most beneficial from the American point of view. President Roosevelt's pronouncements in the summer of 1940 were no guide: they were determined by the imperatives of the election campaign and these dictated repeated vows to stay out of the war and to do everything possible to prevent the spread of the conflict to new areas.

Were these pronouncements sincere? If so, the essentially neutral policy chosen for Yugoslavia by Prince Paul was in the American interest. On the other hand, neutrality meant accommodation with Germany, and Lane could not visualize how this would benefit the United States. In response to his attempts to obtain elucidation from the State Department he received meaningless generalities. To his cable of May 13, requesting the president's authorization to officially commend Prince Paul for his "earnest efforts to maintain peace," Hull promptly replied by telling him to express Roosevelt's appreciation of "efforts made by all political leaders who are endeavoring to maintain peace." One week later, however, under the impact of the German invasion of France, the secretary of state seemed to have abandoned all hope for maintaining peace, or even for localizing the war. After ignoring for months Lane's earlier requests for instructions as to what the legation should do in the event of an enemy invasion of Yugoslavia, Hull suddenly took the initiative. In a long cable on May 20, he instructed Lane that in such a case the minister was to remain in Belgrade

"for the protection of American interests," while his senior
secretary at the legation was to follow the Yugoslav government wherever the latter went. "You are accordingly authorized," wrote Hull, "if Belgrade is occupied by foreign military
forces, to establish contact with the military authorities of the
occupying country and to use your good offices in alleviating
the situation as far as may be practicable. . . The Department
leaves to your discretion and judgment," added Hull, "the
ways of meeting various contingencies, as it is obviously impossible at this time to give specific instructions in this regard."[10]

A sense of considerable urgency and alarm enveloped the
American legation. Lane reported on May 22 that "the news of
the Allied military reverses has had a very depressing affect on
official and public opinion here. . .The General Staff is in a
state of demoralized dejection and disgust over the apparent
defeat of the French army which has always been considered
here as the ideal. . .Yugoslav officials no longer hide their apprehension that the reported debacle in France and Belgium
will merely accelerate the arrival of German troops here. . .For
the first time, the public at large, as well as the officials, felt
that grave danger to Yugoslavia is posed by Germany, and
many diplomats have applied for visas to send away their fami-
lies." He ended this dispatch on a pessimistic note: "Until now
we have been of the opinion that Yugoslavia would resist an
invasion. We are now in doubt, however, in view of the feeling
indicated above. . .whether any effective resistance will be
made." And Lane apologized that if the tenor of his reports
changed from day to day, "it is merely because the morale of
the people and the government changes, chiefly due to developments on the Western front."

As France was nearing the end of its agony, Lane concluded
that the time had arrived to forget about peace and perhaps

---

10. There was curious inconsistency in Hull's instructions: at about the same
time he ordered Ambassador Bullitt in Paris to follow the French government which started preparing for evacuation on May 14. Always independent, Bullitt disobeyed, staying behind and contributing substantially
to the tacit German-French agreement to avoid street battles in Paris. Hull's
indignation notwithstanding, there was little Bullitt could have accomplished dealing with the fleeing French government. See Robert Murphy,
Diplomat Among Warriors, chapters 3 and 4.

start playing for higher stakes. On the assumption that the efforts to salvage the Balkans from German domination were doomed anyway, he proposed a course of action which at that time must have appeared to his superiors in Washington nothing short of radical but which within a few months was destined to become a cornerstone of Roosevelt's policy in the region. On June 6, 1940, Lane suggested in a cable to Hull that "if it is true . . . that it is in the interest of the Axis Powers and the Soviet Union—the quasi-ally of Germany—to keep peace in the Balkans, the corollary suggests itself . . . that it is in the interests of the Allies to disturb that peace thus diverting Italian and German forces from other parts of the Mediterranean." This suggestion, for which Lane cautiously gave the credit to his military attaché, Colonel Louis L. Fortier, drew at that time no response from the State Department.

The drastic change in the strategic picture in the Balkans brought about by the German victories in the West was further accentuated by a new outburst of Soviet aggressiveness. The Soviet annexation of the Baltic states and Bessarabia, and the Second Vienna Award by which Rumania—Yugoslavia's closest ally—lost a large part of its territory to Hungary and Bulgaria, showed that the Balkan region had become an arena of the Great Powers' maneuverings. Although Moscow outwardly continued to cooperate loyally with Berlin, there were signs of a certain tension in Soviet-German relations. This tension was duly registered in Belgrade, injecting a note of hope into the otherwise gloomy picture. In July, Prince Paul told Lane that he had received a report from his extremely capable military attaché in Berlin that the over 40 German divisions which had been concentrated in Austria were intended for possible use against Russia. In reporting this sensational news, however, Lane skeptically commented in his July 19 cable to Hull and Welles that the Yugoslavs were "extremely naive" in everything concerning the Soviets. As an example he cited the speculations in Belgrade that the Soviets were negotiating with Bulgaria over military bases in Varna and Burgas, and that they "intend to push through Rumania and Bulgaria through diplomatic and military means to obtain control of the straits and possibly to seize Istanbul" and Prince Paul's conviction that Rumania "could take no other course than to follow German

dictates." These speculations were, of course, well-founded—
as was Prince Paul's conviction—another proof that leaders of
smaller nations often possess sensitivity denied to those of
great powers.

Rumors and speculations aside, there was little in the way of
meaningful information Lane could pass on to Washington.
The legation's usefulness as a "listening post" was greatly
reduced as a result of German victories. The internal developments in the countries dominated or occupied by the Axis
were of no interest to the State Department, and, besides, were
almost impossible to follow from Belgrade because of the
breakdown of communications. A number of legations in Belgrade closed down or greatly reduced their operations; of all
friendly missions, only the British remained active. But Lane
had never been close to Ronald Ian Campbell, the minister (or,
for that matter, to his predecessor, Ronald Hugh Campbell)
and, besides, he assumed that there was nothing that he could
learn from the British in Belgrade that the Department could
not find out directly from London. There was one bit of original
information which Lane obtained and hastened to report to
Welles: Prince Paul had asked to help out in a transfer to the
United States of some of his personal funds. Lane obliged
(utilizing for this purpose his personal contacts at the Chase
National Bank in New York), but in a private letter to the
Assistant Secretary he stressed that on the basis of his experience in Latin America, he considered this transaction "extremely significant."

With most of his sources of information dried out, Lane was
confined to the rather boring routine of following local developments utterly without significance for the United States.
Mindful of the morale problem at the legation, however, he
took pains not to betray his own depressed state of mind. He
scrupulously appeared at the office every morning, making sure
that everybody was at his post, that the incoming coded messages—mostly repeats of the cables sent to the Department
from other capitals of Central and Southeastern Europe—were
prompty decoded. This was a laborious job in which all members of the legation, including Lane himself, participated. The
outgoing mail and telegrams had to be similarly taken care of,
the few visitors had to be received, and a few calls on government officials were made from time to time.

For a while, Lane tried to focus his attention on economic matters. He had always considered the protection of American commercial interests an integral part of diplomatic function. In Belgrade, he went to considerable lengths in trying to make the Yugoslav government pay its debt to the United States and permit repatriation of the earnings of the few American companies operating in the country. And although he knew that Yugoslavia's currency reserves were extremely limited, he made repeated attempts to drum up some orders for American industry.

The Yugoslav government was interested in purchasing some trucks and aircraft for its armed forces — on credit if possible, for cash, if necessary — to supplement the rather meager supply of such equipment which it could obtain from Germany. Expecting that Yugoslavia would preserve its neutrality, Lane recommended that the State Department approve these sales. Eventually permission was given to sell Yugoslavia one thousand trucks, to be paid for in cash, but the request for aircraft was turned down. Lane's attempts to talk the Yugoslavs into buying other American goods were unrewarding and probably little appreciated by the Department, which in the end advised Lane to stop pressuring Belgrade officials into trade concessions.[11]

All the unpleasant and depressing events of that summer and fall noticeably affected Minister Lane's personality and his ways of dealing with the people around him. He was always attentive to the personal needs of his staff, securing for them housing, supplies, or favorable rates of exchange. He also took seriously his role as principal tutor and advisor of the younger members of the legation, introducing them to the techniques and art of diplomacy. But at the same time he was a strict disciplinarian with little patience for poor performance or errors in judgment, tolerating no arguments and demanding both

---

11. Hull to Lane, October 8, 1940. With his usual aggressiveness Lane tried to obtain for the Standard Oil Company of New Jersey a concession for the exploration of oil in Yugoslavia, but here he ran into powerful competition: the Germans, who had infinitely greater influence in Belgrade, were anxious to expand their oil resources and easily succeeded in "outbidding" the Americans. Lane's reports to the Secretary of State of October 25 and November 2, 1940, and of February 12, 1941, are quite illuminating on the fashion in which American oilmen dealt with Yugoslav officials.

loyalty and obedience from senior members of his staff. Now, with so many adverse developments taking place, he grew irritable and more impatient; even minor manifestations of ineptitude could provoke his sarcastic remarks and reprimands. Inevitably, the cohesiveness of the tiny American colony suffered, and there was considerable concern in the legation every time the minister sent periodic efficiency reports to the Department.

This concern was not entirely unjustified. Although Lane doubtless meant to be fair, he did not lavish praise on everybody, and in one instance he virtually destroyed the career of his senior aide, Robert P. Joyce, a young and capable foreign service officer, for what he regarded as a lack of personal loyalty and because of an incident which, at least in retrospect, appears as a rather insignificant indiscretion in the performance of Joyce's duties. Having learned that Joyce "leaked" some confidential information to C. L. Sulzberger, the *New York Times* Balkan correspondent, Lane requested Secretary Hull to recall Joyce from Belgrade forthwith. The Secretary complied, but the step was so unusual that he dispatched Inspector Avra M. Warren to investigate the case. In the end, the Department backed the head of mission, perhaps more because tradition in the foreign service required that the Number One and Number Two men in a legation be at all times fully compatible, than on any other grounds. But among those who were familiar with the particulars of the episode, both in Belgrade and in Washington, the feeling persisted for a long time that the punishment of Joyce was unnecessarily severe.

Lane's relative aloofness at the office did not mean that he withdrew into total seclusion. It was true that as outside official and semi-official contacts became less important for the purpose of political reporting, Lane's participation in Belgrade's social life considerably dwindled. Nevertheless, he retained warm personal relations with a circle of friends in whose company he could find a degree of relaxation. He had abandoned tennis some time before and played golf only infrequently and only when somebody insisted on taking him to a golf course. But he still enjoyed weekly poker games — he was a superb poker player — at his residence. These sessions had become a sort of institution and were usually attended by two

or three members of the legation's staff who were closer to
Lane than the rest; by Sulzberger; by George H. Schellens, a
soldier of fortune who had spent years in the Balkans in search
of ways to become rich; and by Francis Smith, a Zagreb-based
American oilman who often visited Belgrade. On occasion, a
visiting American diplomat or a newspaperman (or a news-
paperwoman, such as Dorothy Thompson, Lane's old friend)
would join this group. The game was played at table stakes and
had a great deal of excitement, even if the losses at times were
greater than the players could afford. Yet no matter how late
the game ended or how much liquor was consumed, the next
morning the minister would be in his office, efficient, cool-
headed, exacting, and prepared to handle any matter which
came to his desk.

Lane was not a man who shared his innermost thoughts with
anyone, and nobody around him suspected his deep dissatisfaction with his assignment. Feeling the need to apply his
energy to the accomplishment of tangible goals, and anticipating grave developments in Yugoslavia, he wrote, on July 13,
1940, a letter to Sumner Welles, his highest personal contact in
the Department. He typed it himself and handed it personally
to the diplomatic courier the next time one showed up in
Belgrade. In this letter Lane asked Welles "if a vacancy existed in some post near the United States, to bear me in mind."
He reminded Welles that he had wanted to be transferred for
some time and said that "it is more than ever desirable to make
such a change." To justify his request he advanced reasons,
which, even at the time, sounded odd. He wrote that if German pressure brought former Prime Minister Stojadinović back
to power, his usefulness in Belgrade would be considerably
curtailed because, unlike other foreign envoys in Belgrade, he
steadfastly refused to associate "with the persons of the opposition." Lane concluded that he had reason to believe that
Stojadinović "may resent not only my failure to call on him but
my friendship with Prince Paul as well, Stojadinović's dislike
for the Prince as well as the Prince's contempt for him being
well known."

One month later, Welles replied that he had Lane's request
"very much in mind," but that "it would be very difficult to
find a successor who could do the work you are doing," espe-

cially since "your reports from Belgrade have been so ex-
ceptionally helpful and useful to the Department during these
past months." Welles also pointed out that after the Nazi conquest of Europe, "too many of the American career service
ministers were left without posts."

Flattering as this reply was, it did not lift Lane's spirits.
Moreover, an entirely new development which soon came to
his attention greatly intensified his desire to leave the Balkans.

The Plot

Few weak governments base their foreign policies on more
than a short-term prognosis in times of crisis, and as things
stood in the second half of 1940 the Yugoslav government
concentrated its efforts on avoiding any involvement in the
European war. Once the fear of an imminent invasion abated,
the corollary to this policy became the need to accommodate
Germany. This accommodation had to be limited. Prince Paul's
dislike for the Axis remained deep and intense; his sympathies
were with the British; and he had complex internal factors to
consider. Among the latter were the activities of the passionate
pan-Serbian nationalists who loudly professed love for France
and England and hatred for Germany; of the Croat elements
who toyed with the idea of Croatia's independence under Hitler's protective hand; of the leftist intellectuals and the communists who looked to Russia for guidance and salvation; and the
increasingly questionable loyalty of the military. Prince Paul
still controlled the government, but the ability of the government to control internal developments had yet to be put to a test.

Having once chosen his precarious path, Prince Paul tried to
improve Yugoslavia's position in minor ways. One of his acts
was the conclusion of the Treaty of Friendship with Hungary,
which he negotiated personally with Admiral Horthy, who also
strove to maintain a neutral course for his country against
heavy opposition. At the same time, by establishing diplomatic
and trade relations with the Soviet Union, Prince Paul sought
to make available for Yugoslavia whatever potential benefits
the visible strain in Soviet-German relations could yield. But
he accepted as inevitable the policy of weakness as truly reflecting the country's position. This policy appeared in-

glorious—if not outrightly pathetic—to the Serb patriots and their friends abroad. As Prince Paul saw it, the danger of the moment was not a foreign invasion, but the possible activization of the divergent internal forces whose violent collision could easily produce consequences of utmost gravity for Yugoslavia.

The key to stability lay in the loyalty of the people, and especially the Yugoslav army, to the government and the dynasty. But the army was a traditional preserve of pan-Serbian nationalism steeped in the heroics of World War I, and it regarded with suspicion Prince Paul's efforts to bring the Croats—regarded as traitors—into Yugoslav political life. Prince Paul took these sentiments into account to a great extent. Although from time to time he reshuffled some key officers—in January 1940, for instance, he replaced an ambitious general, Dušan Simović, chief of the Yugoslav General Staff (who had been at odds with War Minister Nedic), by the old and colorless but loyal Kosić—Prince Paul took great care not to aggravate the situation further. Simović was appointed commander of the Yugoslav air force, a post from which he could continue his political activity, even if on a reduced scale. In an effort to placate the Serbian establishment in the army, he never tried to promote Croatian or Slovenian officers to high positions. He accepted the existing military structure, with all its intricate relationships, approving without questioning military budgets and closing his eyes to the widespread corruption imbedded in the army's procurement practices. Moreover, he pretended not to notice either the hobnobbing of some of the principal generals with members of the British legation or the activities of undercover British agents in Zagreb, where pro-Allied sentiments were widespread among leftist intellectuals, and in the capital itself. In spite of the danger of political repercussions, he did not try to stop the traffic of British agents and weapons through Yugoslavia into Albania (which in October, 1940, became Italy's base of operations against Greece), facilitated "privately" by military chiefs anxious to help the Allies.

The military were only a part, albeit a crucial one, of the problem with which the Yugoslav government had to deal. After the *Sporazum* of 1939, the Ustaše from across the Italian border resumed their trouble-making in Croatia, finding an ever-growing response among the members of Maček's Peasant Party. Members of the educated Serbian classes gave vent to their anti-German feelings through the influential *Politika* and the Serbian Cultural Club. Two minor Serbian parties, the Agrarian and Democratic, both left-of-center, were strongly on the side of the democracies in the European war, as well as repositories of the vague spirit of Slav solidarity which caused them to regard Soviet Russia with admiration and respect.

The government, headed by the colorless Cvetković, consisted of men unquestionably loyal to Prince Paul and was technically representative of all major national groups of the country. But it was a weak government, and in his holding operations Prince Paul counted essentially on intangibles: on the still strong prestige of the dynasty; on the support of the pan-Yugoslav — as distinct from the pan-Serb — politicians; and on the army officers' realization that Yugoslavia was in no condition to fight a war.

Arthur Bliss Lane, who was beginning to understand these complexities, appreciated Prince Paul's determination to keep the army in check. His distrust of the military dated back to his Latin American days. He disapproved of military takeovers, no matter how nobly motivated. And he instinctively feared internal disorders, believing that no sound and strong policy could conceivably emerge from chaos. So long as there was no conflict between the objectives of the United States and those of the Yugoslav government, the status quo and stability were preferable to any drastic change. In this frame of mind, Minister Lane watched with growing concern the suspicious machinations of the British agents in Belgrade as well as the signs of surreptitious activities on the part of certain key generals and leaders of the opposition.[12] The idea which he advanced in July that it would be "in the interests of the Allies to disturb peace" in the Balkans, did not appeal to him any longer. Moreover, as if anticipating a possible shift in the State Department's attitude from its current disinterest in Balkan affairs to

---

12. Earlier in the year, Lane reported with evident disapproval the rumors that British agents were mining the Iron Gate on the Danube, the narrowing banks of the river where the Carpathian arc joins the Balkan range, to prevent oil deliveries from Rumania to Germany.

some excessive expectations, Lane repeatedly warned Washington that under no foreseeable circumstances could a strong anti-Axis stand be expected of Yugoslavia, that in case of war the Yugoslav army would offer no resistance, and that there was an utter lack of moral and material preparation for war.[13]

Lane was not the only one who noticed the commotion in Serbian military circles. Another diplomatic observer in Belgrade, German Minister von Heeren, reported on October 25 to his government:

> Rumors which are again circulating regarding plans by Serbian generals to make a Putsch in order to set up a military dictatorship—if necessary, by replacing the prince regent with the young king—are characteristic of the profound dissatisfaction in the army and in Serbian circles in general with Yugoslavia's present situation. The reason for this is the growing criticism directed against the prince regent's policy of conciliation toward the Croats, which is considered as weakening and endangering the unity of the state and there is also the concern over the deterioration of Yugoslavia's military and political situation because of Rumania's new course, also because of the impenetrable character of Bulgarian, and above all Italian, intentions with respect to Macedonia. The view is widely held that this danger can be mastered only by a strong policy which neither the prince regent nor Minister President Cvetković is capable of conducting; to establish a military dictatorship and have the king who is already 18 years old ascend the throne before the appointed time undoubtedly seems to some elements in the army the best way out. I therefore do not consider impossible an evolution in this direction, particularly in the case of a further aggravation of military and political tension.[14]

What Lane's German colleague reported as rumors, Lane himself soon learned for fact, mainly through his military attaché, Colonel Louis L. Fortier. Fortier was on friendly terms not only with his British counterpart, Lt. Colonel C.S. ("Nobby") Clarke, but also with a number of high Serbian officers

---

13. See, for example, Lane to Hull and Welles, October 14, 1940. In this message Lane added that, "I endeavored to be most careful in not giving the impression to my foreign diplomatic colleagues or to Yugoslav officials that I view the situation with pessimism as I feel that the United States, being Yugoslavia's only present hope, should lend all encouragement to the assertion of moral courage on the part of the highest authorities here."
14. GFP, D, XI, 396.

who, like himself, had graduated from the Ecole Supérieur de Guerre in Paris and belonged to a kind of informal international fraternity. While avoiding personal involvement in the conspiratorial politics of Belgrade, Fortier managed to obtain enough information about what was going on to be able to reconstruct the scope and appreciate the grave significance of the conspiracy.[15] Lane, whom Fortier informed about his findings, became immediately alarmed. The question of what to do with this knowledge was urgent.

Under normal circumstances, Lane would have placed the problem at the doorstep of his superiors in the State Department, for he realized that it was too hot to handle on his own authority. In this instance, however, he was reluctant to send a full report because of the gnawing suspicion that his communications with Washington were being read by unauthorized eyes. Like all the other American missions abroad, the legation in Belgrade used for coding its dispatches antiquated cipher systems that could not assure the security required in sensitive situations. Although there was no positive proof that the American codes had been broken, Lane had been warned by Prince Paul himself, as far back as the summer of 1939, not to use the telegraph for transmitting the secret information which the prince occasionally gave to the American minister. According to Prince Paul's sources, at least some coded messages were intercepted and deciphered by the Germans. By the end of 1940, incontrovertible evidence had been obtained that such indeed was the case.[16]

---

15. For the most authoritative account of the military plot in Belgrade see Hoptner, Chapter X. The more recent book by Dragisa N. Ristic, *Yugoslavia's Revolution of 1941*, suffers from a distinct lack of candor on the part of the author, who himself participated in the conspiracy and thus apparently felt obligated to protect the record of his associates. Many interesting facts and observations related to this story are found in C.L. Sulzberger's memoirs. The *New York Times'* man in the Balkans seems to have been on excellent terms with all prominent antifascist and antigovernment figures in Belgrade, and knew more about the plot than any other observer.

16. For a long time, the American legation used Brown and Gray codes which were so old that they did not even contain the word "Yugoslavia" in them. Since the State Department stressed frugality in communications, even the later ciphers were so simple that in spite of their periodic changes they could be broken with ease. When in June, 1944, upon entering Rome, the OSS seized Carabinieri files, it was established that for several years before Italy entered the war, true readings of Lane's decoded dispatches

If Lane had to exclude the telegraph, the only way he could send his message to Washington was by diplomatic pouch. But the couriers made their rounds of the American legations in the Balkans only infrequently and any query sent by the pouch took up to two months to be answered, making this means quite useless in emergencies. In the end, not without misgivings, Lane cabled on October 15 that there were rumors of a "forthcoming military dictatorship." In a separate cable, trying to attract more attention to his report, he named General Borivoje Mirković, chief of staff of aviation, as his source. If anybody in the State Department noticed this important point, the official files contain no record of it, and there was no folow-up to Lane's report.

Yet the problem of how to regard the conspiracy remained. Lane found himself caught between a certain sympathy for Prince Paul's predicament and the general awareness that in the European war Yugoslavia was rapidly turning into an asset for the Axis, precisely at a time when his own government was backing Great Britain with growing firmness. Although less frequently than before, he continued to see Prince Paul, a man he had come to know intimately, all the while wondering how long the present regime was going to last. Whatever his feelings were, Lane remained essentially an observer, above all anxious not to be caught off guard. A great expert in playing his game close to the chest, he kept a poker face in his conversations with local officials and foreign diplomats, listening to everything and saying nothing.

Italy's attack on Greece brought the war for the first time into immediate proximity with Yugoslavia. It created in the country an atmosphere of acute crisis by threatening Yugoslavia not only with complete encirclement by the Axis and its allies but

---

were placed on the desks of Mussolini and Ciano within 24 hours after they were sent from Belgrade. Both Italian and German agents penetrated the city's central telegraph office and could easily obtain copies of outgoing and incoming messages. The pattern repeated itself elsewhere. For instance, when in Bern, Allen W. Dulles made contact with a sympathetic German diplomat, the latter warned him that he would do no business with him if other ways could not be found for Dulles' communications with Washington. The German proved his point by showing Dulles several copies of his cables, which the German legation in Switzerland routinely received from Berlin.

also with direct involvement in the war, since under the terms of the Balkan Entente, Greece was Yugoslavia's ally. However, because the Yugoslavs were obligated to come to the Greeks' aid only if Greece were attacked by another Balkan power, the officials in Belgrade could regard the new war merely as a further extension of the conflict between Great Britain and Italy,[17] fearing all the while that Bulgaria—against whom the Balkan Entente was primarily directed—might be tempted to join the aggressor. During the first week of the war the atmosphere in official circles in Belgrade was one of confusion, indecision, and fatalism. Lane, after a visit to Prince Paul, reported on October 31 that "the Prince's morale is so low that he is in no condition to resist external pressure. He admitted to me that his wife—who is a sister of King George of Greece—is on the verge of collapse."[18]

If Lane had hoped that the external danger would help pull patriotic forces in Yugoslavia together and result in greater cohesion for the nation, he was soon disappointed. The Croats and Slovenes vociferously and uniformly insisted on nonintervention. On the other hand, the sounds of the raging battle across the frontier greatly excited Serbian patriots. This should not have been surprising in a nation which annually celebrated the day of its greatest national disaster—the collapse of the medieval Serbian kingdom in the battle against the Turks at Kossovo—as its greatest national holiday. The excitement was particularly noticeable among the military.

Before long, the American legation accumulated so much

---

17. Mussolini, who gave Hitler barely one week's notice of his new adventure, justified his action as follows: "Greece is one of the main points of English maritime strategy in the Mediterranean. The king is English, the political classes are pro-British, and the people are immature but trained to hate Italy. Greece has ordered the mobilization of her armed forces and, as early as last May, has made air and naval bases available to Great Britain . . . in short, Greece is to the Mediterranean what Norway was to the North Sea, and must not escape the same fate." Mussolini to Hitler, October 19, 1940. GFP, D, XI, 333.

18. It is interesting to note that Lane, a professional diplomat and personal friend of Prince Paul, mistakenly refers to the prince's wife as a sister of George II of Greece (she was his cousin) and errs elsewhere in reporting that Prince Paul was a relative of the Russian imperial family. His only relationship to the Romanoffs was by his marriage to Princess Olga of Greece.

information about the conspiracy in the army that Lane decided to find out what the Yugoslav government knew about it. On November 4, he visited the minister of war, General Nedić, and asked him point-blank whether the rumors had any foundation. Nedić appeared quite worried, asked a few questions, and finally declared that "there is no trouble whatever in the army," that the officers "have shown no sign of dissatisfaction," and that "any report to the contrary is humbug." But the very next day the minister of the court, Milan Antić, Prince Paul's confidant, sent for Lane and asked him to repeat the information he had relayed to Nedić. Lane innocently assured him that he really had discussed only "disquieting reports circulating in the capital," and having received General Nedić's assurances he had telegraphed them to his own government. But describing his talk with Antić in his message to Washington that night, Lane commented: "It is evident from Nedić's excited attitude yesterday, his having reported the conversation to his superior, and my having been summoned this morning (the second time in three years) that a situation exists in army circles which is more serious than the government heads admit." And he again pointed out the high rank of General Mirković, Fortier's main source of information, as highly significant.

On November 7 Lane learned that Prince Paul had dismissed the minister of war for being too sympathetic to the disgruntled military. The regent confirmed this news during the conversation he had with Lane at the palace the same day. Lane reported that Prince Paul was "bitter in denouncing 'bigoted' Serbs like Nedić whose racial and religious hatreds affect their patriotism." Asked what he knew about the military plot, Lane answered that "our information regarding defection in the army came from such a reliable source that I felt certain there was something in it," adding that General Nedić's excitement proved this to his satisfaction. He declined to reveal his sources, and the fact that Prince Paul did not insist further convinced Lane that a very dangerous situation was indeed in the making.

This ominous development, so highly significant to Arthur Bliss Lane, was treated by the Department with stony silence, indicating to him its complete indifference to the destinies of

Yugoslavia. Acutely aware of his limitations in influencing the situation one way or another, Lane nevertheless wished his superiors to take cognizance of his forewarnings. The deep involvement of the British in this affair promised to bring the United States into the picture. As the tension increased, the memories of Managua plots and counterplots began to haunt Lane again, causing an uneasy feeling that he might once more find himself in a bloody mess which could ruin his career irreparably. In this mood, he reached the point of seriously considering abandoning the foreign service for good. He could afford to do it, especially since the latest uptrend on the stock market in the United States assured him, as he wrote to a friend, "a financial independence I have not enjoyed since 1929."

After further consideration, however, Lane abandoned this idea. At the age of 46 he was too young to retire, and he could not picture himself in any other line of activity: after more than two decades, the diplomatic service had become a way of life for Arthur Bliss Lane. Yet something had to be done, and the most obvious thing was to get transferred to another post. Suspecting that neither Hull nor Welles would cooperate, he resorted to the rather unorthodox move of addressing President Roosevelt directly. Shortly after Roosevelt's election to a third term, he wrote him on November 18 a personal letter (which he again typed himself) and sent it with the next courier. He wrote that although in the past he believed that "career chiefs of mission should not tender their resignations on termination of the presidential term of office," he had now come to the conclusion that it was their duty "to enable the president, with the least embarrassment to him, to get rid, without asking for their resignations, of chiefs of missions who are not best serving the interests of the United States." He concluded that "it is for the foregoing reasons that I am today sending you, through the Secretary of State, my formal letter of resignation as minister to Yugoslavia."

The idea of having career ministers submit their resignations automatically on termination of the president's term of office (soon to become official policy) was too novel in 1940 and the secretary of state's resentment was evident in the action he took. Hull advised Lane to continue his invaluable service as

minister to Yugoslavia; the Department contemplated no trans-
fers in the area for the time being. Disappointed with the
outcome of his undertaking, Lane noticeably curtailed his activities; for a while, the flow of dispatches from the American
legation in Belgrade to the State Department all but dried up.
None of them contained references to the military plot.[19]

As the year of 1940 drew to a close, Lane found little to
cheer about. Belgrade had evidently lost, in the Department's
view, its importance as a "listening post." It was not an attractive enough place to permit the minister to simply enjoy living
there. For one reason or another, Lane could envy his colleagues elsewhere in Southeastern Europe. Hungary and Rumania had passed under the German tutelage the preceding
fall. Their problems were beyond solution, and the American
diplomats in Bucharest and Budapest could relax. Ambassador
MacMurray in Ankara did not have much to worry about, since
the spotlight there was occupied by the British and the Germans; besides, his was a prestigious post because Turkey was
considered a strategically important country. Lincoln Mac-
Veagh in Athens also played a subordinate role, but Greece,
valiantly resisting Italy, was very much in the news, and
presented an interesting scene for observations. George H.
Earle III, former governor of Pennsylvania, who, by whim of
the president, had become a notoriously incompetent minister
to Bulgaria, was totally oblivious to the world around him.
Engrossed in pursuit of happiness with a voluptuous Budapest
cabaret dancer, he paid little attention to the crosscurrents of
Sofia's politics. Since he could not bear to be away from his
darling for too long, he would periodically leave his post to
travel "incognito" to Budapest. Lane, who was rather prudish
when it came to romantic adventures of this sort, did not treat
Minister Earle well on his stopovers in Belgrade, even though
the affair—known to the diplomats throughout the Balkans—was an inexhaustible source of jokes and anecdotes
which Lane relished more than anything else.

Comparing the relative advantages and disadvantages of

---

19. Fortier, however, continued to explore cautiously the scope of the conspiracy and report his findings by courier to G-2 in the War Department.
Whether his reports ever reached the secretary of state or the White House
is doubtful.

various Balkan capitals, Arthur Bliss Lane could come to but
one conclusion; namely, that Belgrade was just about the worst
place to be in. Yugoslavia's position was most precarious. Its
complete encirclement by the Axis appeared inevitable, pre-
determining the direction of its policy. On the other hand,
there was a clear danger that an internal explosion due to the
military conspiracy would throw the whole country into a state
of chaos, with consequences impossible to predict.

American Neutrality Crumbles

Relief came around the middle of January 1941, when Lane
learned through the British legation that Colonel William J.
Donovan, a Republican politician and successful Wall Street
lawyer known to be close to President Roosevelt, was coming
to the Balkans and the Middle East on an important mission.[20]
From its inception, Donovan's mission was shrouded in controversy. It was officially announced in Washington that Donovan was traveling on behalf of his personal friend, Secretary of
the Navy Frank Knox, who desired to obtain reliable information about what was going on in the region. Simultaneously, newspaper accounts, inspired by the White House
and Downing Street, hastened to inform the world that in
actual fact Donovan had been dispatched by the president
himself with the specific purpose of announcing to the governments of Southeastern Europe the American determination to
support Great Britian against the Axis and to provide aid to
those countries which would resist Nazi aggression. The truth
lay in between: in a private conference with Knox and Secretary of war Henry L. Stimson Donovan volunteered to go on
this "fact-finding trip"; he was very pleased with his trip to
London the previous summer, and hoped to accomplish more
in the way of involving the United States in the European
crisis. President Roosevelt gave his blessing; Churchill was
delighted, and upon Donovan's arrival in London assigned his
aide, Brigadier Vivian Dykes, to accompany the American en-

---

20. For a summary of Donovan's mission see Langer and Gleason, *The
Undeclared War*, Chapter XIII. See also Allen W. Dulles, *The Second Sur-
render*, 7-8; Constantin Fotitch, *The War We Lost*, 41-44; and Corey Ford,
Donovan of OSS, 98-106.

voy in his trip. With all the ostensible "secrecy" surrounding it, the press was kept well informed about his movements: Churchill needed all the help he could get.

The State Department was immediately flooded with inquiries from American envoys abroad and foreign embassies in Washington about the true nature of Donovan's mission. Secretary Hull ordered the uniform reply that Donovan was strictly an agent of Secretary Knox and was to be treated as such. Hull considered American involvement in the Balkans totally uncalled for, steadfastly declining British requests to put pressure on Balkan governments in order to prevent their drift into the Axis camp. He refused to treat American interests as identical to those of Great Britain, and regarded any promises of aid while Congress had not even started the hearings on the Lend-Lease Bill (proposed by Roosevelt on January 6, 1941) quite irresponsible.

Hull's attitude was no secret in the White House, thus ruling out utilization of the State Department's machinery for the kind of help which Roosevelt wanted to give the British. An attempt to prevail upon the strong-willed secretary of state would have involved Roosevelt in a major battle, with a distinct risk of endangering the passage of the Lend-Lease Bill and of causing adverse public reaction, inevitable in view of the still predominant sentiment in favor of keeping America out of the war. Besides, assigning this important mission to a man who was liked and trusted by both Churchill and himself appeared to Roosevelt a much more dramatic (and hence more effective) way of handling the task than relying on traditional diplomatic means. Differences in policies aside, the dispatch of a special representative provoked Hull, who resented White House incursions into the field of foreign affairs.

Most career diplomats abroad shared Hull's dim view of Donovan's mission. Perhaps typical was the reaction of MacMurray, who wrote to the Secretary on February 10, 1941, that Donovan's visit to Turkey was "a matter of very considerable embarrassment to me in my relations with both the Turks and the British, by reason of my being altogether in the dark as to what it was about." He complained that he was given "no indication except certain negatives as to the nature and degree of the cooperation and confidence which this embassy should

proffer under the circumstances"; that not only his British colleague, Sir Hughe Knatchbull-Hugessen, but even the Turkish
government knew more about the visit than he did; and that,
worse still, Knatchbull-Huggessen was warned from London
not to take him, the American ambassador, into his confidence
in this matter "prematurely." MacMurray was prepared to cooperate with Donovan (although he had to "stake my representative capacity upon my unguided faith in a man I had never
happened to meet"). At the same time, he found it hard to
explain, if the purpose of the mission was so confidental, "the
rather short-sighted publicity given to Colonel Donovan's visit
by certain British quarters." He added that he could "conceive
of no good results — nothing but provocate effects" — to be expected by the BBC's publicizing Donovan's presumed assignment (which MacMurray found impossible to believe), to help
the British in confronting the Axis with a major challenge in
the Balkans.

A detailed analysis of British policies in the Balkans early in
1941 is not a part of the present story. In retrospect, it appears
obvious that neither Colonel Donovan nor President Roosevelt
knew much about the situation in the region either before or
after Donovan's trip. The reason is equally obvious. During the
entire three-and-a-half-month trip, Donovan depended almost
entirely on the secondhand information given to him by British
officials of all ranks and positions. They themselves knew little
about political conditions and relations among the countries in
the region and were floundering a great deal, unable to decide
exactly what they wanted to accomplish. In general terms, the
British sought to create a "Balkan front" against the Axis. But
nobody had a clear idea of how to go about it.[21] Opinions
differed within the British cabinet and at General Sir Archibald
Wavell's headquarters in Cairo. There was an almost continuous disagreement between the government and the military
in the field, with the latter alternately trying to bring Churchill's ambitious plans into some balance with their meager

---

21. For the story of British endeavors in the Balkans, see Winston S. Churchill, *The Second World War*, vols. II and III; Anthony Eden, *The Reckoning;* I.S.O. Playfair, *The Mediterranean and the Middle East;* J.R.M. Butler,
Grand Strategy; and Alexander Papagos, *The Battle of Greece.*

capabilities and pressing for a totally unrealistic policy. In November 1940, responding to the chiefs of staff's demand "to bring Turkey in as a belligerent at once," London subjected Ankara to considerable pressure. The Turkish government, for a number of perfectly valid reasons, refused to be drawn into the war. It was at this point that the British cabinet came up with its more far-reaching "Balkan front" scheme. It decided to take advantage of the Greek army's successes in Albania and to induce Turkey, Yugoslavia, and perhaps Bulgaria to join in a common front with Greece against German aggression. What form this common front was supposed to take, nobody quite knew; moreover, in view of the massing of German troops in Rumania, which accelerated in December, none of the proposed members of the common front wanted to take the risks involved in siding with the British.

Even the Greeks were wary of the scheme. When in early January the British cabinet offered to send Greece five air squadrons to be based near Salonika (mainly in order to establish air bases within range of the Rumanian oilfields), Ioannis Metaxas, prime minister of Greece, declined the offer on the grounds that "such a reinforcement would merely provoke a German attack without being enough to repel it." Metaxas felt that while, given luck, Greece could hope to settle its conflict with Italy on acceptable terms, it would be inviting disaster to take on Germany: it was a common assumption in Athens that Hitler would not tolerate a British foothold in Greece.[22]

This assumption was well founded. Anticipating that sooner or later the Greeks would bow down before British pressure, and considering the safety of the Rumanian oilfields of the utmost importance, Hitler ordered, on November 13, 1940, the preparation of contingency plans for the occupation of Northern Greece. The sudden death of Metaxas on January 29, 1941, apparently removed his last doubts, and he issued orders to

---

22. Still obsessed with the desire to bomb Rumanian oilfields, the British cabinet towards the end of January offered ten British-manned air squadrons to the Turks and expressed the opinion that if the Germans should attack, the Straits might serve as "a useful anti-tank ditch." The Turks, who had no quarrel with Hitler, evasively answered that they might consider military action only if and when German troops invaded Bulgaria, although they would really prefer to limit themselves to the defense of their own territory. Butler, 384.

invade Greece, fixing the date for the crossing of the Danube into Bulgaria at March 2, and the date of the attack itself at about April 1, 1941.[23]

Colonel Donovan Appears on the Scene

After a month-long briefing in London by the British Intelligence Service and members of the cabinet, Colonel William J. Donovan arrived in Cairo on January 7, 1941, accompanied by Brigadier Dykes. In Cairo Donovan conferred with the top British commanders and made a tour of inspection in the western desert. On January 15, Donovan flew to Athens with Wavell, Air Chief Marshal Sir A. Longmore, and other members of the British delegation, to take part in the negotiations with Prime Minister Metaxas and Field Marshal Papagos. He was also received by King George II. During his various meetings in Athens Donovan spoke forcefully and eloquently, stating the United States' firm determination to assist the British in securing the defeat of the Axis; urging the Greeks to form a united front with other Balkan states and Turkey; and taking copious notes of Greek needs for military equipment which could be filled by American aid.

Having spent a busy week in Athens—he barely had time to talk with Minister MacVeagh—Donovan took a train to Sofia where he had an important task to accomplish. The British feared that Bulgaria was on the verge of reaching an accord with the Germans on the passage of German troops through the country and hoped that Donovan's intervention would forestall this development. Minister Earle was less optimistic. He reported to Secretary Hull on January 23, 1941, that Donovan's "forceful declaration to the king and his ministers that America, exerting all her enormous force will ensure ultimate victory for England, has had a tremendous effect," perhaps insufficient "to prevent the unmolested passage of German troops through Bulgaria" but hopefully strong enough to "prevent cooperation

---

23. *Ibid.*, 388. It is worth noting that salvaging Mussolini's ill-fated adventure in Greece was not an overriding consideration with Hitler. Initially, dispatch of a mobile formation into Albania was part of the plans for the invasion of Greece. Later, however, Hitler countermanded this order, probably thinking that his partner should pay the full price for his excessive independence.

between Bulgarian and German troops." In turn, Donovan, judging by his report to Secretary Knox on January 24, was quite impressed by the shrewd king whom he found "idealistic" (so much so, as to have an over-belief in the virtue of peace), "honest and shy, although somewhat over-confident of his ability to maneuver in a difficult international situation." Donovan wrote that when he predicted to the king that "you will permit Germany to come through, although you will not participate with her," the king "looked me straight in the eye and smiled."

On January 21, having spent three days in Sofia and feeling that he had grasped the situation in Bulgaria sufficiently to proceed to Belgrade, the next stop on his itinerary, Donovan was about to leave Earle's residence to go to the railroad station when he discovered that his briefcase, containing letters of introduction, a few hundred dollars in cash, and, above all, his passport, had vanished. A thorough search was immediately launched but produced no result, except for world-wide publicity by the press (especially German), publicity which somewhat detracted from the high purpose of the colonel's mission. Although the circumstances of the disappearance of the briefcase remained shrouded in mystery, it seems that it was stolen from Donovan's room by Earle's Hungarian sweetheart who, perhaps not by accident, was visiting her boyfriend at the time of Donovan's visit. The briefcase then appeared at the Gestapo headquarters in Sofia where the local operatives of this organization, moved by natural curiosity, thoroughly examined its contents. After that, the briefcase passed into the hands of the chief of the Bulgarian secret police who, on February 15, proudly returned it, with all its contents, to Earle, stating that it was found somewhere in a trash can, wrapped in an old newspaper.[24]

---

24. Later, when the German troops moved into Bulgaria, Minister Earle pulled strings at the White House to get appointed naval attaché in Istanbul, anxious to be reunited with his sweetheart, and in the meantime drowning his sorrow in gay parties in the city's night clubs. The girl eventually arranged for her transfer to Istanbul and was investigated there by a British intelligence officer who, according to Sulzberger (Earle's old friend), established that she was employed simultaneously by "both the Abwehr and Sicherheitsdienst, the principal Nazi intelligence services." Earle, however, wasn't terribly upset: by then he had fallen in love with a Belgian girl whom

Meanwhile Colonel Donovan, greatly annoyed by the unexpected delay and the equally unexpected publicity, telephoned Minister Lane in Belgrade and asked him to make sure that he would be admitted into Yugoslavia. Lane quickly settled the matter. As he reported to Washington on February 1, "Thanks to the prompt action kindly taken by the Yugoslav authorities, Donovan encountered no difficulties at the border as a result of the theft of his passport in Sofia."

Lane met Donovan at the Belgrade railroad station on the evening of January 22 and took him directly to his residence. There he was closeted with the presidential envoy for several hours, listening to his outline and evaluation of the current British strategy in the Balkans. By skillfully questioning Donovan, Lane obtained a fair idea of the role the British assigned to Yugoslavia in their plans. This role was infinitely more important than that envisaged by the State Department or anything Lane himself had imagined. Lane could no longer doubt that Roosevelt had decided to throw the full diplomatic weight of the United States behind the British policy, thus reversing a much more cautious State Department policy. It may also be assumed that during this conversation Donovan told Lane that the British had a spare trump to play in Belgrade in case Prince Paul persisted in his pro-Axis orientation: his regime could be overthrown with the help of the Serbian military clique headed by Generals Mirković and Simović.[25]

Minister Lane had recognized the importance of Donovan's mission from the very beginning: a man who had access to the highest councils of the United States and Great Britain and enjoyed the confidence of President Roosevelt and Churchill was no ordinary VIP. Lane realized that the organizational

he later married. According to some evidence, the Hungarian dancer eventually arrived in the United States where she had a succession of highly lucrative marriages and a career in the performing arts.

25. Donovan by then had become quite an expert on fifth column activities: after his trip to England the preceding summer, he wrote (in collaboration with Edgar A. Mawrer of the *Chicago Daily News*) a series of articles on this subject, and had been in close contact with the officials of the Special Operations Executive both in London and Cairo who maintained a day-by-day contact with the military conspirators in Belgrade. Donovan's accumulated knowledge of secret operations behind the enemy lines eventually led to his appointment as director of the Office of Strategic Services, the American equivalent of the SOE.

aspects of the mission were in British hands but was resolved that at least in Belgrade such was not going to be the case. Although he had consulted with Campbell, he had worked out Donovan's schedule by himself, paying attention to every minute detail. And he made sure that the envoy of his president would be his house guest for the duration of his visit.

For the next two days, Donovan was engaged in a whirlwind of activities in Belgrade. On January 23, accompanied by Lane, he met Prime Minister Cvetković, had a press conference for Yugoslav newspapermen, had lunch with Prince Paul, visited the tomb of the Unknown Soldier at Avala, and had conferences with the Croatian leader Vladko Maček and Foreign Minister Cincar-Marković. All events went smoothly except for the meeting with Cincar-Marković, and Lane recorded, not without annoyance, that the latter's attempt to snub Donovan was due to his commitment to the pro-Axis orientation for Yugoslavia. At the end of the day Colonel Donovan was entertained at an elaborate dinner at Lane's residence, followed by an enjoyable poker game.

The next day, this time accompanied by Fortier, Donovan visited General Pesic, minister of war; General Kosić, chief of the general staff; General Simović, chief of aviation; and Admiral Luterotti, chief of naval operations. He inspected the military academy and the general staff school, as well as the 6th aviation regiment, chief preserve of General Mirković who, together with Simović, was at the head of the conspiracy. After that he had a prolonged lunch with British Minister Ronald Campbell and his aides, gave informal interviews to American newsmen accredited to Belgrade, and joined the Lanes at a late dinner party. Early next morning, accompanied by the inevitable Brigadier Dykes, Donovan boarded the train for Salonika.

Once again in Greece, Donovan was taken to the Albanian front where, according to Minister MacVeagh's report of February 3, 1941, "he obtained a quick and comprehensive view of the Greek army in action," and was astonished to hear the soldiers enthusiastically shout (in Greek) "Long live President Roosevelt!" Upon his return to Athens (where he stayed at the British legation) Donovan found time to share with MacVeagh his overall impressions. "He said he believed that Germany

would refrain from making any attack on the Balkans," reported MacVeagh to the State Department, "if she were convinced
of united opposition on the part of Bulgaria, Yugoslavia, and
Turkey, and that despite the forces tending to keep their nations apart, their common desire for American moral support
and material assistance might well be sufficient to bring them
together should a move in this direction be made by the president. Doubtless such an idea will seem ingenuous to those
who have had long experience in Balkan affairs," added Mac-
Veagh cautiously, "but even in the Balkans circumstances alter
cases, and the immense interest taken hereabouts in the colonel's visit may be a sign that he is not altogether wrong."

Donovan's further travels took him to Ankara; he would
have visited the French possessions in the Middle East and
North Africa as well if it had not been for the refusal of the
Vichy French authorities (attributed by the British to German
pressure) to give him a visa. Undismayed, he flew to Egypt,
stopping on the way in Jerusalem long enough to observe
"battalions of Arabs and Jews serving together, their political
differences submerged in the need of common defense." After
a night's rest in Cairo, Donovan made a whole-day inspection
tour of the British front in Libya, sending a long message to
Roosevelt on February 20, summarizing his impressions and
conclusions. He wrote that the British "simply must" retain
and widen their foothold in the Balkans because this might
force Germany to "abandon the attempt at invasion of England" and instead "gamble on over-running in a short war not
only all the Balkans but Turkey as well." In this attack, Germany would be likely to employ a new secret weapon ("such as
huge land mines parachuted upon square-mile areas and
self-propelled barges of soldiers three lines in width, guarded
by submarines and canopied by an armada of planes") and
finish the job quickly because the Reich "wants tranquility and
security in the Balkans so as to maintain uninterrupted her
supplies of oil, food, and raw materials." His conclusion was
that the British should not be discouraged by such a threat of a
German attack; that, on the contrary, Yugoslavia, Greece, Turkey, and, if possible, Bulgaria, should be induced to stand
together with England. "Such a joint venture would result in
economy of time, of force, and of administration," Donovan

pointed out gravely, and advised the president to cooperate with the British in their endeavor to form a "Balkan front."

Forging the "Balkan Front"

Donovan's visit to Belgrade provided Arthur Bliss Lane with the answers he had long awaited. He carefully prepared a detailed report on Donovan's activities in Belgrade to be dispatched by courier. Simultaneously he cabled to Washington his quick overall appraisal, saying that "while Donovan's visit may have been distasteful to the appeasement group, it had a good effect on the military element which now appreciates that the material assistance we are giving Great Britian and Greece is because these nations did not surrender without a struggle." The optimistic and unambiguous tone of this message and of the detailed report dated February 1, 1941, represented a striking difference from anything Lane had previously written from the Yugoslav capital.

There is every indication that the weeks immediately preceding and following Donovan's visit saw a crucial change in the way of thinking of Arthur Bliss Lane. It was during this period that, for the first time in his career, he departed from his loyalty to the close-knit fraternity of the foreign service and became in fact a representative of the president, more responsive to the broad political interests of the United States than to the wishes of his immediate superiors in the State Department. This change first manifested itself in Lane's reaction to the Donovan mission. Formerly, he would have reacted to it as other career ministers and ambassadors did, strictly negatively. He would simply have been more forceful than the rest. Once having detected the considerable cleavage that had developed between the White House and the State Department on the issue of aiding the British in the Balkans, he would have instinctively sided with the Department, and he would have been guided by more than loyalty to the foreign service. Lane had a very low opinion of British diplomacy in general; in one of his letters to Roosevelt he referred to Ronald Ian Campbell, his British colleague in Belgrade, as a "poor little man." He rated British chances of staging a comeback through a landing in Greece—a move widely discussed in Belgrade—as nil. He was equally skeptical about America's ability to turn the tide of the war by vocal endorsements of the Allied cause; as an experienced diplomat, he knew that the United States was woefully lacking any effective leverage for dealing with Balkan governments, while Germany dominated politically, if not militarily, the whole region except for Greece and perhaps Turkey.

Yet in spite of all this, the decision to follow Roosevelt's lead came naturally to Lane. His pragmatic evaluation of the Balkan situation clashed increasingly with his emotional involvement in the greatest conflict of his time. He sincerely despised Mussolini, and his feelings toward Hitler were little short of hatred. Although he had been out of the United States for almost four years, he was attuned to changes in public opinion at home. In Belgrade, he had unusually close relations with a group of top-flight American correspondents, most of them passionate anti-Axis crusaders who had converged upon the Yugoslav capital in the expectation that the Balkans were about to become a major theater of war. These men had been fighting the Axis long before Roosevelt decided to place the United States on the side of the British. They represented the "Fourth Estate," the most influential single force in American politics, reflecting as well as forging public opinion. Their enthusiasm was highly contagious, and it easily affected Lane, who was predisposed to join the battle.

Another factor was the change in Lane's attitude towards Yugoslavia. Again, under normal conditions, he would have been inclined to do whatever he could in order to protect the interests of a friendly country. He had been loyal to Prince Paul, sympathizing with his predicament, and abstaining from dealings with the opposition elements beyond the need of being aware of what was going on. Although never a victim of "localitis"—a disposition not uncommon among diplomats to advance the interests of the countries in which they served—Lane would never have considered causing harm, or even discomfort, to a government which was on good terms with his own. In the specific situation of Belgrade at the beginning of 1941, however, his attitude in this respect was changing. On the one hand, several months of expectation of a military coup d'état gave the regime of Prince Paul a certain unreal quality: it had not been overthrown yet but could be at any moment. On the other hand, as the European war entered into its critical stage, Yugoslavia looked increasingly like a minor pawn on the great chessboard, a pawn which had to be played before it was too late. Prince Paul was entitled to feel that Yugoslavia's best course lay in accommodating the Axis; even the State Department could feel the same way, mainly because of its aloofness and ignorance of the great stakes of the game.

It was more than by accident that at this juncture Lane was not kindly disposed toward the Department: it had ignored his many warnings about the deteriorating situation in Yugoslavia, and it had stubbornly assigned that country (and, consequently, the American minister in Belgrade) a negligible role in United States foreign policy. So long as there was no duality in Washington's position, Lane, a disciplined career diplomat, had no choice. But the Donovan mission indicated that there actually was an alternative, that he in fact could serve his government in the most active and even dramatic way. Of course, this involved a risk of annoying Cordell Hull and Sumner Welles: departures from the fraternity spirit of the foreign service were not easily forgiven. But this risk appeared small, especially since Lane anticipated that Roosevelt would in the end bring the Department around to carrying out his wishes.

There is no question that Lane's new attitude was in no small degree affected by the fact that Colonel Donovan, a man so close to the president, had taken him fully into his confidence in outlining plans designed to change the course of histroy. It was true that these plans were based on very general political considerations and were only distantly related to Balkan realities; Donovan's ignorance at times must have appeared appalling to Lane. But this aspect somehow seemed unimportant. Lane was prepared to follow Roosevelt's directives, which, in practical terms, amounted to an unqualified support of whatever the British wanted'to accomplish.

Lane's personal dislike of the British minister in Belgrade ruled out close cooperation with him, and besides, he did not want to appear in the role of a mere assistant to Campbell. But that was not really necessary so long as he conformed to the overall understanding which Donovan told him had been established between Roosevelt and Churchill. As Lane saw it now, Yugoslavia's fortunes had become intertwined with those of the democracies, and its drift toward neutrality and isolation under the protective wing of Germany had to be reversed.

The task ahead loomed formidable. Lane was aware that beginning with the talks that Cincar-Marković had held with Ribbentrop and Hitler at Berchtesgaden the preceding November, Yugoslavia had again come under pressure to join the Axis by acceding to the Tripartite Pact. Both Hungary and Rumania had done so, and Bulgaria was expected to follow suit at any time. Hitler promised Yugoslavia what nobody else could: peace, trade, security against the encroachments of Italy and Bulgaria, and the coveted outlet to the Aegean Sea in Salonika, which the Yugoslavs considered vital to their commerce and which the Serbian military regarded of paramount importance.

But, reasoned Lane, on the other side of the balance sheet was Prince Paul's strong dislike of the Axis, a dislike shared by Yugoslav intellectuals and especially by the Serb-dominated armed forces. The elements in the government which were inclined towards greater accommodation with Germany had to be very careful. There was no immediate threat from abroad: so long as Greece continued to fight, Prince Paul did not have to fear Italy, and on the assumption that Hitler did not want to become embroiled in a Balkan campaign, the possibility of a German attack could be dismissed. As Lane reported to Washington earlier in December, Prince Paul was "more than ever the master in his own house" and "his determination to resist" German demands was impressive.[26]

In retrospect, it appears that Arthur Bliss Lane badly misread the picture by assuming that the joint Anglo-American diplomatic effort might be sufficient to offset the pressure which the Axis could apply to the Yugoslav government. Alternatively, he might have counted on a successful overthrow of the government by the army conspirators in case it were tempted to yield to the Axis demands, and on Hitler's continued reluctance to

---

26. Prince Paul had repeatedly turned down German requests for making Yugoslav railroads available for transportation of supplies to the Italian army in Albania, and would not even consider signing the Tripartite Pact. His attitude was fully appreciated by Hitler, who, on December 13, 1940, wrote Mussolini that Yugoslavia for the time being should be left alone, and that no further pressure on their part "would be promising before the psychological situation has been generally improved once more by [your] military successes." GFP, XI, 993.

attack even a pro-British Yugoslavia. On the other hand, it is at least equally plausible that Lane simply avoided thinking about the ultimate outcome of the Anglo-American political offensive he was about to take part in, and concentrated upon its immediate aspects.

On January 25, the day after Donovan departed for Greece, Lane cabled several messages to the Department, reversing his earlier evaluation and suggesting: (1) that Yugoslavia was determined to fight if attacked; (2) that if Turkey and Bulgaria would take a similar attitude, a general agreement on policy might ensue; (3) that although Prince Paul distrusted Bulgaria and felt sure that German troops would be permitted passage to Greece, Donovan's forceful appeal to King Boris might make him hesitate; and (4) that "positive action" be taken to allay mutual distrust of the three countries. Lane also quoted Prince Paul, who in reply to his question whether Yugoslavia would fight if German troops entered Bulgaria answered that although there was no unanimity in the government on this issue, faced with encirclement by the Axis Yugoslavia might take a military initiative since "the time has come to act on principle, to abandon expediency."[27]

Lane's optimism caused no inspiration in the Department. To his proposal to take "positive action" Hull replied that it was "not the practice of the Department to initiate directly such a policy." A few days later, in reply to a British request to encourage the Yugoslav and Turkish governments to start direct negotiations in view of the impending German offensive, Hull evasively answered that "we were closely observing the situation. . .together with related conditions in that area from day to day," and that "we would continue to keep every phase of the matter in mind and give it such attention and consideration as might be practicable from the standpoint of promoting and preserving peace and opposing further military activities in that area."[28]

The British initiatives in creating a Balkan Front were slowed down by reports that upon his return to the United States, Colonel Donovan would write a series of articles in the *Chicago Daily News* (Secretary Knox's newspaper) about his mis-

---

27. Lane to Hull, January 25, 1941, FR, 1941, II, 939.
28. *Ibid.*, 941.

sion. Alarmed envoys of the Balkan governments in Washington rushed to the State Department asking for assurances that the confidence which their respective chiefs of state had placed in Donovan not be betrayed. Wallace Murray, chief of the Division for Near Eastern Affairs, wrote a memorandum to Sumner Welles on January 30, pointing out that Donovan had repeatedly been referred to as the president's representative and had been accorded in Athens, Sofia, and Belgrade, "extraordinary facilities which would never have been granted had his true [?] status been known." Murray emphasized that Donovan's present mission, "far from 'improving' the situation in the Near East, might greatly worsen it and play into the hands of the Germans if this journalistic aspect of his mission is allowed to materialize."

Lane, who was equally dismayed by these reports, had an additional problem. On the evening of February 3, he was called by the prime minister to hear the news that Cvetković's confidential remarks to Donovan had somehow become known to the Yugoslav legation in Moscow. Lane hastened to assure him that his legation had given out nothing on the matter to anybody. Having returned home, he wrote a formal letter to Prince Paul in which he boldly stated that "Colonel Donovan has asked me to reassure your Royal Highness that he has no intention of writing his impressions, even in a general way, for the *Chicago Daily News* or for any other newspaper." He also sent a cable to Donovan (then in Ankara) urging him to disavow his alleged journalistic ambitions.

"Resisting German Aggression"

If Colonel Donovan had any plans for writing up his experiences in the Balkans, he was discouraged from proceeding with them. But although the concern of Balkan leaders over possible disclosures of what they had told Donovan soon disappeared, the episode probably made them regard American appeals and assurances more cautiously. This, however, was a minor factor in the sharp deterioration of the overall political situation in the region which took place during the month of February, resulting from the pressure which Berlin brought to bear on the Balkan governments. Bulgaria displayed every sign of aligning itself with Germany, while Turkey was more than ever determined to remain neutral. Minister Lane in Belgrade however, was resolved to do everything in his power to swing this pivotal country to the Allied camp regardless of what Bulgaria or Turkey did.

In practical terms, "Yugoslavia" was Prince Paul, who thus became the principal target of Lane's diplomatic offensive. The first step, it appeared, was to make the regent at least consider the possibility of military action against Germany. In this, Lane did not make much headway. As he reported to the Department on February 8, Prince Paul told him "with seeming despair" that Yugoslavia's position had become hopeless and that "no pretext must be given the Axis" for making it worse, insisting that war with Germany must be avoided at all costs. The minister warned the secretary of state that this might easily become the case "despite his previous assurances to Donovan and me" unless the regent's "low morale" improved.

Not easily given to discouragement, Lane paid a visit to the foreign minister with the idea of neutralizing the man rated as the most pro-Axis member of the cabinet. Lane explained to him Roosevelt's statement of January 6, 1941, about integrating America's needs with the British war effort until final victory over the Axis was achieved, and expressed his "personal opinion that countries which do not resist aggression are not worthy of independence and need not count on our support when political and geographical readjustments are made after the war." Cincar-Marković was so unimpressed by this threat that Lane felt he had to have his hand strengthened by Washington. In his message to Hull he suggested that "if the Department could see its way clear to making a similar statement . . . that we are committed to full support of all people who resist aggression, I believe, even at this late hour in the present critical situation in the Balkans, the result would be salutary."[29]

Within three days Lane obtained proof that his ability to perceive his own government's thinking was intact. On February 14 Secretary Hull cabled that "in conformity with the desire of the president" he had informed the Yugoslav minister in Washington that "any victory on behalf of the predatory powers

---

29. Lane to Hull, February 11, 1941, FR, 1941, II, 943.

if it only be in the diplomatic field would but pave the way for fresh demands accompanied by threats of force against the very independence of the nation thus menaced" and that the Lend-Lease Bill then before Congress permitted the president "to supply the materials of war to those nations that are now the victims of aggression."[30]

This cable was delivered to Lane on the evening of February 15, as he was attending an official concert at which Cvetković and other members of the government were present. As he read it, he could note with satisfaction that Secretary Hull, however grudgingly, had been compelled to accept Roosevelt's position. The message contained a combination of warning and promise which, Lane felt, would not fail to impress the Yugoslav government. Somewhat hastily, he attempted to see Cvetković during the intermission but was not allowed to enter the prime minister's box. Annoyed with this brush-off, he visited the minister of the court the following morning and requested an audience with Prince Paul. Antić told him that the prince was very busy and that he had already read the president's message cabled to him by Minister Fotitch from Washington. Lane insisted, threatening that otherwise he would be "obliged to telegraph my government that it was not possible to approach the Chief of State."[31]

Lane's desire to see Prince Paul was prompted by an additional, much more serious development. He had just learned that the day before Hull's message arrived, Cvetković and Cincar-Marković had made a secret pilgrimage to Berchtesgaden where they had met with Hitler and Ribbentrop. The secrecy surrounding this trip indicated that the Yugoslavs had come under renewed German pressure, and Lane felt that it was imperative to counteract it. The audience with the regent was finally granted on February 18.

Prince Paul assured the American minister that Yugoslavia continued to refuse to adhere to the Pact. He assumed that Roosevelt hoped that Yugoslavia would resist German aggression. This it would do, if attacked, but if resisting aggression meant attacking Bulgaria in the event that German troops en-

---

30. Hull to Lane, February 14, 1941, *ibid.*, 944.
31. Lane to Hull, February 18, 1941, *ibid.*, 945.

tered it, the answer was No: Germany could then invade Yugoslavia from several directions and the country's resistance would collapse in less than two weeks. German forces could be augmented by those of Italy, Hungary, and Rumania, which would create a hopeless situation for Prince Paul since, for political reasons, he could not remove troops from Croatia and Slovenia and concentrate on the defense of Serbia.

The mood of the prince regent was very pessimistic. Two days earlier he had talked with the British minister, trying to find out the probable extent of British aid to Yugoslavia if it clashed with Germany. Campbell's replies were anything but reassuring. All he could promise was some supplies at some future date. Prince Paul listened, made no comment, and dismissed Campbell. Now, talking to Lane, he said twice that he wished he were dead. He was responsible for King Peter and the country's survival, and was prepared to live up to his responsibilities no matter how unpopular his course of action might be. He pointed out the futility of American promises of aid which could not possibly arrive in time. Bulgaria was lost to the Allies, he felt, largely through the stupidity of British diplomats in Sofia; Turkey had just concluded a pact of friendship and non-aggression with Bulgaria and was closer to the Axis than ever before. Although Prince Paul believed that England would eventually win the war, the immediate prospects were bleak. The Germans were ready to move into Bulgaria and finish off Greece. Yugoslavia's only course was to stay neutral, relying on Hitler's assurances and accepting his protection.[32]

It is impossible to say whether Lane realized how far the Yugoslav government was prepared to go in its desire for neutrality, but those concerned with the situation in London, Washington, and Cairo had little choice but to hope that the Yugoslavs' backs could be stiffened. The situation in Greece was rapidly approaching a critical stage as the German attack appeared imminent. It was deemed imperative for Yugoslavia to attack the German army the moment it entered Bulgaria, with a simultaneous offensive against the Italian forces in Albania. Given the disposition of the Yugoslav government, these actions were out of order at least until its relations with Berlin

---

32. Lane to Hull, February 18, 1941, *ibid.*, 945-946.

had been brought to a breaking point. Since Prince Paul was evidently unwilling to undertake anything of that sort, the Anglo-American strategists conceived a way of provoking Hitler's wrath against Yugoslavia by securing the latter's categorical refusal to sign the pact with the Axis, thus defeating Hitler's primary objective. In the polite language of diplomacy, the political-military challenge to German supremacy which the Allied strategists sought to bring about in Belgrade was termed "resisting aggression."

The British effort was directed by foreign Secretary Anthony Eden and General Sir John Dill, chief of the Imperial General Staff, whom Churchill sent to the Middle East in mid-February with instructions to organize the landing of British forces in Greece and to bring Turkey and Yugoslavia into the war on the Allied side. The Greeks, after the death of Metaxas, went along. The Turks refused to abandon their neutrality—to the relief of the British Mediterranean command, which regarded the ill-equipped Turkish army as a military liability. The Yugoslavs declined even to enter into high-level discussions with the British which, as Prince Paul explained to Campbell, would only unnecessarily provoke the Germans.

In their effort to prod Yugoslavia into "resisting German aggression," the Americans followed the British lead. By mid-February, President Roosevelt had succeeded in persuading Secretary Hull that the United States ought to become concerned with the outcome of the British plans for the Balkans. Sumner Welles, who was more privy to Roosevelt's thinking, assumed an overall, albeit informal, supervision of the State Department's operations in the area. When Minister Lane's cable of February 18, describing his dramatic meeting with Prince Paul, found its way to Welles' desk, the latter immediately brought it to Hull's attention. Hull promptly forwarded it to the White House. Two days later, Roosevelt reacted by a lengthy memorandum which spelled out broad guidelines for the United States' approach to the problem.

"In the case of Yugoslavia," read the pertinent passage of the memorandum, "we should find some means of getting across to the Prince Regent and others that the United States is looking not merely to the present but to the future, and that any nation which tamely submits on the grounds of being quickly overrun would receive less sympathy from the world than a nation which resists, even if this resistance can be continued only for a few weeks." Roosevelt then cited examples of other heroic nations, and concluded that "our type of civilization and the war in whose outcome we are definitely interested, will be definitely helped by resistance on the part of Yugoslavia and, almost automatically, resistance on the part of Turkey—even though temporarily Yugoslavia and Turkey are not successful in the military sense." And Roosevelt asked Hull to get these thoughts across to Prince Paul.

Hull called in Ray Atherton, then in charge of the Division for European Affairs, and told him to draft a message to Prince Paul, basing it on Roosevelt's letter. Atherton went to work, taking into account a memorandum prepared at this request by one of his chief aides, Robert D. Coe (to whom he showed Roosevelt's letter), in which Coe cited various examples of American rejection of Yugoslav pleas for assistance. Coe recommended a broader and more meaningful approach. "I have constantly urged," he wrote, "that we release whatever we could for the Yugoslavs in an effort to demonstrate our real sympathy for the country in its present situation." Coe pointed out the high degree of understanding of American aims manifested by Belgrade officials, called attention to the fact that "we have not demonstrated in any sense, beyond words, our desire to help Yugoslavia," and suggested following the proposed message from the president "by immediate and effective aid to Greece" which would have "its repercussions in Belgrade and might stiffen the morale of the Yugoslav government in resisting diplomatic or military pressure."

Atherton, who considered Coe's ideas sound, modified some of the points made by Roosevelt in his draft, and took it to Sumner Welles. Welles took strong exception to most of Atherton's modifications. In a memorandum to Hull, dated February 21, he wrote that he was "not particularly happy about this draft telegram. Why should we redraft the President's message and, in particular, in our redraft omit what, in my judgment at least, are the most significant portions of the message as he phrases it?" After giving the matter further thought, Welles sent another memorandum to Hull the next day. He agreed now that some passages needed to be altered and others omitted altogether (he specifically indicated which ones). But he stressed that the general tone and the phrasing should be left the way Roosevelt had written it. Welles was particularly emphatic that the message should contain no specific American commitments.

Hull did not argue. He accepted Welles' objections and the message went to Lane the next day as follows:[33]

Having read your 115, February 18, 8 P.M., the President wishes you to seek an immediate audience with the Prince Regent and state the following:

"I am addressing this message to Your Royal Highness with a view to emphasizing the interest of the United States in the outcome of the war. I fully appreciate the difficult and vital problems facing you and the Yugoslav government, but I most earnestly wish to point out that the United States is looking not merely to the present but to the future. I wish to convey to you my feeling that the world in general regards with very real sympathy any nation which resists attack, both military or diplomatic, by the predatory powers.

"The examples of Abyssinia, China, and Greece are in point. Abyssinia won world sympathy by a brief though unsuccessful resistance and Abyssinia will be restored.

"China seemed capable of making no resistance in the modern sense of the word but after 4 years China is still resisting and has the sympathy of the world with an excellent chance of being reconstituted in her independence in some way at some date.

"The Greek cause looked completely hopeless in view of an Italian army and air force of overwhelming proportions. The cause of Greek independence will win in the end.

"The rear guard action fought by Norway for 2 or 3 months means that all of us will work for the restoration of Norwegian independence.

"I am convinced that our type of civilization and the war in whose outcome we are vitally interested will be definitely helped by resistance on the part of the nations which suffer from aggression."

Reading this message, Lane was elated. It looked as if the president fully accepted his recommendation to use a promise of supporting Yugoslavia's political and geographic claims at a

33. Hull to Lane, February 22, 1941, FR, 1941, II, 947.

future peace conference as an additional diplomatic weapon in dealing with Prince Paul. He rushed to the palace to deliver Roosevelt's message to Prince Paul, but the regent's reaction was disappointing. Prince Paul reiterated that for Yugoslavia to attack Germany would be sheer folly. At the same time, he assured Lane that he "[would] not sign any political agreement with Germany derogatory to Yugoslav sovereignty." This statement Lane interpreted in his subsequent report as a promise "under no conditions to sign the Tripartite Pact" or "join the new order which is the same thing." To Lane's question as to whether he could inform the president that the prince would "resist aggression," the latter emphatically answered yes.[34]

It seems obvious that the meaning which Prince Paul put into this catchword differed substantially from the way Lane interpreted it. It is also possible that both men were aware of the difference but preferred not to go into semantics; Prince Paul, because this would have meant admitting that under no foreseeable circumstances would Yugoslavia join the Allies in an active struggle against the Axis; and Lane, because he felt compelled to sound more hopeful than the situation warranted. It was simply too hard for him to admit the futility of the president's appeal.[35]

This conversation took place on February 23, when the over-all picture in the Balkans still had the deceptive appearance of being relatively static, thereby inviting diplomatic maneuvering with a promise that something significant could come out of discussions of this sort. What both the British and the Americans overlooked was that the Germans held all the trump cards

---

34. Lane to Hull, February 23, 1941, *ibid.*, 947–948.
35. Another possibility is not excluded, namely that Prince Paul did actually sound more optimistic in this conversation. At this moment he hoped to get some good news from Italy where he had played his last card: his private emissary, a Belgrade lawyer, V. Stakić, who had carried out on his behalf negotiations with Mussolini and Ciano the preceding November and early in February, was again in Rome. He was authorized to ask the Duce to join Prince Paul in a statement reaffirming the old Pact of Friendship of 1937 between the two countries, thus making it unnecessary for Yugoslavia to sign the Tripartite Pact with the Axis, as Hitler demanded. Mussolini received Stakić on February 24, 1941, and stated that he would intercede with Hitler only if Yugoslavia signed a formal treaty of alliance with Italy and declared war on Greece. This price Prince Paul, who did not trust Mussolini anyway, refused to pay.

and that their initiatives were based on power rather than the
intangibles and abstractions which filled the arsenal of the
Allied camp. Within 24 hours, however, reports were received
in both Belgrade and Athens that German troops had started
pouring from Rumania into Bulgaria. According to the British
scenario, this move was supposed to trigger an action on the
part of the Turks and the Yugoslavs. Nothing happened. One
week passed, and on March 1, 1941, as the Germans entered
Sofia, Bulgaria announced that it was joining the Tripartite
Pact, thus casting its lot with the Axis. Yet the British continued to cling to the hope of swaying at least Yugoslavia. On
March 3, Campbell returned from a trip to Athens and brought
to Prince Paul Eden's personal letter. The foreign secretary
described in most optimistic terms the progress of Anglo-Greek
plans, reminded the regent that German occupation of Salonika
would isolate Yugoslavia entirely, and requested that a Yugoslav general staff delegation be sent to Athens immediately in
order to discuss plans for mutual defense. Prince Paul did not
reply. Instead, on March 4, in great secrecy, he left for a
prearranged meeting with Hitler in Berchtesgaden.

In their five-hour talk, at which nobody but Ribbentrop was
present, Hitler formally invited Prince Paul to join the Axis,
pointing out that this was the only way to guarantee Yugoslavia's security against Italy. He mentioned that Salonika
would go to Yugoslavia after the war and said that Germany
would attack Greece shortly. This was not something Hitler
relished doing (in a fit of frankness he told Prince Paul that he
would launch an invasion of Russia in June and that the Greek
campaign was an undesirable distraction), but he could not
take chances that British airfields would be established within
range of the Rumanian oil fields. Because of this timetable, the
Greek campaign had to be swift, and he needed assurances that
Yugoslavia would be on his side.

Prince Paul mostly listened, overwhelmed by the unfolding
picture. He remarked that if he agreed to sign the pact, he
would not last six months in his present position. To this,
Ribbentrop ominously suggested that "the reverse might happen," that is, "that he would no longer be here in six months if
he did not take our advice and thus let a unique opportunity

slip by."[36] Although Prince Paul reserved his decision, he apparently appeared impressed enough for Ribbentrop to telegraph von Heeren, German minister in Belgrade, to make sure that the Yugoslav government signed the Pact within two weeks. Because of the military timetable, no further delay was possible. Ribbentrop also warned von Heeren that the whole affair was to be handled in total secrecy so that nothing would interfere with the favorable decision of the Yugoslav government. A similar stiff warning was sent to Mussolini.

On March 6, Prince Paul called a meeting of the Crown Council, the executive committee of the cabinet, and reported the essence of Hitler's demands. After long and heated argument the question boiled down to whether or not Yugoslavia could take an anti-Axis stand and survive the German attack which, in this case, had to be taken for granted. The minister of war's report was gloomy. After more discussions, a consensus was reached to sign the Pact if the Axis would accept certain conditions. These conditions were to have the Axis guarantee in writing the sovereignty and territorial integrity of Yugoslavia; to formally promise not to request any military assistance from, or passage of troops through, Yugoslavia; and to restore after the war Yugoslavia's privileged position in Salonika which it had enjoyed since 1929. These terms Cincar-Marković passed on to von Heeren.

Arthur Bliss Lane Acts

By the beginning of March the American legation in Belgrade looked more like a battle station than a "listening post." The phones rang all the time. Visitors kept pouring in and out. News kept coming in from local and foreign diplomatic missions; from friendly government, military, and political circles; and especially, from the excited American newsmen who had descended upon Belgrade from other Balkan capitals where, due to German pressure and local censorship, they had found little they could report. The Yugoslav government, which effectively controlled the local press, in its desperate effort to preserve an appearance of neutrality was reluctant to interfere

36. GFP, D, XII, 230–232. Cf. Hoptner, 218; and FR, 1941, II, 973.

with the intelligence-gathering efforts of these newsmen or to
censor the outgoing stories, bitterly critical of Yugoslav policy
as they were. The newsmen's attacks on the Axis and the
publication abroad of various news (and rumors) aimed at en-
cumbering political and military moves of Berlin and Rome
were a source of continuous embarrassment for the Yugoslav
government. German and Italian protests were frequent, complicating the delicate negotiations over the terms of Yugoslavia's accession to the Tripartite Pact—which was precisely
the goal of the American newsmen.[37]

The American legation did not limit itself to the gathering
and relaying of information to Washington. A great deal of what
the minister learned from Yugoslav officials he passed on to
American correspondents in Belgrade who were all too happy
to mobilize public opinion at home against the Yugoslav government's pro-Axis orientation. Abandoning his professed dislike for dealing with the opposition, Lane expanded his contacts with the political adversaries of Prince Paul and Prime
Minister Cvetkovic. The more apparent the drift of the government into the Axis camp, the more energy Arthur Bliss Lane
put into his campaign aimed at arresting this drift. He worked
around the clock, keeping track of all developments, and
coordinating every aspect of the legation's operations. His staff
and the rest of the American colony in the Yugoslav capital,
equally inspired and excited, followed Lane's direction as never before. Gone were the relaxing evenings of poker with a
glass of Scotch at the minister's residence; and many of those
who observed Arthur Bliss Lane in action during those days
marvelled at his limitless energy.

Lane pinned most of his hopes on his ability to influence
Prince Paul, whom he considered rather weak. Although there
was no more informality in their relations, and although Lane
began to encounter difficulties in securing audiences at the
palace, Prince Paul was still willing to listen to Lane's argu-

---

37. For a good recollection of the newsmen's activities, see Ray Brock's, *Nor
Any Victory* (New York: Reynal & Hitchcock, 1942). Brock aided Sulzberger
in "covering" the Balkans for the *New York Times*. See also Sulzberger's
memoirs.

ments and to state, with apparent sincerity, his own position. Therefore, the inaccessibility of the regent during the first week of March caused Lane considerable concern. He sensed that something was going on unfavorable to his cause. Unable to see the regent, he redoubled his efforts elsewhere. He saw practically everybody of prominence in Belgrade, trying to advance the now crystallized American policy in every conceivable way. He obtained more favorable coverage in the Yugoslav press of the congressional debates over the Lend-Lease Bill, in which some of the speeches of the isolationists played clearly into German hands. With Hull's permission, Lane acquainted top government officials and leaders of the opposition with the contents of Roosevelt's personal message to Prince Paul, stressing the long-range advantages of an anti-Axis posture for Yugoslavia and the grave consequences of the alternative course. Fortier devoted much of his time to seeing Yugoslav military leaders, especially Mirković and Simović of the air force, the citadel of the Serbian patriotism. He listened to their passionate declarations of hatred for the Axis and resolutions to fight to the last ditch. He inspected secret hideouts and caches of arms and munitions in the mountains, and studied the Cetnic organization of Colonel Draža Mihailovic. In the end, the normally cautious Fortier was won over. He abandoned his previously skeptical evaluation of the Yugoslav capacity to resist the Germans and concluded that Yugoslavia could, after all, contribute significantly to the Allied war effort.

Prince Paul finally received Lane on the evening of March 7. The ruler of Yugoslavia was reserved. He did not tell Lane about his meeting with Hitler or about the Crown Council's decision. But he admitted that he was "wavering" in the face of German encirclement of the country. There were two choices open to him, said Prince Paul: "(1) to resist, at the cost of two or three hundred thousand lives and devastation of the country and the establishment of slavery as in Poland until the end of the war, and partition of the country between Germany, Italy, Hungary, and Bulgaria; or (2) to keep quiet and permit the country to be occupied with some conditions of slavery but without loss of life." Anticipating Lane's objections, he said he knew the arguments about national honor, but he also had a duty to turn the country over to the king intact and not in ruins. To attack Germany would be suicide.[38]

There was a certain air of finality in the tone of his voice, and Lane, who knew Prince Paul well enough to be able to tell how his "wavering" would end, could see the writing on the wall. Yet in reporting this conversation, he could not bring himself to face this bleak prospect and to share his forebodings with the State Department. To predict the likely outcome of Yugoslavia's adherence to the Pact was to acknowledge the failure of his efforts to carry out the wishes of the president. It did not matter to him that the State Department was more than satisfied with his performance. Determined to obtain tangible results and refusing to back down in the face of the adverse developments he was witnessing, he focused all his attention on the attainment of the single objective of preventing Yugoslavia from signing the Tripartite Pact.

He did all he could, perhaps all that was humanly possible, during those first weeks of March to prevent Yugoslavia's alignment with the Axis. The first ominous sign that he had failed came on March 8 when he learned from his private informers that Prince Paul had met recently with "Ribbentrop or some other high German." The second sign followed almost immediately. As if by command, the government officials, hitherto so communicative, suddenly became reticent, refusing to discuss Yugoslav relations with Germany in any shape or form. Sensing the meaning of these signs, and more than ever convinced that the Yugoslav government was following a wrong course, Arthur Bliss Lane came to the conclusion that a great betrayal was in the making; that Prince Paul had gone back on his promise to "resist German aggression"; and that the Yugoslav nation had to be rescued in spite of its government.

It was not easy for Minister Lane to arrive at this conclusion. Ever since he had learned about the officers' plot to overthrow

---

38. Lane to Hull, March 7, 1941, FR, 1941, II, 949–950. According to Hoptner, who had at his disposal Prince Paul's notes, this conversation "had something of the atmosphere of the interrogation of a criminal or of one suspected by the Holy Office of heresy. The American minister, even more than his British counterpart, questioned, insisted, beseeched. Both used every means at their disposal to coerce Prince Paul and others in the Yugoslav government into bringing their policies into line with the dogma of strategy enunciated in London and Washington." Hoptner, 222-223.

the government, he had hoped that this drastic step would not be necessary. The available record contains no indication that he saw any merit in such an act. So long as he could hope that Prince Paul and his ministers would be persuaded to follow Anglo-American advice, he could also hope that the differences between the regency and the conspirators would not break into the open; that, on the contrary, in the face of the external danger national unity would be accomplished. Now he realized that the Allies' last recourse, the military coup d'état, could no longer be avoided.

This conclusion, no doubt painful to Lane, was made easier to arrive at by Prince Paul's lack of candor in regard to his dealings with the Germans. Resentful and suspicious, Lane resolved to exacerbate the regent's relations with the opposition, giving the latter all possible encouragement and thereby making the government's dilemma even more difficult.

Much as Arthur Bliss Lane tried to act discreetly, his vigorous activities could not remain secret for long in the gossip-ridden capital. On March 11, the minister of the court called him in and reprimanded him for violating diplomatic ethics by taking his cause to the disgruntled Serbian oppositionists. As Lane reported to the Department the same evening, he replied (without giving any specifics) that for this he had Prince Paul's permission. Then he aggressively countered with a complaint to Antić that he had been unable "due to the reticence of local officials," to give his government "official information as to what is transpiring here" and had been forced to transmit to Washington nothing but unconfirmed rumors. He inferred that the Yugoslav government was "terrified by Germans and consequently afraid to discuss the situation openly with us." To this, Antić replied that he would inform Lane "at an appropriate moment." Lane finished his report about this encounter by repeating that rumors persisted that "a non-aggression pact" would be executed with Germany during the coming weekend: he apparently felt that the time had arrived to start preparing his government for the bad news.[39]

Two days later Lane was called in by the foreign minister, who pointedly asked him about American "guarantees" to ·Yu-

39. Lane to Hull, March 11, 1941, *ibid.*, 952. Also Lane to Hull, March 13, 1941.

goslavia ("presumably in the event of resisting Axis pressure") which Lane reportedly made in his talks with several cabinet ministers and opposition leaders. These promises had started a chain of rumors which reached as far as Washington: the Yugoslav minister there had cabled Cincar-Marković asking for information about such guarantees. Lane denied "having promised any guarantees of any nature" but, in his report to Hull of March 13, cautiously added that he received the impression that Cincar-Marković "wished to ascertain whether my talks here took place with the approval of the Department."

There is no evidence to indicate that Lane did in fact have such approval. Secretary Hull firmly opposed any further involvement of the United States in Yugoslav affairs. On March 12, in response to new demands from the British Embassy to put full diplomatic pressure on Belgrade and Ankara (and in disregard of the president's expressed viewpoint on this matter), Hull stated that "we have already done everything this government can possibly do in the present circumstances." It can also be surmised that Hull was none too pleased with Minister Lane's highly unorthodox tactics. Having read Lane's cables of March 11 and 13, the Secretary responded on the 15th by warmly thanking Lane for his "most helpful" reports, phrasing his message in such a way as to suggest that reporting was really all he expected from the minister, and that perhaps it would be better for Lane not to undertake the impossible. It is unlikely that Lane, who had been well versed in the art of diplomatic phraseology, missed this hint, but he probably attributed Hull's lack of enthusiasm to the secretary's inflexibility and disapproval of the president's policy. At any rate, in the following days Lane's participation in the activities of the Serbian opposition continued unabated.

In the meantime, the secret German-Yugoslav negotiations over the conditions laid down by the Crown Council continued, with the Yugoslavs clearly stalling. Prince Paul had faint hope that if the decision were delayed long enough, the immense problems which Germany faced in its forthcoming invasion of Russia might change Hitler's mind so that he would decide to leave Yugoslavia alone. Accordingly, his negotiators insisted that all the conditions exempting Yugoslavia from any military obligations under the Pact be met by the Axis.

Ribbentrop was exasperated. Germany needed Yugoslavia's accession to the Pact more than ever because the forthcoming invasion of Russia was already threatened with delay by the necessity of resolving the conflict in Greece. Yugoslavia, with its weak government, could not be permitted to become a source of trouble as a ground for intrigue and subversion for the Anglo-Americans. On March 14 Ribbentrop threw up his hands. He telegraphed von Heeren, accepting all Yugoslav demands. Written guarantees, amounting to recognition of Yugoslavia's continued neutrality in the war in spite of its adherence to the Pact, would be given in separate notes, wrote Ribbentrop. These could then be made public, except for the one containing the Axis promise regarding Salonika: to keep it secret was in the Yugoslavs' own interest. Making these concessions, Ribbentrop stressed that "there was no foreign policy interest at all *in favor of doing this*, but exclusively domestic policy considerations of the Yugoslav government." He instructed von Heeren to present to Cincar-Marković the modified German position "in a friendly but urgent form," leaving him "in no doubt that it is now up to the Yugoslav government to make up its mind as to whether or not it wants to accede to the Tripartite Pact on the basis as outlined." "You can also tell the foreign minister," added Ribbentrop, "that we have been as accommodating to him as we possibly could be." And he insisted on a speedy answer.[40]

With Germany having thus met their terms, the Yugoslavs could not drag their feet any longer. On March 15, Cvetković told Campbell that although no decision had yet been made, Yugoslavia would probably sign a "non-aggression pact" with Germany which would guarantee its neutrality. To Campbell's suggestion that "Yugoslavia should take a positive stand," he replied, "Do you want us to attack Germany?" Campbell left, "puzzled by the inconsistency of Cvetković's remarks."[41]

The "Capitulation" of Prince Paul

On March 15, 1941, Anthony Eden cabled Churchill from

---

40. Ribbentrop to von Heeren, March 14, 1941, GFP, XII, 291-294. For a detailed account of these negotiations, based on both German and Yugoslav sources, see Hoptner, 225 f.
41. Lane to Hull, March 15, 1941, FR, 1941, II, 955.

Cairo that he was doing all in his power "to encourage Yugoslavia and to stiffen Turkey, so that she in her turn might stimu-
late Yugoslavia. The hand is an extraordinarily difficult one to
play. Commanders-in-chief, while anxious that Yugoslavia
should fight with us, are of the opinion that Turkey's entry into
the war at this stage would constitute a military liability which
they do not wish to incur," that "only if a Turkish declaration
of war proved essential to bring in the Yugoslavs . . . we should
press for one."[42] Acting on these assumptions, Eden made
arrangements for a meeting with the Turkish foreign minister,
and sent to Belgrade Terence Shone, British minister in Cairo,
a close personal friend of Prince Paul. In a letter to Prince
Paul, Eden wrote that coming to terms with Germany at that
point would be "to sacrifice the strong position you have built
up and would lead step by step to Yugoslavia suffering the fate
that has already overcome Rumania and Bulgaria." Eden suggested that "valuable munitions of war and supplies of all
kinds" were awaiting the Yugoslavs in Mussolini's Albania,
and asked Prince Paul to receive Sir John Dill, chief of the
Imperial General Staff.

Prince Paul refused to meet Dill. From an officer of the
Yugoslav general staff, Major Peričić, whom he had reluctantly
sent to Athens on March 8, Prince Paul had already learned
that the British could offer no help to the Yugoslav army and
that he could not take seriously the promise of supplies which
were to be captured in Albania. He told Shone frankly that the
action suggested by Eden would be suicidal for Yugoslavia.
Having received this information, Eden was "more sorry than
surprised." He felt he had done all he could "to persuade the
Prince to resolve his dilemma, cruel, and admittedly none of
his making, in the way which would best have served his
people and his dynasty."[43]

Secretary of State Hull by this time seemed to have adjusted

---

42. Eden, 256. The Turks refused to be pressed into the war, in spite of a
promise of "complete understanding and neutrality" which they had received from Moscow, their continuing source of worry. Similarly, they declined the British suggestion of making a declaration that they would regard
a German attack on Salonika as a *casus belli* if Yugoslavia would do the
same. The reason, of course, was that they had accepted Hitler's promises
(renewed on March 4) to respect Turkey's neutrality.
43. *Ibid.*, 259.

to the prospect of Yugoslavia's adherence to the Tripartite Pact or its speedy occupation by Germany. On March 15, he cabled Lane that the previous day the National Bank of Yugoslavia had requested Secretary of the Treasury Henry Morganthau to convert 22 million dollars worth of its gold, deposited in the Federal Reserve Bank (out of a total of about 60 million), into dollars and immediately transfer half of this amount to its account with the Bank of Brazil. Since the American policy had been to freeze all the assets of governments which had fallen under the political control of the Axis, Hull expressed concern. He felt that "in the face of an overwhelming of the government or country by force" the freezing of the funds in the United States should be appreciated by all who wished to prevent the possibility of their seizure by the Nazis. "In order to protect Yugoslav interests," wrote Hull, "it may be necessary to consider a freezing order."

Lane, who was desperately searching for ways of influencing the Yugoslav government, contrived to use the promise of letting Yugoslav funds go to Brazil as an additional means of pressure in Belgrade. His plan did not work. Prince Paul said he knew nothing about the gold deal and suggested that Lane see the minister of finance. Prime Minister Cvetković, whom Lane visited immediately afterwards, also claimed to be ignorant of the order to convert the 22 million dollars worth of gold into a dollar account and, like Prince Paul, proposed to meet jointly with the minister of finance. Discussing other points, Cvetković emphatically stated that no German troops or war materiel would be allowed in Yugoslavia, and that the army would resist a German attack. But he also said that the government had decided not to interfere with a German occupation of the port of Salonika.

These two conversations—which took place on March 16—gave Lane a fair idea about the terms on which the Yugoslav government was prepared to join the Axis in the Tripartite Pact. It appears that for a brief moment the American minister wavered. Recognizing that a deal with Germany was inevitable, he felt that perhaps it would be wise, as well as realistic, to settle for less than the officially stated American goal. If Belgrade could succeed in remaining militarily neutral, this would be somewhat to the Allies' advantage. At any rate, after a conference the next day with Cvetković and the ministers of justice and finance during which he received further assurances of Yugoslav neutrality, he sent Hull a "triple priority" cable recommending the transfer of the Yugoslav funds "in the interest of friendly relations."

The mood in Washington, however, was not favorable to compromise solutions of any sort. Sumner Welles, who had just returned from a vacation, took the matter of Yugoslav gold into his own hands. He discovered that the Yugoslavs had just made an additional request: they now wanted another 11 million dollars from their gold account to be transferred to Argentina. This looked so ominous that he went to see Roosevelt. Both concluded that "the Yugoslav government has already taken the path which will ultimately lead to capitulation." Having returned to the State Department, Welles called in the Yugoslav minister and told him, with considerable annoyance, that President Roosevelt "regarded the Yugoslav insistence on transferring these funds, after having received our assurances that there was no intention on our part to freeze" as an indication of "a lack of confidence in the expressed attitude of this government." After Fotitch told Welles that he would recommend that Belgrade cancel the new order, Welles said that the sale of the requested amount of the Yugoslav gold would be allowed to go through, but that the rest of it should not be touched. In the end, quite irritably, he added that "we feel that in view of our determined attitude to be of every assistance we can to the government of Yugoslavia in support of its efforts to maintain the independence and integrity of the country, we are entitled to enough consideration of our own problems here to warrant some notfication and discussion of any major operations in the financial field contemplated by the government of Yugoslavia with respect to its funds in this country."[44]

Welles' message describing this encounter indicated to Lane that Roosevelt had taken an everything-or-nothing attitude towards Yugoslavia, and that therefore his own task still

---

44. Welles to Lane, March 19, 1941. Fotitch, 61-64. The State Department approved the sale of the Yugoslav gold to the Treasury on March 18; $11,225,000 was transferred to the Chase Manhattan Bank for the Yugoslav account with the Banquo do Brazil while another $11 million remained in the Yugoslav dollar account with the Federal Reserve Bank.

was to prevent a political rapprochement between Belgrade and the Axis. But what else *could* he do? For several weeks he had been acting at his top capacity, living under a tension which would have been unbearable to anyone of lesser purposefulness, energy, and determination. He had seen all the important members of the government, most forcefully presenting to them all conceivable arguments in an effort to forestall the inevitable. He had violated the diplomatic code by encouraging the opposition elements to press the government for a firm anti-Axis stand. It was to no avail. Much greater forces were at work, and the task which President Roosevelt had assigned him was clearly beyond his power. Although he still refused to admit his failure, he was beginning to recognize it. On March 19 he cabled Welles a carefully worded message, reminding the under secretary that he had warned the Department not to take Prince Paul's promise not to sign the Pact literally, since the regent was likely to be "so overwrought by the seriousness of the situation as to be inclined to forget the gravity of his former promises. I fear that this is the situation as it is today" concluded Lane. He informed Welles that he was dining with Prince Paul the next evening and that he would do his best "to strengthen his resistance, even though it may be too late." And he asked for a personal message from the president "for whom Prince Paul has the greatest admiration."[45]

We do not know what went on in Lane's mind during the dinner on the evening of March 20 at his residence at which nobody but Prince Paul, Princess Olga, and Mrs. Lane were present. The atmosphere recalled the old days of their intimate friendship, but this time it was almost unbearably depressing. There were no jokes; Princess Olga was in tears most of the evening. There is no question but that Lane fully appreciated the drama of the occasion: he was essentially a sensitive and even sentimental man. But whatever his inner thoughts were, he remained true to his mission to the end. Perhaps in a somewhat friendlier manner than had been his way in recent weeks, but with the same singlemindedness, he recapitulated

---

45. Lane to Welles, March 19, 1941, FR, 1941, 957. Welles immediately cabled back, informing Lane that Roosevelt was on vacation but that he could state "as emphatically as you consider desirable" that the president was "following every development with the keenest interest."

his old arguments. He pointed out that the Yugoslavs in the United States would feel that Prince Paul had let them down if he adhered to the Pact; that the Pact itself would be no guarantee against later German encroachments; that the thing to do was to protect the long-range interests of Yugoslavia which would be taken care of after the war. Lane accused Prince Paul's advisers of selfish pursuit of their own material gains. And with calculated cruelty, he suggested that joining the Pact would be a treacherous act against Greece, the native country of Princess Olga.

Prince Paul, tired and melancholic, listened to the admonitions of his former friend. He repeated his counter-arguments, saying that to fail to sign the Pact now that the Germans had accepted all his demands would mean war; that the country was politically disunited, with the Croats and Slovenes opposing any action against Germany; and that the army was incapable of offering any significant resistance. The immediate prospect, if he were irresponsible enough to follow Lane's advice, would be a quick defeat, military occupation of the country, and its partition between Italy, Germany, Hungary, and Bulgaria. This he could not allow to happen. In reply to Lane's remark that the most important thing was to preserve Yugoslavia's integrity and to maintain its position among the Allies, Prince Paul merely shrugged his shoulders. "You big nations," he said bitterly, "are hard. You talk of our honor but you are far away."[46]

Lane's report of this conversation crossed with the message from Welles. If Lane was inclined to accept the inevitable, his government was not. "I am so impressed with your able handling of the present delicate situation," cabled Welles, "that I desire you to make a further attempt to clearly impress upon Prince Paul that the Italian debacle in Albania is such that there is no threat from that region to Yugoslav safety; that the landing of British forces in Greece is ahead of schedule and that the terrain there would allow them to withstand any thrusts the Germans may be able to make." Welles further wrote that the attitude of the Turkish government "is now clear" (he did not say in what way), and emphasized that the

---

46. Lane to Hull, March 21, 1941, *ibid.*, 962-963. Cf. Hoptner, 235-236.

United States was prepared "to offer all facilities under the Lend-Lease Bill." As extra bait, Welles added that "those Yugoslav assets which are now on deposit in the United States will remain at her disposal as long as in the interpretation of this government Yugoslavia remains a free and independent country."[47]

In order to make sure that there would be no misunderstanding in Belgrade, Welles repeated the same arguments to Fotitch, the sympathetic Yugoslav minister in Washington, who came to show him the latest explanatory cable from the foreign minister. Both heartily agreed that the cable "explained nothing" and that it was of the kind of which "a schoolboy would be ashamed." Then Welles officially declared that "if the government of Yugoslavia entered into any agreement with Germany which either diminished the complete sovereignty or autonomy of Yugoslavia, or facilitated in any way by means of Yugoslav connivance or concessions for a German attack upon Greece or upon the British forces in the Mediterranean region, or which in any way assisted the Axis powers in either a naval or military sense, this government would immediately freeze all Yugoslav funds within the United States and would refuse to consider any request for assistance under the terms of the Lend-Lease Bill." The United States, said Welles, "might conceivably understand and palliate an agreement between Yugoslavia and Germany which was purely and solely a non-aggression agreement and nothing more"; anything beyond that "would place Yugoslavia outside the pale of the sympathies of the United States government."[48]

This combined presentation had no effect in Belgrade. On the same day, March 21, the Yugoslav cabinet resolved to sign the Pact. Lane, who learned about it "from a reliable source," reported to Hull all the supplementary terms upon which the cabinet had insisted and which the Axis had accepted. Although realizing that this was final, Lane visited the prime minister and Prince Paul to show them Welles' message. Both pointed out to him gross inaccuracies in the allegations of the undersecretary, and restated the reasons which compelled Yu-

---

47. Welles to Lane, March 21, 1941, *ibid.*, 961-962.
48. Memorandum of conversation, *ibid.*, 959-961.

goslavia to adhere to the Pact. Lane warned that the signing
would provoke "public hostility" in Yugoslavia, but the threat
was shrugged off by Prince Paul who had other things to worry
about. "I have never seen the Prince so upset," reported Lane,
"and, unless he is an excellent actor, almost without self-
control. . . He ranted on about Bulgarian perfidy, British stupidity, and opposition of the Croats, but he refused to consider the
possibility of not signing the Pact and capitulating to Germany."[49]

The Coup d' État

The world learned about Yugoslavia's accession to the Tripartite Pact from a public announcement made after the appropriate ceremony took place on the afternoon of March 25, 1941,
at the Belvedere Palace in Vienna. Cvetković and Cincar-
Marković, who had left Belgrade in secret the previous day,
signed the protocol for Yugoslavia; Ribbentrop and Ciano represented the Axis. Simultaneously, the Yugoslavs received four
notes from the German and Italian governments, exempting
Yugoslavia from certain provisions of the Pact and recognizing
Yugoslav interest in the outlet to the Aegean Sea in Salonika.[50]
After the ceremony, Cvetković and Cincar-Marković were received by Hitler. In a long-winded speech, the Führer described the advantages gained by Yugoslavia through its adherence to the Pact, assuring the newcomers that they would
always find him "an honest, loyal mediator, broker, and
friend." He said that he understood very well the aversion of
many Yugoslavs, including Prince Paul, to taking the present
step and that he himself was "not free of sentiment in this
respect." But, added Hitler, "reasons of state and the interests
of the people had precedence," just as he, Hitler, after cool
consideration, often had to take steps of a military nature which
were not pleasant for him from the human point of view. He
fully realized, "that certain decisions in the last few days had

49. Lane to Welles, March 23 and 24, 1941, *ibid.*, 966-967.
50. For the texts of the notes see GFP, D, XII, 313-314. On the role of the
Salonika question in the Yugoslav negotiations with the Axis, see the exchange between R.L. Knejevitch and D. Cvetković in *International Affairs*,
January and October, 1951, which also reveals the background of official and
opposition thinking in the spring of 1941.

been difficult," but was confident that "in the developments as a whole it would certainly prove to be correct ... although perhaps the youth did not everywhere understand the realistic decisions of the statesmen."[51]

Within two days Hitler's hopes were shattered. Not only "the youth" failed to understand the realistic decisions of the statesmen, but the Serbian military plotters in Belgrade took full advantage of the unpopular step taken by the government and in a single stroke, in the early hours of March 27, overthrew the regency and arrested the key ministers. General Dušan Simović, acting as the "strong man" of the new regime, proclaimed King Peter II the ruler of Yugoslavia. The king, in turn, appointed Simović prime minister. Prince Paul, who was in Zagreb when the coup d'état took place, rejected all suggestions to organize resistance. He returned to Belgrade in the evening of the same day, signed the documents of abdication, and by midnight had left for Greece — and exile — accompanied by his family.

The coup d'état, the brainchild of General Mirković and his British advisers, was completely bloodless and carried out with utmost efficiency.[52] Nobody in the capital attempted to rally forces to the defense of the government. As one author summed it up:

> The complete success of the *coup* was due to the coalescing of a number of different elements. With the exception of a few individuals, the Serbs — specially the "old generals," the intelligentsia and leftist students, the opposition, the army, the air force, and Orthodox church — and some Croats and Slovenes be-

---

51. Later in the day, talking privately to Ciano, Hitler expressed satisfaction with the accession of Yugoslavia to the Pact. With Belgrade's uncertain attitude thus ended, Germany could now complete the preparations for the attack on Greece early in April. Hitler was confident that the presence in Greece of the 20 to 40 thousand British troops that had landed near Athens and Salonika could not possibly prevent a quick and complete German victory; in fact, the more English ships in Greece, the more crushing would be the defeat he was about to administer. GFP, D, III, 354–357, *ibid.,* 357–361.

52. The mechanics of the Belgrade coup d'état are described by Ristic, chapters 8-10; some interesting recollections can be found in King Peter's book, *A King's Heritage;* V-VI; in Brock's, *Nor Any Victory;* and Robert St. John's, *From the Land of Silent People.* By far the best analysis is provided by Hoptner, chapters VIII-X.

lieved the signing of the Pact betrayed old alliances and doomed
Yugoslavia to dishonor and penalty after the inevitable Allied
victory over Germany. Moreover, they were convinced it would
encourage Croat separatism and Italian territorial claims, and thus
bring an end to the Yugoslav state.[53]

While the success of the coup d'état can adequately be
explained in these terms, it is doubtful that the Serbian opposition would have developed and carried out the "revolution" of
March 27, 1941, on its own. Everybody was so much aware of
the terrible danger of Hitler's retaliation that only very few
men could bring themselves to consider what amounted to a
national suicide for the sake of noble principles. Perhaps, more
importantly, the opposition was far from uniform in its objectives, and its diverse elements needed a catalyst—a unified and
determined leadership. Ostensibly, the latter was provided by
the Serbian officers. In actual fact, these officers were merely
tools in the hands of the British military agents in Belgrade.
This link between the conspiracy and the British legation (and
to a much lesser extent, the American) was one of the most
secret components of the plot, the existence of which was
vehemently denied in the following years by all involved.
Even a quarter of a century later, the evidence is scant, and
more disclosures are required before the whole story can be
reconstructed.

It is well known that six days before the coup d'état, on
March 21, British Minister Campbell cabled Eden (who was
then in Cairo) asking whether he should threaten to break off
relations with Yugoslavia if the government signed the Pact,
and to "encourage the opposition to overthrow the government
and annul their signature." Eden, whose knowledge of the plot
had apparently been insufficient (or so it appears from his
memoirs), ruled against breaking off relations but agreed that
the "suggested *coup* would have to be staged at the moment of
reaction caused by the signature." On March 22, Eden sent
additional instructions, telling Campbell that "rather than allow Yugoslavia to slip by stages into the German orbit, we are
prepared to risk precipitating the German attack" on that country. On the eve of Cvetković's departure for Vienna, Eden sent

---

53. Hoptner, 255-256.

yet another message authorizing Campbell to "proceed at your discretion by any means at your disposal" to meet the situation, and to take "any measures that you may think it right to take to further change of government or regime, even by *coup d'etat*."[54] We also know that having learned about Cvetković's trip to Vienna, Churchill himself immediately telegraphed Campbell to "continue to pester, nag, and bite" Prince Paul and his ministers, and to "not neglect any alternative to which we may have to resort if we find the present government have gone beyond recall."

Many of those who witnessed the events in Belgrade recall that the British legation was extremely busy during the month of March. Its task was to build up the morale of the opposition to Prince Paul in the face of the growing German pressure. To this end, British agents resorted to spreading rumors about the extraordinary dimensions of the forthcoming landings in Greece. While in fact no more than 7,000 airmen and supporting personnel were located in Greece by the end of the first week of March, with perhaps twice that number of Australians and New Zealanders disembarking in the following two weeks, the rumors had it that hundreds of thousands of troops with plenty of tanks, planes, and munitions were ready to back up the brave Greeks and Yugoslavs. One source of such "information" was a Greek journalist secretly in the British employ by the name of Pappas, who constantly shuttled between Athens and Belgrade, excitedly whispering the latest "news" into the ears of the scores of eager Western journalists in the Yugoslav capital. When confronted with the "news" that the Mediterranean waters off the shores of Greece were crowded with British ships carrying a mightly Balkan army of the empire, officials at the British legation smiled significantly and denied the tale but readily vouched for Pappas' reputation, stressing that because of his important connections he certainly was in a position to know what was going on. This was enough for many a newsman. Robert St. John, an Associated Press correspondent, later recalled: "I sent a story about one hundred thousand British troops in Greece with planes, tanks, and munitions. Then I sent a story about the blue Mediterranean

---

54. Eden, 262-264.

being black with British ships. Later I boosted the number to
two hundred thousand and eventually to three hundred thousand, all on the say-so of the Greek Pappas and on the
unofficial confirmation (but official denial) of the British legation in Belgrade."[55]

These "stories," carried by the Allied and neutral press and
amplified in foreign broadcasts, inevitably reached the Belgrade public. The leaders of the plot probably knew better but
were anxious to hear such encouraging accounts. It can be
safely surmised that those Britons who had been commu-
nicating with the rebellious generals had resorted to promises
of speedy and overwhelming aid in case of a crisis. This fan-
ning of Serbian enthusiasm was accompanied by more pragmatic measures. From at least the beginning of the year, the
British legation had been quietly distributing substantial
amounts of money among patriotic Serbs, sometimes even
without the knowledge of General Mirković. The whole leadership of the Serbian Agrarian Party had apparently been
placed on the British payroll. And although some dextrous
Balkan politicians simply pocketed the money, the bonds thus
created proved to be strong enough to cause three ministers
from the Serbian Agrarian and Independent Democratic parties
to resign on March 21 in order to demonstrate a split in the
government over the issue of the accession to the Pact. At a
meeting in the palace on March 23, General Simović forcefully
warned Prince Paul and the prime minister that if Yugoslavia
signed the Pact, he could not guarantee that his officers would

---

55. Diplomats in Athens estimated the number of troops landed in Salonika
and Piraeus by March 25 as between 80,000 and 120,000, which only proves
the success of the British in creating an impression of a truly large-scale
operation. Hitler's estimate, based on extensive intelligence reports from
Greece, placed it, for the same date, at 30,000 to 40,000. Berlin instructed
German embassies abroad to make the British military effort in Greece look
as large as possible: "The more bragging the English have done, the more
effective will be their defeat from the standpoint of propaganda," stated one
memorandum (GFP, D, XII, 349). In actual fact, on April 6, the day the
Germans invaded Greece, the British had about 62,000 men there, most of
them landed after mid-March. They also had about 80 aircraft and some
tanks and artillery against an enemy force at least ten times as powerful.
About 50,000 men (apparently including many Greeks) were eventually
evacuated from various beaches between April 24 and 29, when the war in
Greece ended in a German victory. See Butler, 457; Sulzberger, 124-126.

not revolt and overthrow the government and the regency. The warning was disregarded, mainly because Simović was known to have limited intelligence and was rated incapable of doing anything significant.

There is no question that the British maintained tight control over the moves of the plotters. The military and air attachés, Clarke, MacDonald and Mapplebeck, were in constant touch with General Mirković and Colonel Mihailović. The overall strategy of the coup had probably been in the hands of Thomas S. Masterson, an old intelligence officer, "oil man," and an expert on Balkan affairs, who appeared at the British legation in November 1940 under the cover of a "temporary secretary," but actually represented Lord Dalton's Special Operations Executive (SOE). This organization (a branch of the Ministry for Economic Warfare which Churchill jokingly called the "Ministry of Ungentlemanly Warfare") was extremely active later in the war using all sorts of covert means, including clandestine propaganda, bribery, kidnapping, and murder, to undermine the enemy; it played a major role in the organization of resistance movements and guerrilla bands in the Axis-occupied areas, providing them with arms, munitions, and operational guidance, and coordinating their activities with the needs of the British armed forces. And although the technical details of the coup d'état had been worked out almost entirely by General Mirković, political guidance and the timing of the event was doubtless provided by Campbell, Masterson, and their associates.[56]

The news of the coup d'état elated Churchill. Delivering an address to the Conservative Party leaders that day, he declared:

> Early this morning the Yugoslav nation found its soul. A revolution has taken place in Belgrade, and the ministers who but yesterday signed away the honor and freedom of the country are reported to be under arrest. This patriotic movement arises from the wrath of a valiant and warlike race at the betrayal of their country by the

56. See Hugh Dalton, *The Fateful Years, Memoirs 1931–1945*, 373–375; Sulzberger, 126–127; Hoptner, 242–243. Masterson later moved to Cairo, the operational base of the SOE in the Middle East, and from there to its London headquarters. For SOE exploits in Western Europe, see E.H. Cookridge, *Set Europe Ablaze*. Ristić, in his tale of the "revolution," chose not even to hint at the British role.

weakness of their rulers and the foul intrigues of the Axis powers. We may therefore cherish the hope . . . that a Yugoslav government will be formed worthy to defend the freedom and integrity of their country. Such a government in its brave endeavor will receive from the British Empire, and, I doubt not, in its own way, from the United States, all possible aid and succor. The British Empire and its allies will make common cause with the Yugoslav nation, and we shall continue to march and strive together until complete victory is won.

Churchill also telegraphed Eden, who by then had reached Malta on the way to London, ordering him to return to Athens, and expressing confidence that "now is surely the chance to bring in Turkey and form a joint front in the Balkans."

There was no official reaction in Moscow to the news from Belgrade. Milan Gavrilović, the Yugoslav minister, had been trying for weeks to reach agreement on a treaty with the Soviet Union. He was pro-Russian and pro-British, and a patriotic leader of the Serbian Agrarian Party. He was anxious to strengthen Yugoslavia's independent posture and attached great importance to a rapprochement with Russia which could counterbalance the Axis pressure. But the Soviet government was aware that such a step would be frowned upon in Berlin, further complicating the already uneasy Soviet-German relations. In view of the massing of German troops along the Soviet border and numerous reports of Hitler's intention to attack Russia — which by mid-March had begun to worry Stalin — the government preferred to proceed with caution. Nevertheless, the growing coolness in relations with Germany made Stalin more receptive to the idea of playing a more important role, an idea which Stafford Cripps, the British ambassador, had tried to implant in the minds of Soviet officials ever since his arrival in Moscow in March, 1940.[57] On March 22, Cripps visited Vyshynsky, deputy foreign minister, and told him that it was imperative to encourage the Yugoslavs to refuse to sign the Tripartite Pact. This, he suggested, would provoke Hitler's attack on Yugoslavia, which in turn would upset other German

---

57. In his first long talk with Molotov, Cripps suggested (a) a common policy of self-protection against Germany; (b) the establishment of Soviet leadership in the Balkans; and (c) the creation of Soviet military bases in the Straits. But at that time, the Soviet government loyally passed information about this overture to Hitler. See *Nazi-Soviet Relations, 1939-1941*, 166-168.

plans with a resulting gain not only for England but also for the Soviet Union.[58]

For a few days, Stalin hesitated. Although he still refused to believe that Hitler intended to invade Russia, he seemed to like the idea of embroiling his German partner with Yugoslavia. The coup d'état in Belgrade, universally greeted as a great British success, ended Stalin's hesitation. Negotiations with the Yugoslav mission resumed on April 3, 1941. The next day, Molotov informed the German ambassador in Moscow that the Soviet Union, in its desire to preserve peace, and in view of Yugoslavia's adherence to the Tripartite Pact, had decided to accept Belgrade's offer to sign a treaty with Yugoslavia. The following day the Treaty of Friendship and Non-Aggression was drafted and the list of Yugoslav requirements in planes, arms, and munitions was approved. In the early hours of April 6, the treaty was signed in the Kremlin. It was never ratified.[59]

The news of the coup d'état in Belgrade started a chain reaction in Berlin. At 1 P.M. on March 27 at the Reich chancellery, Hitler called a conference of his top military leaders. He grimly expressed satisfaction that the coup had taken place now rather than during the forthcoming attack on Greece or the invasion of Russia. To end all uncertainties, he ordered that necessary preparations be made for the destruction of Yugoslavia, "without waiting for possible loyalty declarations of the new government . . . which cannot anyhow be trusted in the future." The attack was to begin as soon as the means and troops were ready; Hungary and Bulgaria were going to participate in the invasion; and the Croats would be promised political autonomy. Hitler further announced that the campaign against Greece would proceed as scheduled, but that Operation Barbarossa, the attack on Russia, would now have to be postponed for up to four weeks. The Führer stressed that in order to deter Turkey from intervening and to create a favorable political climate for the Greek campaign, it was "especially important that the blow against Yugoslavia be carried out with

58. Eden, 262.
59. Hoptner, 281-282. See also MS of Žarko Popović, then Yugoslav military attaché in Moscow, with recollections of the negotiations with the Soviets and the dramatic night in the Kremlin. The Yugoslav mission in Moscow was expelled early in May, after Stalin, frightened by Germany's prowess, embarked on a series of measures aimed at placating Hitler.

inexorable severity and that the military destruction be carried out in a lightening-like operation."[60]

If the purpose of the new Belgrade regime was to put Yugoslavia on the side of the Allied powers, it did not manifest itself in the night-long conference of the political leaders (the military stayed away) called by General Simović at the war ministry immediately after the coup. Everybody except Miloš Tupanjanin, deputy leader of the Serbian Agrarian Party (who later escaped to Istanbul with $35,000 of British money), spoke for peace. In fact, the group appeared more scared of the German might than members of the Cvetković group had been. Fully realizing the significance of the events which had brought them into positions of influence, these men were overwhelmed by fear of what was now likely to happen. Simović, a man distinctly lacking in intelligence, let alone leadership qualities, seemed to be no less frightened than the others; his feeble attempts to reassure his civilian colleagues were unconvincing. Responding to the demands of the politicians, Simović readily agreed to include in the new cabinet ten non-Serbian ministers of the defunct government. Much as they were compromised, Croats, Slovenes, and Bosnians had to be retained for the sake of national unity because the minorities they represented had no leaders of stature who had a record of opposing the alignment with the Axis. The key foreign minister post was given to a non-controversial former diplomat, Momćilo Ninčić, who seemed to be acceptable to everybody, including the Germans and Italians. The Croat Maček, anticipating German retaliation (and already in secret contact with German agents in Zagreb) refused to join the cabinet.

The retention of some old faces, however, could not conceal an overall anti-Axis coloration of the new government. Although both Simović and Ninčić hastened to assure von Heeren that the revolution had purely internal political causes and had resulted from the unpopularity of Prince Paul, the Germans could hardly be expected to believe it. Churchill's speech of March 27, immediately broadcast by the BBC, set the tone for enthusiastic headlines throughout the British Empire and the neutral world. In the United States, the daily radio

---

60. GFP, D, XII, 372-375. Cf. Churchill, III, chapter IX.

broadcasts in Serbo-Croatian by a leading antifascist expatriate, Dr. Petrovitch, started on March 21 under the "private" auspices of two short-wave radio stations in Boston, had called for the overthrow of the regency and the Cvetković government. Petrovitch's impassioned appeals to the Serbs to rise up in arms against Germany intensified after the coup d'état; the reaction of the American press to the stories pouring in from Belgrade, together with Cordell Hull's statement that the Yugoslav assets in the United States were now unfrozen, only underscored the real meaning of the event.[61]

If the Germans had any doubts as to the real meaning of the developments in Yugoslavia, these were effectively dispelled by the outbursts of popular emotion following the coup d'état. Pro-Allied demonstrations, which began on March 27, continued. On the 28th, after the solemn ceremonial service at the cathedral in the presence of the king, the patriarch, the court, and the diplomatic corps, Campbell and Lane were nearly mobbed. At the same time, the German and Italian diplomats, as well as the members of the German, Italian, and Hungarian minorities throughout the country, did not dare appear in the streets.

Such demonstrations could not be restrained by the British strategists in Belgrade whose paramount task was to gain time, as much time as possible. It was on their instructions that Mirković and his military associates withdrew from the political scene immediately after the coup. In their well-reasoned judgment, nothing could return Yugoslavia to a position of neutrality under the Axis tutelage. Hitler's vengeance was obviously forthcoming and Yugoslavia was bound to be drawn into the war regardless of the equivocations of the Simović regime.[62] Whether the Serb military seriously believed—as they later claimed they did—that at least fifteen British divisions and hundreds of British planes would rush to protect

---

61. See Dr. Svetislav-Sveta Petrovitch, *Free Yugoslavia Calling* (New York: Greystone, 1941), Part IV. The book is full of factual inaccuracies but is very representative of the general spirit of the time.
62. On March 29, Eden, back in Athens, told American Minister MacVeagh, "I don't care if the Yugoslavs don't actually repudiate their signature on the Tripartite Pact if only we can get together now and formulate some sort of common policy after which we can take it to the Turks." MacVeagh to Hull, March 29, 1941, FR, 1941, II, 668.

Yugoslavia from the German onslaught, must remain a moot point. The new regime did precious little in the days following the coup d'état to put the Yugoslav armed forces in a state of readiness, and probably could not have done much even if it had tried.

As has been shown, in the weeks preceding the coup d'état in Belgrade, the activities of the American legation paralleled those of the British. While Minister Lane in his efforts to forestall Yugoslavia's accession to the Tripartite Pact concentrated on politicians, Military Attaché Fortier did his best to bolster the fighting spirit of the military leaders. Although the British role was much more important, the overall American contribution to the success of the coup d'état should not be underestimated. With the British military fortunes at a low ebb, the American prestige in Belgrade had increased enormously. The passage of the Lend-Lease Bill in congress early in March had considerable impact on the public. To many excited friends of the democracies it was almost mandatory to think that lavish American aid was already underway and that between them, the United States, the British Empire, Yugoslavia, and Greece, would easily crush the Axis; the Serbs had no way of knowing how slowly the American machinery would move into action.

Sumner Welles, who by now had fully assumed charge of the "Yugoslav situation," was inclined to regard the new developments optimistically. His evaluation of the events was based on enthusiastic reports coming mainly through British channels. On March 28, Welles wrote a memorandum to the president saying that "the estimate from excellent Yugoslav sources in Belgrade is that the coup d'état establishing the government of General Simović and overthrowing the regency makes war between Serbia and Germany 95% certain." Although the eventual attitude of the Croats and Slovenes was unpredictable, wrote Welles, "war preparations are being rushed, troops have been sent to battle stations," while, according to reports from Bulgaria, "the Germans have reversed the southward direction of the flow of troops and guns." The Yugoslavs had no illusions about withstanding the German attack indefinitely, continued Welles, "but hope to hold up the German advance towards Greece for two months, to inflict tremendous losses and crush the Italian army in Albania." Welles added that the British were very pleased with General Simović, regarding him "as a man of special force and decision."

The strategy emerging in Welles' mind called for further efforts to strengthen the morale of the new men in Belgrade. He instructed Lane to deliver to King Peter the president's "sincere and genuine wishes for the health and well-being of Your Majesty and for the freedom and independence of Yugoslavia." On a more prosaic level, Welles informed Lane that Roosevelt suggested telling the Belgrade government that the United States would consider revoking the freeze on the Yugoslav funds "as soon as the situation becomes clear." In a separate cable, Welles instructed Lane to tell Simović that "every liberty-loving man and woman" in America was pleased by the coup, and that, thanks to the Lend-Lease Bill, the president was now enabled "to provide assistance to Yugoslavia like all other nations which are seeking to maintain their independence and integrity and to repel aggression."[63]

Despite the great excitement Arthur Bliss Lane had gone through during the previous days, greeting crowds of Serbs milling in front of the legation, checking on the safety of American citizens, and keeping track of the fast-moving developments, he realized that things had gone well beyond the control of anybody in Washington, London, or Belgrade. The job was done, Hitler was challenged, Yugoslavia's adherence to the Pact was effectively invalidated together with its neutrality, and the German attack was only a question of time, and of a short time at that. On the evening of March 27, concluding his very brief report to the Department, Lane warned that "we may shortly be compelled to destroy all codes and ciphers except Gray" and suggested the use of this code until further notice.

It was not easy for Lane to adjust to the idea that Yugoslavia's days were numbered. Sumner Welles could have his own sources of information, but to the American minister in Belgrade his optimism looked silly. If the Yugoslav army was capable of offering a meaningful resistance at all, it would have to resist without Lend-Lease supplies; any fool knew that this

---

63. Welles to Lane, March 27, 1941, FR, 1941, 969.

assistance could under no conditions arrive in time to make a difference. The unfreezing of the Yugoslav funds could, at best, provide a consolation prize for those Serbs who succeeded in laying hands on them before everything collapsed. The floundering of the new regime, which Lane observed at close range, left no room for hope.

Thus it was inevitable that rather than being pleased with the successful completion of his mission, Arthur Bliss Lane was now besieged by doubts caused by the enormity of the tragedy about to befall Yugoslavia. Easily given to moodiness and soul-searching, Lane was now questioning the wisdom of all he had done since Colonel Donovan visited Belgrade. He sharply curtailed his activities. He made no attempt to press the new regime into the denunciation of the Tripartite Pact or to urge it to prepare the armed forces for the impending German attack. What had appeared to him crucial so recently had suddenly lost importance. Moreover, evidence indicates that during the days following the coup d'état Lane tried to dissociate himself—and the United States—from the consequences of the act which had created a mortal threat to the very existence of Yugoslavia.

This evidence is found in two messages to the State Department which Lane wrote following his meeting with Simović and Ninčić, the tone of which was sharply at variance with the enthusiasm expressed by Sumner Welles. Lane reported that he had told the new prime minister that, unlike the British, the United States had never urged the previous government to take offensive action against Germany, and that his own efforts "had been solely to prevent Yugoslavia from relinquishing her independence." This American policy, Lane pointed out, was correct; proof of it lay in the public enthusiasm in the streets of Belgrade. If this policy was now shared by the Yugoslav government, Simović could count on the United States to help both materially and morally. Having made this statement, Lane became reticent. When Simović declared that although the government wished to avoid taking a position on the Pact, it would resist by force any attempt to take Salonika—exactly what both Washington and London had wished the Yugoslavs to do—Lane made no encouraging comment. Moreover, as if to discourage Simović from any such move, he remarked that, according to his information, there was a distinct lack of enthusiasm for the new regime in Croatia.

Lane's report about his talk with the foreign minister is also suggestive of the American minister's inner feelings. He listened to Ninčić's assurances that Yugoslavia "will never permit what has happened in Rumania and Bulgaria," without comment. Nor did he argue (as he had done before in his many talks with Prince Paul and Cvetković) when Ninčić said that the Croats, the Slovenes, and the Bosnians desired faithful adherence to the Pact, and that its repudiation was impossible. Lane sympathetically listened to Ninčić's complaints about the embarrassment the street demonstrations in favor of the democracies and, particularly, the inflammatory British broadcasts caused the government. And he pointedly told Ninčić that the United States "had never urged Yugoslavia to be the aggressor in any conflict despite rumors to the contrary."[64]

This was, of course, manifestly not true, and Lane could make such statements only because he surmised that none of the new leaders of the government had been privy to the foreign policy developments under the old regime: Ninčić as much as admitted that he was not familiar with the documents relating to the Tripartite Pact and with Yugoslavia's actual commitments under the terms of the Pact. Much more interesting, however, is the question of why Lane took this line. Although the Serbs were not asking the United States for any specific favors, they sought, rather eagerly, expressions of sympathy and understanding for their precarious position. The only plausible explanation for the distinct lack of enthusiasm for the coup d'état which the American minister displayed in his conversations with Simović and Ninčić seems to be that he had concluded that the American involvement in Yugoslav affairs had not been a good policy to begin with. If such were the case, to Arthur Bliss Lane this would not be merely a question of an error made by the impersonal government of the United States which he represented in a country of marginal significance to America's destiny. Though he regarded the Axis, particularly Nazi Germany, as a major source of evil in the contemporary world, his standards of morality were such that he could not accept a premise that any and all means fostering the eventual victory of the democracies were justifiable. Although he had never seen war and destruction with his own eyes, he

---

64. Lane to Hull, March 28 and 29, *ibid.*, 970-972.

could imagine the horrible sacrifice which was about to be made by the people of a small country utterly incapable of resisting the German war machine. He could not dismiss the impending disaster as yet another minor episode in the great struggle of virtuous democracies against the forces of tyranny; nor could he place the responsibility with his president and say to himself that he was a mere executor of Roosevelt's will. His activities since January, 1941, had not quite been those of a detached diplomat. He had unjustifiably altered his own well-founded evaluation of Yugoslavia's potential contribution to the Allied war effort; he had not warned Washington sufficiently about the grave consequences for this friendly nation of the course charted for it by Roosevelt; and no matter how limited his own role was in the momentous developments of the preceding months, in his own mind he was an accessory to an evil deed which was about to result in death and ruin.

All this is essentially conjectural. Lane shared his inner thoughts with no one, including his wife. Many years later, on his deathbed, but still hoping to be able to write his autobiography, he pondered over his Belgrade experiences and remarked that "the Yugoslav chapter would be most difficult to write." But at the time, he maintained an appearance of satisfaction with the way things were going. He was not about to spread doubts among the members of the legation as to the righteousness of the Allied cause, or, for that matter, the impeccability of his own judgment. None of these men knew about the involvement of Lane and Fortier in the Belgrade conspiracy. All of them were carried away by the popular enthusiasm caused by the coup d'état and Yugoslavia's apparent move to the Allied camp. They were prepared for the consequences — everybody had emergency suitcases packed and ready — and searching questions were out of order. Mentally and emotionally, Americans in Belgrade were already at war. A slap administered to Hitler by the Serbian patriots was in itself a victory. The consequences were beyond their control and, anyway, could only prove the infinite evil of the Nazis.

Although proof is lacking, Lane's thoughts as described above offer the only conceivable key to his behavior in the days following the upheaval. He had one talk with General Simović and one with Foreign Minister Ninčić. He had an audience with the new head of state, the boy King Peter, which he described in detail in a message to Roosevelt, perhaps sarcastically terming it "the most encouraging thing I have experienced since the crisis started."[65]

After this visit Arthur Bliss Lane lapsed into almost total passivity. Of the few dispatches he sent to Washington, only two were meaningful: he reported his discovery that Hitler had told Prince Paul during their last meeting that he was going to attack Russia "in June or July"; and he conveyed the warning which the departing German military attaché (almost all German and Italian diplomats were then leaving Yugoslavia) issued to his porter: "If any of his effects were damaged or interfered with during his absence from Belgrade, he would have the porter hanged when he returned in three weeks." Beyond that, Lane found nothing worthwhile to tell the State Department. He left without reply to Welles' inquiry as to whether the Yugoslavs had any plans, in case of hostilities with Germany, to destroy the canal circumventing the Iron Gates on the Danube (known to any apprentice strategist the world over as the number one target in Serbia), or for the sabotaging of bauxite mines in Croatia. Likewise, he ignored Hull's message relaying his public statement that "every American citizen would be grateful to see the inclusion of Dr. Macek in the new cabinet" as "concrete evidence of unity in Yugoslavia," and that Croat-Americans were particularly anxious to see this unity accomplished. The feelings of Croat-Americans about Yugoslav unity had hardly any bearing on the situation.

Lane's silence is the more significant because there were in fact interesting developments taking place around him. He learned about Simović's clash with other members of the cabinet: the prime minister demanded that the Yugoslav army occupy Salonika even as German motorized divisons were about to start pouring into Greece. He was informed that the Yugoslav mission, which Simović had sent to Moscow, was about to sign a treaty of friendship with the Soviet Union. He was aware that General Sir John Dill had arrived incognito from Greece for talks with Simović. He knew that Foreign Minister Ninčić, on behalf of the frightened government, desperately begged

65. Lane to Roosevelt, March 31, 1941, *ibid.*, 973-975.

the German chargé d'affaires to allow him to go to Berlin to explain to the leaders of the Third Reich Yugoslavia's passionate wish to reach an understanding with Germany.

Lane reported none of this news. His diplomatic mission was over. Nothing really mattered any more; insofar as he was concerned, nothing could save Yugoslavia.

One nagging problem remained, that of evacuation of the legation. Watching the extreme confusion in government circles, Lane realized that to depend on the Yugoslavs in this matter would be folly. The government and the military intended to abandon the capital the moment the Germans attacked. Several legations intended to follow the government: the British, Polish, Czech, Belgian and Dutch legations had little choice since their diplomatic status would not be recognized by the Germans. For a short while, Lane toyed with the idea of following the king and his government—Secretary Hull had given him full discretion in this matter—but then decided to remain in Belgrade.[66] The prospect of running away to the hills of Southern Serbia chased by Stukas and motorized German columns demanded much more energy than Lane, close to total exhaustion after the unbearable pace of the previous weeks, could muster. He decided to send Colonel Fortier and Secretary Macatee to represent the United States at the government and army headquarters in the hills, and reasoned that by staying behind he would be able to evacuate the American colony in one way or another after the arrival of the Germans. After all, the United States was still a non-belligerent and its legation was entitled to diplomatic privileges.

Not all Americans were willing to stay. Most newsmen demanded Lane's help in enabling them to follow the government. Lane did whatever he could in making arrangements for transportation for a few of them. Some, including Sulzberger, prudently decided to leave for the Greek or Albanian border without waiting for the German assault. Others agreed to stay temporarily, using a downtown hotel, the *Srpski Kralj*, as their headquarters, and to gather at the American legation for a roll call and a final war council in the event of bombing or invasion.

---

66. Hull changed his instructions on April 6, when he ordered Lane to follow the government, but Lane never received this cable due to the interruption in communications.

This matter settled, there was nothing for Lane to do but wait for the unknown, for the disaster, for the terrible blow to fall.

The Reckoning

At 4:30 A.M. on Sunday, April 6, 1941, the Reich's Foreign Minister Joachim von Ribbentrop began reading a statement over the Berlin radio. He accused "the clique of conspirators in Belgrade" of making common cause with Germany's enemies, of unleashing terror against German nationals residing in Yugoslavia, and other "outrageous acts." At the end of his speech, Ribbentrop declared that the Reich government had ordered German troops to "restore peace and security" in Yugoslavia "by every possible military means." As he spoke, over 30 motorized German divisions entered Yugoslav territory from Bulgaria, Rumania, and Austria; Hungarian troops began to mass north of the border.[67] The German armies advanced as fast as their vehicles could move and their communications be secured. The Yugoslav army offered little resistance; Croatian units mutinied one after another, in several instances attacking their Serbian comrades-in-arms rather than fighting the enemy. The government and the General Staff (which lost contact with field commanders on the first day of the invasion) concentrated on the task of getting out of Yugoslavia as quickly as possible.

The first wave of German bombers appeared over Belgrade at 5:15 A.M., while other Luftwaffe squadrons attacked Yugoslav airfields, methodically destroying planes which did not even try to get off the ground. Of the three hundred thousand inhabitants of the Yugoslav capital, only a handful of officials, diplomats, and newsmen knew in advance that it was to be bombed that morning. The rest were awakened by air-raid sirens barely half an hour before the bombs began to fall. As the waves of Heinkels, Stukas, and Messerschmitts unloaded their deadly cargo upon the defenseless city, clouds of dust and smoke from explosions and fires enveloped Belgrade. Several thousand people perished under the ruins. Men, women, and children ran from one place to another searching for shelter,

---

67. The Hungarian invasion started on April 11. It was limited to the occupation of a region, with a large Magyar population, which had been claimed by Hungary ever since the Treaty of Trianon.

crawling over piles of rubble from destroyed buildings, filling the air with shouts and shrieks.

Occasional planes could still be seen in the sky—bombing continued intermittently through April 8—when a group of Americans began to gather at the minister's residence. These were members of the legation, newsmen, and a few civilians seeking help and protection. Unshaven men and hastily dressed women, mostly without luggage, milled around in the three-story building badly damaged by several bombs which had fallen nearby. With a few exceptions, they were terrified by this first encounter with war. Lane, who had stayed awake most of the night awaiting the air assault, and had spent several hours under the grand piano in his living room while the bombs were falling, was as badly shaken as anyone. In addition, he was covered with soot and ashes: in between the raids he was burning secret papers in the kitchen. Mrs. Lane was about the only person who fully retained her composure and presence of mind. She consoled those who were most upset, suggested taking a stiff drink from the minister's supply of Scotch, and cheered bewildered men and women with a suitable comment or joke. Colonel Fortier soon came from the legation chancellery where he was destroying codes and files of classified documents. About 10:00 A.M. the legation's official car arrived with Outerbridge Horsey, a young vice-consul reassigned the day before from Budapest, who delivered to Lane a large diplomatic pouch for the British.[68] The car was quickly taken over by Fortier and a couple of newsmen who immediately left for a pre-arranged rendezvous in the mountains with the Yugoslav general staff. Shortly thereafter Secretary Macatee and other newsmen left in another car to follow the Yugoslav government. The British minister stopped by to say goodbye on his way out to ask Lane to protect British interests in Belgrade, and to pick up the bag brought by Horsey which

---

68. Anticipating the air attack on Sunday morning, Lane had telephoned the legation in Budapest on Saturday instructing Horsey to leave the train at Subotica, near the Yugoslav-Hungarian border, and to continue to Belgrade by a car which would meet him at the station. Lane had requested Horsey's transfer because the latter knew Hungarian and could be useful in establishing contact with Budapest, the nearest neutral capital, after the German attack.

contained, among other things, a substantial amount of money in dollars and gold coins.

By noon the crowd began to disperse. Lane told them all to take care of themselves the best way they knew how and to keep in touch. Because the residence was uninhabitable, it was decided that the Lanes would move to the house of Commercial Attaché Karl Rankin in Dedinje, on the western outskirts of Belgrade. With the help of friends and servants, Mrs. Lane packed whatever belongings could be readily collected, making sure to take every scrap of food and every bottle from the fortunately undamaged wine cellar. By late afternoon the Lanes had abandoned their home of four years.

Having received the news about the invasion of Yugoslavia, President Roosevelt issued the following statement to the press:

> The barbaric invasion of Yugoslavia and the attempt to annihilate that country by brute force is but another chapter in the present planned movement of attempted world conquest and domination. Another small nation has been assaulted by the forces of aggression and it is further proof that there are no geographical limitations or bounds of any kind to their movement for world conquest.
>
> The American people have the greatest sympathy for the nation which has been thus so outrageously attacked and we follow closely the valiant struggle the Yugoslav people are making to protect their homes and preserve their liberty.
>
> This government, with its policy of helping those who are defending themselves against would-be conquerors, is now proceeding as speedily as possible to send military and other supplies to Yugoslavia.

Evacuation

The six weeks which Arthur Bliss Lane spent in Dedinje were the unhappiest of his life. Someone else in his place would have sat back and waited for a better turn of events, riding out the adverse situation. But Lane could not. He was a warrior; he had fought hard as long as he could, sustaining immense pressure as he fulfilled his major assignment, helping to draw Yugoslavia into the war. Now suddenly the pressure was off, there was nobody and nothing to struggle against, and the world was falling to pieces around him. The effect of this enforced idleness on Lane was nothing short of disastrous.

Time and again he asked himself what had gone wrong, and whether or not he had served a good cause to begin with. He was overcome by a feeling of helplessness and frustration, and this feeling was unbearable, the more so because he could not bring himself to share his thoughts with anyone.

For the first days Rankin's house resembled a railroad station. The numerous house-guests were coming and going, bringing and arranging suitcases and trunks from their abandoned apartments and houses in the city, securing water supplies, getting candles, and searching for food. Two or three times Lane drove downtown in order to establish the whereabouts of several prominent Americans and to salvage some more clothes from the ruins of his old residence. What he saw was depressing. The municipal government and the gendarmerie still functioned, but there was no other authority. The city had neither electricity nor water; many of the dead were still buried under debris, and corpses could be seen lying in the streets. He was shaken by the misery of the population of the burning city, and in an effort to alleviate it he encouraged his energetic and resourceful friend, George H. Schellens, to organize a string of kitchens to feed the people. This operation was placed under the auspices of the American Red Cross, which Lane created on the spot for the purpose, appointing the same Schellens as chairman and advancing him some funds from the legation's treasury.[69]

Arthur Bliss Lane's first encounter with the ugly face of war

---

69. In his first post-invasion message to the State Department, which reached Hull on April 12, Lane requested authorization of an initial allocation of $100,000 to sustain Schellens' operation. Hull answered by authorizing the spending of $25,000 which the American Red Cross deposited with the Department, instructing Lane to submit a separate accounting of this expenditure. Upon Lane's further insistence, the amount was increased to $50,000, which Lane augmented by his personal contribution of $20,000 to the Red Cross relief in Yugoslavia. See Lane to Hull, April 12, and G. Howland Shaw's memorandum of April 23, 1941, in FR, 1941, II, 977–978; also Hull to Lane, April 12, Harrison to Hull, April 28; Lane to Norman Davis, April 29; and Davis' memo, May 19, 1941. This haggling over a relatively small sum, so badly needed for clearly charitable purposes, as well as the personal contribution by Lane—who was far from a rich man—may appear incredible in retrospect. It suggests that the U.S. government was in fact much less concerned about the fate of Yugoslavia than it publicly had claimed to be.

left him almost paralyzed, unable to think clearly or even to attempt to comprehend the significance of the new situation. He was still the head of mission, but he had no mission to perform. Only yesterday he had been one of the most important men in Yugoslavia. Now few people cared whether he existed or not. The government to which he had been accredited was gone, and was trying to get out of the country as quickly as possible. The members of his staff were still around, some of them crowded under the same roof in Rankin's house, but there was absolutely nothing for them to do. The chancellery of the American legation downtown was not seriously damaged but the files and codes had all been burned.[70] Even if they had not been, neither telephone nor telegraph functioned, no cables were coming in and none could be sent out. There was no point in pretending that business could be conducted as usual, not even in a small room in Rankin's house designated as the legation's temporary quarters. Nobody reported for duty or was asked to. Lane himself stayed in his own room, not wishing to see anyone and dulling his senses with whiskey.

Lane was not the only head of mission in Belgrade who was in such a depressed state. Several other ministers and ambassadors, representing for the most part neutral and non-belligerent nations, who for one reason or another did not escape together with the Yugoslav government, were in the same condition. Most of them either had lived in Dedinje or moved there after the bombing. They were fearful of new air raids and trembled at the thought of what would happen to them when the German troops started storming the city! That this would happen very soon was obvious from the radio reports, their only source of news. Cut off from the rest of the world, they could expect no help from anywhere. Accustomed to a free and easy life as members of European high society, they were both physically and emotionally unprepared for the trials of war.

These men soon located each other and formed a group, resurrecting the diplomatic corps which, under the circum-

---

70. The abandoned chancellery was locked and boarded up, with a notice posted on the door that it contained property of the United States of America. When the first American officials arrived in Belgrade at the end of the war, they discovered to their surprise that apparently nobody had entered the chancellery during the preceeding four years.

stances, had little meaning and much less influence. Except for their profession, nothing truly united them. Politically, they were extremely diverse, ranging from strongly pro-German Paul Steiner, the Swiss minister, to implacably anti-German Arthur Bliss Lane. But they had in common the fear for their lives, and the desperate wish to do something. What they did, some of them later preferred to forget.[71]

The first informal gathering of the diplomatic corps took place at the Brazilian legation on the afternoon of April 7, and since the old dean of the diplomatic corps, the Rumanian ambassador, was nowhere to be found, the Brazilian minister assumed the chairmanship. Neither the German chargé d'affaires nor the Italian minister, whose country was also at war with Yugoslavia, showed up; their interests were represented by the Swiss minister. The talk drifted from one subject to another, and the only matter which was formally discussed was the desirability of getting better police protection for the German and Italian legations against possible attacks by outraged Serbs. The need for it was questionable: nothing had happened except for an attempt by a drunken Yugoslav soldier to break into the German legation. Nevertheless, the diplomats agreed that it would be useful to request the authorities to furnish special protection for the diplomatic representatives of the Axis. Lane offered his services, feeling that he "might have more influence with the Yugoslav authorities in view of the known friendly attitude of the United States towards the Yugoslav government, to endeavor to persuade the competent Yugoslav authorities to give every possible guarantee regarding the safety of the personnel of the two legations." He declined to go alone on this mission "on the ground that it was not my duty to protect German or Italian interests" but said that he would go with the others "in the interests of sparing the lives of our colleagues of these two countries."

Lane and his Swiss and Brazilian colleagues spent several

---

71. The following is based on Lane's message to Hull, dated April 8, FR, 1941, II, 976-977, on his detailed reports to the Secretary of State of April 17, 22, and 23, and his memorandum of May 29, 1941, as well as on the documents from State Department files. Several interviews with the persons who were in Belgrade at that time and were aware of the developments described here were greatly helpful in reconstructing a picture.

hours in the city, talking to a retired army general, the commandant of the gendarmerie, and the vice prefect of Belgrade. In the end, they accomplished their mission and a platoon of gendarmes was posted around the Axis legations. Describing this episode in his later report, Lane confessed that he felt somewhat uneasy approaching the Yugoslavs with this request to protect the enemy, "as the city was in flames and intermittent bombing was taking place up to the time we returned to Dedinje at about 10:00 P.M."

The next day, April 8, another meeting of the diplomats was held in which Lane participated together with the Spanish, Hungarian, Swedish, Swiss, and Danish ministers. The Rumanian ambassador showed up but announced that under the circumstances, and due to the questionable status of the diplomatic corps, he would not assume the position of dean. The gathering was also attended by Lane's personal friend from the Italian legation, Guidotti, who came as an unofficial representative of his minister.

Steiner announced that he had been advised by the German chargé d'affaires, Dr. Feine, that the position of the diplomatic corps had become "untenable" and that its members should either evacuate by plane to Budapest, or move by car to Novi Sad "where there would be less probability of a major military engagement." Although this suggestion seemed to have no legal ground and was in fact rather arrogant, the diplomats decided to explore the situation. A discussion followed, Lane declaring that since he was accredited to the Yugoslav government, he "must either remain in Belgrade or go to a place aggreeable to the Yugoslav government." Steiner suggested that perhaps the simplest way out would be to declare "neutral" the suburb of Dedinje where most of them already lived anyway, and thus be protected against German military action. This suggestion was rejected on the grounds that it would be resented by the population of Belgrade. Somebody then proposed evacuating to the town of Ruma, which was considered "safe" because it had a large German minority. In the end, on Lane's insistence, and after considerable discussion, the group resolved to ask the Yugoslav government to formally declare Belgrade an open city, with a promise not to defend it, and simultaneously ask the German government to agree not to bomb the city by air or artillery. Guidotti helped draft the document which, in its final form, read as follows:

Les Chefs des Missions Diplomatiques des pays neutres et non-belligerants se trouvant à Beograd, se sont réunis à la Legation du Brésil et, vu la situation créée par l'ouverture des hostilités, dans le bût de protéger autant qu'il leur est possible les interêts de leurs co-nationaux et en même temps la population de Beograd, ont décidé de soumettre à l'approbation des Gouvernements Yougoslave et Allemand les propositions suivants:

I. Le Gouvernement Yougoslave s'engage de déclarer d'une maniéré cathegorique la ville de beograd ouverte, de ne pas la defendre et de retirer toutes les troupes sauf les forces de police;

II. Le Gouvernement Allemand s'engage de ne plus bombarder la ville de Beograd ni par avion ni par l'artillerie.

Si les Gouvernements Yougoslave et Allemand trouvent plus pratique d'organiser l'evacuation du Corps Diplomatique, de leurs fonctionnaires et de leurs colonies pour une autre ville Yougoslave hors du champs des operations militaires, le Corps Diplomatique se declare pret a accepter cette solution et prie les Gouvernements respectifs de communiquer leur decision le plus tôt possible et de prendre les mesures necessaires pour assurer les moyens d'evacuation.

Jusqu'au moment que I'echange entre les Missions Diplomariques des pays belligerant pourra se faire, les Missions Allemande et Italienne suiront le sort des autres Missions Diplomatiques á condition que les Gouvernements Allemand et Italian prennent les mèmes mesures de protection pour les Missions Diplomatiques et colonies Yuogoslaves dans leurs pays respectives.

Beograd, le 8 Avril 1941

Signe: Victor Cadere
Ambassadeur de Roumanie

     Eduardo Garcia Comim
E.E. et M.P. d'Espagne

     Knut Karl Folke Malmar
E.E. et M.P. de Suede

     M.I.P. Mirner
Chargé d'Affaires de Danemark

     Arthur Bliss Lane
E.E. et M.P. des E.U. d'Amerique

     Le Baron Georges Bakach
E.E. et M.P. de Bessenyey Hongrie

     Le Dr. Paul Steiner
E.E. et M.P. de Suisse

     Carlos Alves de Souza
Ministre du Bresil

The document was signed in duplicate. Lane, who was

apparently the only one capable of doing more than talking, volunteered to organize its delivery to the appropriate authorities. Since Fortier had returned from the hills (finding no useful function for himself in the chaotic situation which he observed in the "temporary seat" of the Yugoslav government), Lane decided to send him back to Prime Minister Simović with one copy of the paper, and to dispatch the other copy to Budapest with Outerbridge Horsey, to be handed over to the German legation in Hungary for transmission to Berlin. There being no objection from the diplomatic corps, both couriers left at once. After a day of chase, Fortier finally located Simović, and had him sign the declaration in which the prime minister agreed not to defend Belgrade and to withdraw all troops except police forces.

The declaration, addressed to the Brazilian legation, went as follows:

PRESIDENT DU CONSEIL
  DES MINISTRES

LEGATION DES ETATS-UNIS DE BRESIL

En réponse à la lettre du 8 Avril de l'année courant du Corps diplomatique se trouvant à Belgrade réuni dans Votra Légation j'ai l'honneur de porter à votre connaissance ce qui suit.

Le Gouvernement yougoslave est complettement d'accord avec la proposition faite dans la dite lettre au sujet de la ville de Belgrade.

De son côté le gouvernement yougoslave ayant déjà proclamé Belgrade comme ville ouverte est consentant de renoncer d'une manière catégorique cette declaration. Si le gouvernement allemande de son côté s'engage de ne plus bombarder la ville de Belgrade ni par avion ni par l'artillerie le gouvernement yougoslave cessers de défendre la ville et retirera toutes le troupes sauf les forces de police, comme c'était d'ailleur sa première intention.

En ce qui concerne les autres propositions dans votre lettre, je vous prie de vous mettre en rapport avec le M. Nintchich, Ministre des affaires étrangères qui a étè chargé par le gouvernement de les régler.

LE PRESIDENT DU CONSEIL DES MINISTRES
GENERAL D'ARMEE
(Signé)   D. T. SIMOVITCH

This declaration was actually a minor concession on the part of the Yugoslav prime minister; by that time there were no troops in Belgrade anyway. The Yugoslav army had ceased to exist, the Germans were rapidly converging on the capital, and Simović himself, together with other top officials, was busily preparing for the last leg of his escape, the flight to Greece.[72]

Horsey's attempt to cross into Hungary on April 8 was unsuccessful: he drove as far as Subotica, but was told that to traverse the frontier would be "absolutely impossible" and returned to Dedinje the same night. Upon Fortier's return from Simović's headquarters on April 10, Lane decided to try again. This time he sent Horsey with Fortier, who convinced Yugoslav officials at Subotica that their mission was of utmost importance. They continued to the border by rail hand-car and discovered that this important crossing point was guarded by a single Yugoslav sentry. As Fortier watched from the Yugoslav side, Horsey walked across no man's land into Hungary. There, with the help of cooperative Hungarian officers, Horsey quickly found a taxi which took him to Budapest where Howard K. Travers, American chargé d'affaires, having been warned by phone from the border, waited for him at the legation. Horsey handed Travers several dispatches which Lane had scribbled in Dedinje to be cabled to Washington. Then both of them, in spite of the late hour, went to the German legation and handed the official on duty the diplomatic corps' proposals, together with the copy of Simović's declaration. The official promised to transmit the documents immediately to the foreign office in Berlin. There was no response from the Reich government, then or later, to this communication.

The bewildered diplomats in Dedinje met once more to discuss various plans for evacuation but were unable to arrive at any decision. Their apprehension was finally dispelled when Belgrade fell to an SS infantry platoon, led by Lieutenant Klingenberg, at 5:00 P.M. on April 12, 1941. The next day, large numbers of troops poured in and German rule in the Yugoslav capital was officially established.

The German high command had some difficulty in finding an

---

72. Four years later, Simović was one of the first Serbs-in-exile to return to Tito's Yugoslavia. He lived in Belgrade for the remainder of his life but took no part in politics. His colleague Marković chose to stay in England, living on a modest British pension.

appropriate Yugoslav authority to sign the document of surrender: the government was already on its way out of the country. After several days of confused negotiations, an armistice was signed in Belgrade by a deputy of Simović, and by Alexander Cincar-Marković, former foreign minister, who was somehow talked into taking on this unpleasant assignment.

Even before the armistice was signed, Feine again put pressure on the diplomatic corps, prodding it to leave Belgrade as soon as possible. Until Yugoslavia officially surrendered, Lane resisted this pressure, stating time and again that he was there to represent the United States in Yugoslavia and that he would not move unless so ordered from Washington or unless the Yugoslav government approved his evacuation. On April 18, however, when the armistice went into effect, he went to see Feine to explore the possibilities of evacuation. Feine told Lane that there would be no difficulty in obtaining exit visas, but that physical facilities for the evacuation of the foreign colony should be provided by the foreigners themselves. He recommended obtaining a river boat from Hungary rather than attempting to go by car, since that would permit everybody to leave together, carrying a maximum of personal belongings. Reluctant to make a decision of this kind on his own responsibility, Lane took advantage of the restored telephone communications with the American legation in Budapest and requested instructions from Washington. On April 23, on Lane's behalf, Travers spoke by telephone with Assistant Secretary of State G. Howland Shaw who suggested that Lane, with the legation's staff, should move to Budapest, leaving in Belgrade several consular officials of his own choosing. Means of transportation were up to Lane to decide upon; extra expenses were authorized.

On April 27, accompanied by three members of the legation, Minister Lane drove to Budapest, encountering no difficulties in crossing the region of Yugoslavia occupied by German and Hungarian troops. The next day he made arrangements with a Hungarian steamship company to send a river boat with a tug and a barge to Belgrade in two weeks. He stayed with his personal friends, appearing at the American legation only once, on April 29, when he sent the following cable to President Roosevelt:

Perhaps I am personally too upset by recent events in Belgrade to report objectively. May I, however, endeavor to impress on our government the imperative necessity of officials and private individuals forgetting their own personal interests and cooperating in the common cause. When I say that the danger for us is approaching I am not exaggerating. I fully realize that you know what our problem is but I wonder whether the American people do. We must, repeat must, wake up to the necessity that we must be willing to give everything we have to save the situation. This is for the sake of religion, democracy, and civilization.

On May 4, Lane drove back to Belgrade expecting to proceed with the evacuation as scheduled. This expectation, however, did not materialize. A few days later Travers telephoned from Budapest saying that the State Department frowned on the idea of hiring a steamboat for the evacuation of the American, Brazilian, and Argentine colonies, believing that the cost — $5,000 — was excessive. Hull instructed Travers to "take no action to execute the plan and make no commitments on behalf of the Department with respect to the plan, pending Department's further advice." In the next message, Hull irritably declared that the "need for the boat is not understood since other means of travel are apparently available" and again ordered no commitments pending further instructions. Finally, on May 12, Hull grudgingly authorized the expenditure of $3,300 for the transportation, sternly admonishing that accounting for this expenditure be kept separately. "American citizens in Belgrade," wrote the secretary of state, "who desire to avail themselves of this opportunity to proceed to Budapest, may travel on the steamer, provided there is no extra expense to the government and provided that they understand that the Department can assume no, repeat no, responsibility whatsoever for them after their arrival in Budapest. If they are able to reimburse their share of the hire of the steamer," added the frugal Hull, "they should be requested to do so. It is of course assumed that they will be able to proceed from Budapest without financial assistance from the Department."[73]

---

73. Hull to Travers, May 12, 1941. See also Travers to Hull, May 3; Hull to Travers, May 4; Travers to Hull, May 10, 1941. Actually, $940 was collected in Budapest from the refugees and deposited to an appropriate State Department account. Pell to Hull, June 20, 1941.

While these exchanges were taking place, the Americans in Belgrade, all ready to leave, were getting increasingly nervous. Arthur Bliss Lane, who had hoped that the problem of evacuation was solved, was furious. His mind had been occupied by too many unpleasant things for too long. He could not stop thinking about the catastrophe which had befallen Yugoslavia and Greece as a result of the misconceived and miscarried idea of the "Balkan Front." He was gravely concerned about the possible consequences of the shrill Axis propaganda directed against the United States, ascribing Yugoslavia's fate to American intrigues in Belgrade both before and after the military coup d'état, naming Lane personally responsible for the calamity, and calling the brief Yugoslav campaign "Colonel Donovan's War."[74] In addition to this worry, Lane experienced humiliation in dealing with the German officials in Belgrade, with whom he had several violent encounters over the issue of the protection of British and Belgian interests (which he had assumed in the name of the United States) and over the confiscation of the legation's reserve gasoline supply. The Germans tended to laugh at his diplomatic authority and he had to be his most forceful self in order to get anywhere; whatever he accomplished was done at the cost of great emotional strain. At length, Lane succeeded in securing the German recognition of Karl Rankin as American consul in Belgrade after the legation had officially stopped functioning. He was anxious to get out of this God-forsaken place as quickly as possible, and he found the State Department's silly quibbling over the cost of transportation of the American colony to Budapest not in the least amusing.[75]

---

74. Phillips to Hull, April 13 and 18, 1941. Lane to Hull, May 9 and 17, 1941. Goebbels' propaganda got another shot in the arm in September when, after the departure of the American consulate in Belgrade, the Germans found a small cache of arms and ammunition in the garden of the British consulate over which Rankin had retained official control. This was a left-over of what the SOE agents had not disposed of before their flight. Because of the incriminating nature of such possessions, Rankin, who discovered them in the British consulate building, dug a hole in the garden one night and buried his find. See German Minister Benzler's report to Berlin, No. 605, September 6, 1941. Isolationist papers and writers in the United States happily amplified this propaganda line. Ford, 105-106.

75. Had Lane known what was to happen to the members of the American embassy in Berlin, he would have considered himself lucky; at least his and his aides' salaries were not questioned by the State Department. As George

The river boat finally arrived on May 16. It was loaded with the worldly possessions of some 40 Americans, Brazilians, and Argentines, and at four o'clock the following morning departed for Budapest, arriving there late in the evening of the following day. During the voyage Lane became seriously ill, suffering from uncontrollable hemorrhaging in the nose, and during the week of his stay in the Hungarian capital was confined to bed. On May 25, still quite weak, he left Budapest with his wife by train for Berlin, spent one day there, and then continued the journey through Switzerland and Spain to Portugal. In Lisbon the Lanes boarded an American clipper and on June 6, 1941, landed at La Guardia airport in New York.

Postscript

By the time Arthur Bliss Lane reported to the State Department a few days later, he looked pretty much his old self. The nightmare of the last two months was fading away. He was in the news; the German attack on the Soviet Union had not yet overshadowed the Balkan tragedy. He was hailed by the interventionists, denounced by the isolationists.[76] His many friends hastened to greet the man coming from the battlefields of the war. He received scores of invitations to address various groups across the country; *Life* magazine asked him to write an article describing the debacle in Yugoslavia. At the State Department he had to go through the minor nuisance of explaining, in writing, why he had to hire the Danube steamer to evacuate from Belgrade.[77] But high officials appeared appre-

---

F. Kennan recalls in his *Memoirs*, the Department refused to pay him and his colleagues for the five months they spent in confinement, interned by the Germans following the declaration of war in December, 1941. The reason advanced for this decision was that the members of the embassy, after all, had not been working all that time and thus failed to earn their wages.

76. See, for example, "Our Frontier on the Danube: An Appalling Story of Our Meddling in the Balkans," by Demaree Bess, in *The Saturday Evening Post*, May 24, 1941. Lane was staunchly defended by his admirers from the Belgrade press corps. See Leigh White, *The Long Balkan Night*, 208-209.

77. Describing the episode to Frank P. Corrigan, on June 9, 1941, Lane scoffed at the Department's objections, saying, "all the bridges had been blown up by the Yugoslav army, hence there were no trains; there was no gasoline available in Yugoslavia, hence the automobile was merely a geographic expression; and lastly, if we asked the Germans to furnish us with air transportation, I fear that the raspberry cheer might have been heard all the way to the Bronx—which, I believe, is the land which gave it birth."

ciative of his accomplishments, and he spent several hours with Sumner Welles himself, discussing current political and military developments in Europe. The under-secretary was so impressed that he deemed it necessary to present Lane with an official letter of gratitude. "The Department takes pleasure," wrote Welles, "in commending you for your ability, energy, and the tact with which you handled the difficult situation in Yugoslavia during the early months of this year. Your constant attention to the various problems which arose and the solutions thereto justify the confidence felt in you during your mission to Yugoslavia."

President Roosevelt, who invited the Lanes for lunch at the White House, was friendly and pleasant. He inquired into various aspects of the Balkan situation and listened attentively as Lane narrated his experiences. At the end of the lunch, Roosevelt warmly thanked Lane and assured him that after he had sufficiently rested—the Department had granted him two months of annual leave of absence—he would be reassigned to a post of his own choosing.

Everything seemed to be going so well that Lane was beginning to think that he had been right all along. Did he not do in Yugoslavia what Roosevelt wanted him to? Did he not sacrifice his own judgment and compromise his views in the broader interests of state? Did he not suffer and struggle against tremendous odds, tormented by thoughts and doubts, encountering humiliating reverses, only to come out on top in the end, safely bringing out of Yugoslavia his staff and numerous Americans and other nationals caught there by the momentous events of the war? That Yugoslavia had failed to offer any appreciable resistance to the Axis and that the British were swept into the Mediterranean in Greece was surely not his fault. And it would be only natural if he now received a just reward for his accomplishments in the form of a new important post. Lane hoped it would be truly a good post, perhaps even the embassy in Mexico, which he had coveted all his life.

Some rest was needed, it was true. But with his nervous energy restored, Lane also felt he had to bring his message to the anxious American public which knew so little about the struggle unfolding in Europe. With Welles' approval, he accepted several speaking engagements, and worked tirelessly on the article for *Life*. The article reflected the spirit of the time

and conformed to official policy. In it, Lane fully endorsed
Roosevelt's intervention in the Balkans; depicted Prince Paul
as a weakling, incapable of withstanding Hitler's pressure, and
as a sworn enemy of Soviet Russia. He claimed to be completely innocent of the conspiracy which led to the coup d'état
of March 27, and he vividly described the enthusiastic
pro-American demonstrations in Belgrade, the assumption of
royal powers by King Peter II, and the events following the
German air attack. The article was well written. It assured the
public that the administration was on the right course in its
resolution to aid Great Britain and to resist the evil forces of
aggression.

Then something went wrong. On August 6 Arthur Bliss Lane
returned to Washington after a successful lecture trip and had a
conference with Sumner Welles. Welles wanted to talk to him
about his next assignment. There was a dearth of vacant posts
abroad and an overabundance of unemployed ambassadors, but
it seemed that Lane could get Costa Rica. Of course, Mexico
was vacant too, but the president had not made up his mind
about that post and wanted to keep it open for the time being;
he had certain important political obligations to fulfill. Costa
Rica would be, naturally, only a temporary assignment until
something more significant opened up, and the minister to
Yugoslavia did not have to feel that it would be a step down.

Lane listened, controlling his temper, and asked for a few
days to think it over. Early next morning he left for a planned
vacation in Montebello, Quebec.

At Montebello, on August 8, he received a formal letter,
signed by Sumner Welles and dated August 4, which Welles
had not mentioned to him during their talk on the 6th. An
identical letter, signed by Cordell Hull and sent to his New
York forwarding address, reached Lane the next day. The secretary of state curtly informed Lane that the president had
"appointed Anthony J. Drexel Biddle, Jr., of Pennsylvania, to
be Envoy Extraordinary and Minister Plenipotentiary of the
United States of America, to reside near the present government of Yugoslavia established in England," and that this appointment "will automatically result in the termination of your
status as minister to Yugoslavia." Lane was further told that
upon expiration of his leave he would be assigned to the De-

partment "for emergency duty," with his salary reduced from $10,000 to $9,000, and without any travel expenses or per diem authorized in connection with the new assignment. The transportation of Lane's effects from Budapest to Washington was, however, approved, and he was requested to fill out the enclosed form, giving an estimate of expenses incurred in this connection.

We do not know what went on in Arthur Bliss Lane's mind as he read this letter, but there is little doubt that he took it as a personal offense. From Welles he knew that Biddle's appointment as minister to the Yugoslav government-in-exile (he already had a similar position with the Polish government-in-exile in London) had been considered. But the protocol prescribed a certain ceremonial procedure in such cases, namely, a presentation by the previous envoy of a letter of recall to a chief of state before the new one could present his letter of credence. Lane's abrupt dismissal was only accentuated by his appointment "for emergency duty at the Department." In fact, he was not anxious to go abroad at the moment, but he wanted to regard the stay in the United States as his personal choice. If the secretary of state had any appreciation of his past service at all, he should at least have asked for his consent to this interim assignment. As for the tactless references to the reduction of his salary, travel expenses, and per diem, they might have been a manifestation of some bureaucratic stupidity on the part of an aide who drafted the letter. But it could also have been a calculated affront. In his frame of mind, Lane was inclined towards the latter explanation.

The next day Lane answered Welles. Referring to "the personal intimation which you made to me on August 6" (i.e., to Welles' suggestion that he accept the post in Costa Rica), Lane remarked that "it would not be practicable for me to give you an affirmative answer." In the first place, he doubted the wisdom of his return to Central America where he had had such adverse publicity during and after his service in Nicaragua five years earlier. Secondly, he feared that "the fact that the appointment would be a temporary one would also work against my usefulness." A more important reason for declining this offer, wrote Lane, was that "there seems little of importance to be accomplished there"; in fact, there was no work "which could not be accomplished just as well by a man of lesser experience." Then, with a reference to the Department's letter of August 4, Lane said that he would prefer "to do what I can in this country until such time as the administration feels that it can appoint me to a post which would offer me opportunity for service commensurate in importance to that which I was privileged to render in Yugoslavia."

To the secretary of state, Lane sent a formal reply, acknowledging the contents of the letter received. He stated that he could not submit an accurate estimate of expenses to be incurred in transporting his effects from Budapest to Washington, acidly pointing out that "as the Department is aware, it is impracticable to ship lift vans from Budapest to the United States at the present time." He concluded the letter by requesting cumulative leave of absence as might be due to him.

In addition, he wrote a personal letter to Hull. In it he expressed a desire "to take advantage of my present appointment to the Department of State for emergency duty to travel throughout the United States and talk with responsible persons in different sections of the country regarding conditions in Europe, with a view to acquainting them with the dangers of the international situation affecting the United States." He mentioned that he had had offers from the Foreign Policy Association and the Council of Foreign Relations to sponsor such appearances, especially in the Middle West. He also assured Hull that there would be "no expense entailed to the government in connection with this travel," and that any remuneration he might receive he would turn over to the American Red Cross.

There was no reply to this letter. For the second time within a year, Lane seriously considered resigning from the foreign service. He felt that his public appearances in the United States were important and that they would give him much more satisfaction than diplomatic activities in Costa Rica. He was a good speaker, forceful and witty; he could easily attune himself to the mood of any audience and carry it with him. But Lane also realized that his current success in this activity was due mainly to his official position and to the publicity he had received in connection with his role in the dramatic events in the Balkans. This glamour was bound to wear off sooner or later, and Lane could not visualize himself as a professional lecturer, addressing service clubs and women's organizations across the country, repeating the same things long after new developments would obscure those he had been part of.

After giving the matter considerable thought, he went to Washington. Sumner Welles was apologetic and even solicitous. In their several friendly talks he pointed out that Lane would be in Costa Rica for a very short time, and reminded him that San Jose was, after all, the most pleasant capital in Central America and the Caribbean. Welles also told Lane that early in the next year a vacancy in Colombia would open and that it would be given to him, together with the rank of ambassador. And he stressed that the whole Isthmus region was becoming extremely important for the strategic defense of the Americas in view of the German and Japanese intrigues and manipulations there, an ominous development which required the utmost attention of the United States.

Lane permitted himself to be talked into accepting the assignment and his appointment was announced. But at the end of his leave, on September 29, 1941, he made another attempt to extend his stay in the country. In a "My dear Sumner" letter to the under secretary, he described the great success of his public appearances and of his article in *Life,* and asked to postpone his departure so that he could continue to acquaint "the public in the United States with conditions in occupied Europe and the methods which the aggressors have been employing." He suggested that Costa Rica could easily wait, at least until the end of the year, while he continued with his good work.

Welles was unreceptive. As the country was heading for war, the last ditch struggle of the isolationists against the administration was getting fiercer by the hour. What Lane considered as his advantage—his being "an official eye witness who has no axe to grind in domestic politics"—was in fact provoking bitter complaints from influential quarters that the supposedly non-partisan foreign service was being utilized by Roosevelt for promoting partisan political viewpoints. The more successful Lane was in rallying his audiences to the cause of the democracies, the more frequent were the objections of prominent public figures, including senators from midwestern states, to his activities. To have this controversy continue and grow was a luxury which the State Department could not afford at the moment. On October 1, 1941, Welles replied:

> While I appreciate the importance of what you propose to do and realize, if you were not appointed to a new post, the kind of activity you have in mind would undoubtedly be of value, it is in my opinion by no means commensurate with your value as American minister to Costa Rica. I shall not attempt to go into details since you will appreciate what I have in mind. I hope, consequently, that you will make arrangements to arrive at your new post not later than November 1.

And so it was. The Yugoslav chapter of Lane's life had to be closed, no matter how reluctant he was to abandon the attractions of the noise and glitter of public life, the fight for good against evil which he so thoroughly enjoyed. Duty, as before, came first. By November 1, 1941, the Lanes had moved into the minister's residence in San Jose, Costa Rica.

V

The Defeat in Poland

After one year in Costa Rica, which was pleasant but uneventful, Arthur Bliss Lane was transferred to Colombia and simultaneously promoted to the rank of ambassador. Because of Colombia's proximity to the Panama Canal and because the activities of pro-German, pro-Italian, and pro-Japanese elements in that country were thought to constitute a menace to the security of the Western Hemisphere, the State Department rated the Bogotá post as reasonably important. Ambassador Lane did not feel that such was the case. He privately scoffed at the presumed threat to the American strategic position in the Carribean, and there was nothing new about anti-Yanqui sentiments among Latin Americans. Locally, at least, the situation was pretty much under control. The Conservative government of Colombia, although not very popular, was cooperative. It duly undertook a program of nationalization and confiscation of the property of Axis nationals, which Lane urged upon it on instructions from Washington. By the end of 1943, after some not quite spontaneous agitation following the sinking of a Colombian schooner by a presumably German submarine, the government allowed itself to be pressed by the United States into a declaration of a state of belligerency with Germany.

Lane's dissatisfaction with his post was only partially related to local developments. His mind was occupied by the great struggle developing in the world, to which Colombia contributed next to nothing. The declaration of belligerency could not be interpreted as a serious contribution to the cause of freedom by any stretch of the imagination. With considerable disgust, Lane noted in his November 29 cable to the Department that the public reacted to this important step with apathy. He complained that "there are no flags flying nor any public demonstrations. Having witnessed popular enthusiasm following anti-Nazi action on the part of the Yugoslav and Costa Rican governments, it is almost unbelievable that life in Bogotá can continue without any interruption whatever on the occasion of the Colombian government having taken such a momentous decision."[1]

Ever since the landing in North Africa, when the Allied armies and navies began the long-awaited offensive against the Axis, Lane had become restless, his desire to be in the midst of things growing by the day. Life in Bogotá was too relaxed to satisfy him. He felt that his abilities and energy were not being put to proper use and he wished to move to some other place where he would be able to make a real contribution to the war effort. On a visit to Washington in the summer of 1943, he spent some time exploring the possibilities for reassignment. His talks with old friends at the Department convinced him that these possibilities were quite small. There were still many senior foreign service officers around waiting for vacancies. His most important connection, Sumner Welles, was of little help: he was about to lose his own job due to his growing frictions with Secretary Hull. Moreover, Lane discovered, the State Department itself had been relegated to a rather insignificant position within the government. The tremendous concentration of power in the White House brought about by war needs had all but destroyed the established administrative channels. The conduct of foreign policy, as well as important appointments, appeared to be in the hands of a small circle of the president's advisors.

Having found no encouragement in the Department, Lane made an attempt to see the president. He did not succeed; Roosevelt was too busy with other things. But Lane managed to contact General Edwin M. Watson, the president's military aide, whom he asked to relay to the Chief his request for reassignment. Watson recorded in his memorandum to the president on July 12, that "Lane feels that because of his experience — twenty-seven years in the service — he could serve better in a more active place at this time." Somewhat unkindly, Watson noted that although Lane had assured him that both

---

1. FR, 1943, VI, 6.

Hull and Welles would have no objection to his being moved, he "told Arthur" that he thought it advisable for Lane "to see Secretary Hull and get his definite recommendation before asking again to see the president."

Lane, who did not really anticipate any immediate results, shrugged off "Pa" Watson's bit of free advice. But he made sure, both during the rest of his leave in the United States and after he returned to Colombia, that his desire to be transferred to a more responsible and challenging post became known to all concerned.

The pay-off came one year later when, owing to a combination of circumstances which had little to do with the foreign policy of the United States, Roosevelt appointed Lane ambassador to Poland, or, more exactly, to the Polish government-in-exile in London. He made this appointment very reluctantly, and would have been happier if he could have avoided it. Ever since the break in Soviet-Polish relations in April, 1943, the whole Polish question had threatened the close cooperation of Great Britain, the United States, and the Soviet Union, a cooperation which Roosevelt cherished above anything else. At Teheran he had gone along with Churchill and Stalin on the vexing issue of the future of the Soviet-Polish frontier which eventually left in Soviet possession almost one-half of Poland's territory. But at the same time, Roosevelt had excused himself from participating in discussions on all matters related to Poland. He told Stalin that although he agreed with his views on the solution of the Polish question, "there were in the United States some six to seven million Americans of Polish extraction and, as a practical man, he did not wish to lose their vote" in the next year's presidential election.[2]

Much as Roosevelt wished it, there was no way of eliminating Poland as a factor in inter-Allied relations. The country was, after all, the first victim of Nazi aggression, and Great Britain, which had declared war on Germany when Hitler

---

2. FR, Conferences at Cairo and Teheran, 1943, 594. On the same grounds, Roosevelt also refused to be commited to a decision regarding the future of Lithuania, Estonia, and Latvia, "adding jokingly that when the Soviet armies re-occupied these areas, he did not intend to go to war with the Soviet Union on this point."

launched his attack on Poland, was morally and formally committed to its restoration. Moreover, the Poles continued to contribute substantially to the Allied war effort, valiantly fighting alongside the British in Italy and sabotaging German lines of communication in the east at a tremendous cost in human lives and suffering. Their underground resistance movement was one of the best organized in Nazi-occupied Europe, and since it maintained close liaison with the Polish government in London, developments in Poland were constantly in the news in the West, evoking expressions of admiration for the heroic struggle of the Polish people. A sensitive politician, Roosevelt realized that the greater the accomplishments of the passionately nationalistic and strongly anti-Russian Poles, the more difficult would be the settlement of Poland's future. Unwilling to incur Stalin's displeasure by appearing to sponsor Polish interests, he assumed a hands-off attitude and let Churchill carry the ball. When Anthony J.D. Biddle resigned as ambassador to the governments-in-exile situated in London in January 1944, he declined to appoint his successor, hoping that such downgrading of this post would further emphasize the reluctance of the United States to become involved in the problems of Eastern Europe.

Stalin did not display any sympathy with Roosevelt's predicament. On the contrary, presenting his Western allies with a *fait accompli,* he ordered the forming of a group composed of Polish communists and fellow-travelers—which became known as the Lublin Committee—and had it declared the sole spokesman for the Polish people. Having created this body, Stalin then embarked on a scheme aimed at undercutting the legal position of the Polish government-in-exile, headed by Stanislaw Mikolajczyk.

Mikolajczyk himself was acceptable to Stalin. This leader of the Polish peasants was known to regard Germany as the principal enemy of Poland; his attitude toward Russia, even communist Russia, was one of accommodation, not unusual among the Poles originating from the western provinces of Poland which, until 1919, had been part of Germany. But among Mikolajczyk's colleagues in the cabinet there were several who viewed the Soviets with deep suspicion and were unwilling to forget either the Nazi-Soviet partition of Poland or the harsh treatment which the Soviets accorded the Poles in the subsequent years. Now, sensing the strength of Russia's position, Stalin suggested to Churchill and Roosevelt that a compromise solution of the Polish question might be effected through purging the government-in-exile of all anti-Soviet elements and by including in it pro-Soviet Poles from the Lublin Committee, from the underground in Poland, and from the United States. This suggestion was rejected by the British. Churchill could not, both because of internal political considerations and because of his concern about the future relations of Great Britain with East European countries, appear to be forcing a legally constituted and officially recognized Allied government to purge itself in order to become acceptable to Stalin. In this regard, he had an ally in Secretary Hull, who differed with the White House in believing that there were limits to what the United States should do by way of satisfying Stalin's wishes. But Hull's influence was on the decline, and in the end, under Roosevelt's pressure, the State Department accepted the idea that the Polish government should be "reconstituted" on terms acceptable to Moscow.[3]

The Warsaw Uprising

Roosevelt's hopes for a compromise solution, one which he could endorse publicly without endangering his standing with the American voters in the election year, were dashed when the leaders of the Warsaw underground decided to launch an uprising against the Germans. The moment appeared appropriate. The Red Army was within a few miles of the Polish capital, and the retreating German divisions were pouring

---

3. After Stalin's repeated requests, and despite the objections of the Polish Ambassador, Ciechanowski, Roosevelt instructed Hull to let three pro-Soviet Americans of Polish origin—a University of Chicago professor, Oscar Lange, a priest from Massachusetts, Stanislaus Orlemanski, and the chairman of the American Slav Congress, Leo Krzycki—go to Moscow for political consultations. The first two gentlemen traveled to Moscow in May, 1944, via Alaska, and met Stalin, Molotov and the members of the Lublin Committee. Stalin liked Lange enough to ask for Roosevelt's consent to the professor's appointment as director of the Committee's foreign relations. To his chagrin, Roosevelt had to withhold his consent to the move, which would have commited him to a politically unacceptable solution of the Polish question. See FR, 1944, III, 1231, 1321, 1399-1422.

across the Vistula bridges. Radio Moscow, which had been accusing the nationalists of inactivity, appealed to Warsaw to rise and help deal the enemy a decisive blow. Churchill and Mikolajczyk were at that time in Moscow, discussing terms for the re-establishment of Soviet-Polish relations. And all the Poles desired to free their capital themselves before it was occupied by the Soviets. In one massive effort, they rose on August 1, 1944, attacking the Germans on every street in the city.

Stalin at first seemed to be understanding: he promised Mikolajczyk to parachute arms to the Warsaw fighters and assured him that the Red army would soon enter the city.[4] However, almost immediately after the departure of Churchill and Mikolajczyk from Moscow, the Soviet government officially termed the uprising "a purely adventuristic affair" and refused to have anything to do with it. No supplies were sent to Warsaw, and the Red Army advance on the whole Polish front came to a dead halt.[5]

As the English-speaking world breathlessly watched the heroic struggle, newspaper editors, radio commentators, and politicians indignantly demanded prompt aid for the embattled fighters of Warsaw. General George C. Marshall, chief of staff of the United States army, who on the fourth day of the uprising had suspended the aid program to the Polish underground army on the grounds that the Soviets had recognized the Lublin Committee as a quasi-government of Poland, issued a directive to organize delivery of supplies to Warsaw. Since supplies had to be flown from England and Italy, and the distance was too great to provide the heavy bombers with a protective fighter escort to Warsaw and back, Harriman was instructed to seek Soviet permission for the planes to land on Soviet airfields after they had dropped arms to the Poles. He got nowhere. In his report to Washington he bitterly remarked that "for the first time since coming to Moscow I am gravely concerned by the attitude of the Soviet government in its refusal to let us assist the Poles in Warsaw," and concluded that

---

4. Harriman to Hull, August 10, 1944, *ibid.*, 1308-1309.
5. Official Soviet historians later argued that the Red army was exhausted and couldn't continue advancing on the Warsaw front.

"this refusal was based on nothing but ruthless political considerations.[6]

Harriman urged Roosevelt to send immediately a "strong
message" to Stalin explaining that the "chances of world security and postwar cooperation would be deeply shaken" if the
Soviets adopted an attitude of indifference towards the extermination of the Poles in Warsaw. Roosevelt's first reaction to
this idea was negative: he guessed that Stalin was annoyed by
the Poles' attempt to assert their national independence, and
did not want to appear to be siding with the elements regarded
as hostile by his Soviet partner. After a barrage of messages
from Churchill (who had come under considerable pressure in
England) Roosevelt finally consented to make a joint appeal,
but made sure that its wording did not hurt Stalin's feelings:

> We are thinking of world opinion if the anti-Nazis in Warsaw are
> abandoned. We believe that all three of us should do the utmost to
> save as many of the patriots as possible. We hope that you will
> drop immediate supplies and munitions to the patriot Poles in
> Warsaw, or you will agree to help our planes in doing it very
> quickly. We hope you will approve. The time element is of ex-
> treme importance.

Stalin, who by then had been roundly denounced in the
world press for his calculated cruelty, was in no mood to cooperate. He called the insurgents "a group of criminals, who have
embarked on the Warsaw adventure in order to seize power";
Molotov would not permit the landing of even crippled Allied
planes on Soviet territory.[7]

In the meantime, the frantic radio appeals of the Warsaw

---

6. Harriman to Hull, August 15, 1944, *ibid.*, 1376.
7. *Ibid.*, 1385-1389, *passim.* George F. Kennan recalls in his memoirs that
Harriman and his military aide, General John R. Deane, returned from their
conference with Stalin and Molotov where this decision was announced,
"shattered by the experience. There was no doubt in any of our minds,"
continues Kennan, "as to the implications of the position the Soviet leaders
had taken. This was a gauntlet thrown down, in a spirit of malicious glee,
before the Western powers. What it meant to imply was: 'We intend to have
Poland, lock, stock, and barrel. We don't care a fig for those Polish underground fighters who have not accepted communist authority. To us, they are
no better than the Germans; and if they and the Germans slaughter each
other off, so much the better. It is a matter of indifference to us what you
Americans think of all this.' "

fighters, along with vivid descriptions of the struggle, found their way into the Western press. The Germans were methodically reducing the Polish capital to a heap of rubble; the number of Poles killed in the uprising was approaching 100,000. By mid-September, after six weeks of fighting, the insurgents still refused to surrender in spite of the hopelessness of their situation. In the United States, the deep public sympathy for the abandoned Poles was beginning to reflect on Roosevelt's popularity and the polls showed that Polish-American voters, traditionally Democratic in their allegiance, threatened to defect to the opposition. Seriously alarmed, Roosevelt tried to direct public wrath against the Germans, but, as the criticism of his failure to aid the valiant ally mounted, in his campaign speeches he spoke more and more often about his unswerving intention to leave no stone unturned until Poland had been restored as a great, free, and independent nation.

Arthur Bliss Lane is Reassigned

It was against this background that Roosevelt decided to appoint an ambassador to the long vacant post accredited to the Polish government-in-exile. Arthur Bliss Lane seemed to be a logical choice. He had an established record of determined opposition to the Axis. He had demonstrated his popularity among ethnic groups in the country in the summer of 1941 when in public speeches he advocated greater commitment by the United States to the cause of freedom in the European conflict. He had served in Poland early in his career, in 1919, under a popular ambassador, Hugh Gibson, an admitted Republican and a close friend of Herbert Hoover. And he was perfectly acceptable to the leaders of Polish-American organizations.

Lane's appointment, announced on September 20, 1944, made news and evoked favorable editorial comment. The next day the New York *Herald Tribune* remarked that this was an indication of "support by the American government of the exiled Polish regime in the conflict with the Soviet-sponsored Polish Committee of National Liberation over which will govern post-war Poland." The White House received a number of letters and telegrams praising the president for making his position known. The Polish-American Congress stressed that Mikolajczyk's government was recognized by the "overwhelming majority of Poles as the legitimate ruling body," and the auxiliary Bishop of Detroit wrote the president a letter, expressing his admiration for Roosevelt's "courage and the true American spirit which prompted you to appoint an ambassador to the Polish government-in-exile at this particular time." The Bishop assured Roosevelt that "fully ninety percent of our citizens of Polish extraction" shared his satisfaction.

In far-away Bogotá, Lane was extremely pleased with the new assignment, giving little thought to what might have brought it about. Secretary Hull also chose to take the appointment at face value. Pleased that it would strengthen the American hand in the diplomatic bargaining with the Soviets, he cabled Lane on October 3, 1944, ordering him to proceed to London as soon as possible, "via the Department for consultation en route." The Lanes quickly packed their belongings and shipped them directly to London, not for a moment suspecting that they would not see their trunks again for more than two years.

On October 16, Hull cabled additional instructions, formally advising Lane to "proceed to your post at the expiration of your period of instruction in Washington, which period must not exceed thirty days." Since no urgent business kept Lane in Bogotá, he wound up his affairs and, on October 20, reported to the State Department, to begin his "period of instruction."

After two or three weeks of hard work, Lane was up to date on matters relating to Poland. He carefully read the dispatches of Rudolph E. Schoenfeld, chargé d'affaires in London, and of Harriman from Moscow, as well as the outgoing cables of the secretary of state. The Polish ambassador in Washington, Ciechanowski, acquainted him with current developments in the government-in-exile and with the critical situation in the parts of Poland which had come under control of the Soviet authorities, where members of the nationalist underground were subjected to arbitrary arrests, deportations, and executions. Lane understood the bitterness of the Poles-in-exile over these developments. He took it for granted that the Soviets would attempt to install their puppet, the Lublin Committee,

as the government of Poland. But he was not emotionally involved in the developing drama. Reflecting what he assumed to
be Roosevelt's views, he did not consider the Polish government in London to be truly representative of the Polish nation
and saw a reasonable ground for give-and-take in the forthcoming negotiations with the Soviets. He anticipated that the interests of Poland would be provisionally represented by a regime based on a broad coalition of groups and parties, agreed
upon by the Big Three, and that this regime eventually would
be replaced by a new government, elected by the Polish nation
in free elections.

False Assumptions

It may appear in retrospect that for a man designated to
represent the United States in Poland, Arthur Bliss Lane knew
woefully little about the true intentions and thoughts of his
president. This kind of ignorance, however, was fully within
the tradition of the time. With the exception of a few personal
and political friends, Roosevelt took no one into his confidence.
He distrusted the State Department as a body, suspecting that
many of his ideas would find a cold, if not hostile, reception
there. The immense problems of the postwar era were to be
resolved personally by Roosevelt, Stalin, and Churchill, without consultation with the junior members of the anti-Axis coalition, no matter how much their interests might be involved. In
due course, they were to be informed of the Big Three decisions and expected to accept them.

It followed that until these decisions had been made, the
United States did not have (and did not need) a defined policy
of its own toward such a country as Poland. If Roosevelt had
immediate objectives, he did not care to share his ideas with
those in the State Department who had been handling Polish
affairs. This assured him a maximum freedom of action and
spared him the possible blame if he failed to sway his partners
toward his point of view. For the time being, meaningless
generalities about a "strong, free, and independent Polish
state" were all Roosevelt had to say on the subject.

General ideas aside, even the specific commitments which
the president had already made to Stalin in regard to the Polish

question were known to very few men in Washington. Until his retirement in September 1944, Secretary Hull had not been allowed to see the minutes of even the formal meetings of the Teheran conference. Only one man in the State Department, Charles E. Bohlen, who acted as Roosevelt's interpreter at Teheran and who became chief of the Division of Eastern European Affairs in January 1944, knew the extent of the president's commitments. But Bohlen was sworn to secrecy and never as much as intimated that the policy of the United States, as reflected in the official cables of the secretary of state, was at variance with the president's true thinking. And not even Bohlen saw the messages which Churchill and Stalin exchanged with Roosevelt after Teheran, messages which were destined to remain completely secret for twenty years or more. Ambassador Harriman, another man who enjoyed Roosevelt's confidence, was similarly discreet. If he had to report from Moscow on some particularly sensitive subject, he directed his dispatches to the White House; if he addressed them to both the president and the secretary of state, he worded them in such a way that neither Hull nor Stettinius (who replaced Hull), nor anyone else, would be able to learn more than he was entitled to.[8]

Roosevelt's secretiveness was deep-rooted. He had learned the lesson from Woodrow Wilson who allowed his vision of world peace and security to be ruined because of his insistence on open covenants openly arrived at. Roosevelt knew that a large segment of the American public deeply distrusted the Soviets, and that the implications of his "Great Design" were so far-reaching that to reveal its ingredients would have caused a furor which would have made the attainment of his goals

---

8. As one example, although Harriman was present at Roosevelt's private meeting with Stalin at Teheran on December 1, 1943, when Roosevelt endorsed Soviet territorial claims, he assumed a look of innocence when Molotov referred to it at a meeting with Churchill and Mikolajczyk on October 13, 1944; in his report, he termed Molotov's statement untrue. Churchill, who was also puzzled by Molotov's revelation, learned the facts next day directly from Stalin. Harriman to Roosevelt, October 14, 1944, and Churchill to Roosevelt, October 18, 1944, ibid., 1322–1326. That Roosevelt lied to Mikolajczyk on this and other points during the latter's visit to Washington in June, 1944, is understandable in view of the overall ticklishness of the subject. See Stettinius' memorandum, June 12, 1944, ibid., 1281.

well-nigh impossible. He believed that by exercising personal diplomacy and by strengthening his ties with Stalin he would in the end be able to produce solutions acceptable to the public; in the meantime he regarded the need for secrecy as paramount.

Understandable or not, the president's ways of doing things had created an eerie situation in which the actual policy of the United States, as conducted by the White House, remained unknown to the foreign policy establishment. Through his correspondence with Stalin, for example, Roosevelt knew that after the Warsaw uprising and the uproar which accompanied it, Stalin would not accept the Polish government-in-exile, or any political fraction thereof, as a basis for the interim regime in liberated Poland. Roosevelt did not share this knowledge with the secretary of state who, in his ignorance, still expected an important role for the London Poles. Acting Secretary of State Edward R. Stettinius recognized that Mikolajczyk's resignation on November 24 "rendered the Polish question much more acute and difficult" and feared that the Soviet government "will be quick to take advantage" of the new situation and proceed "more vigorously with the establishment of the Lublin Committee as the sole representative authority in Poland."[9] Like Hull before him, Stettinius did not suspect that Roosevelt was in no mood to fight Stalin over Poland, even as he was assuring Mikolajczyk upon the latter's departure from Washington that the United States stood "unequivocally for a strong, free, and independent Polish state with the untrammeled right of the Polish people to order their internal affairs as they see fit."[10]

Such declarations were hardly sufficient to guide Arthur Bliss Lane's thinking. Perhaps he did not feel, as George F. Kennan did at the same time, that there was "something frivolous about our whole action on the Polish question." As a politically attuned man, Lane saw his mission in upholding American interests in Poland (whatever they might be) and in fulfilling the overall American commitment, so frequently stressed by Roosevelt, to the restoration of Poland's national independence.

---

9. Stettinius to Roosevelt, November 25, 1944, *ibid.*, 1339.
10. Roosevelt to Mikolajczyk, November 17, 1944, *ibid.*, 1335.

At the same time, Arthur Bliss Lane regarded skeptically
Roosevelt's idea of the great powers' postwar unity. Seeing
Poland as a bone of contention between the Allies, he suspected both Stalin and Churchill of expansionist designs and of
the readiness to strike a deal at the expense of Poland, while
Roosevelt appeared to him the chief protector of Polish interests. Lane could not have conceived that Roosevelt considered the winning of Stalin's trust and affection the key to the
solution of all postwar problems, and that Roosevelt was determined to avoid any step which could make this ultimate goal
more difficult to attain. On the contrary, since the Soviet Union
was emerging out of the war as a strong and dynamic state,
Lane fully anticipated a long series of diplomatic wranglings
over the major issues, including Poland.

Within two months after his arrival in Washington, Lane
learned enough to realize that he would not go to his post at
the Polish government-in-exile, headed after Mikolajczyk's resignation of November 24 by the uncompromisingly anti-Soviet
Tomasz Arciszewski. On December 15, 1944, he wrote Schoenfeld that it would be unwise for him to proceed to London
because it would mean tying the United States to a government
"which in our opinion cannot last, thereby prejudicing our
position with the authorities with whom we shall eventually
deal, whoever they may be." In his mind, this opinion did not
conflict with the American commitment to defend the "untrammeled right of the Polish people to order their internal affairs
as they see fit." Present difficulties had to be overcome, Lane
believed, and before long the will of the people, freely exercised, would create a government in Poland capable of pro-
tecting the nation's interests.

To the State Department, this was a long-range expectation,
which did not mean that the Polish government headed by
Arciszewski should be thrown overboard: such an act would
have violated both the rules of diplomacy and political common sense. In a cable to Harriman, Stettinius explained that
although the department did not contemplate that relations
with Arciszewski would be more than "correct," he did not
wish Lane's prolonged stay in Washington to be "given any
political significance." He instructed Harriman, in his discussions with Soviet officials, to "be guided by the fact that this

government has continued recognition of the Polish government in London." He stressed that if the Soviets accorded full recognition to the Lublin Committee "we would not look favorably on such a step." Stettinius anticipated that the Arciszewski government would soon fall and that "Mikolajczyk may then be induced to form a new cabinet composed of persons who fully support his policies, which eventually might make it possible for us to take a more positive attitude in favor of the Polish government in London."[11]

This stated position did not quite correspond to the realities of the moment. Roosevelt had told Stettinius that regardless of whether Arciszewski's cabinet survived or not, nothing would be done about formulating United States policy toward Poland until the whole issue had been discussed by the Big Three in the forthcoming meeting at Yalta. All the same, Roosevelt knew that time worked against him. Late in December, in an attempt to salvage something of the Western position, he pleaded with Stalin not to rush recognition of the Lublin Committee as the provisional government of Poland "until we have had an opportunity at our meeting to discuss the whole question thoroughly." When Stalin refused to wait, Roosevelt probably realized that the chances for a reasonable compromise solution of the issue had all but vanished.

Yalta

On November 2, 1944, at a conference in the White House, Roosevelt outlined to Lane the difficulties he was encountering and authorized him to remain in Washington on a week-to-week basis. After Lane was officially sworn in as Ambassador to Poland on December 4, Stettinius again told him that he would have to wait at the Department until the situation was clarified at the forthcoming Yalta conference.

Personally, Lane was none too happy about the way things were going. He found the highly unusual delay in proceeding to his destination increasingly irritating. He was compelled to lead a rather secluded life, inventing explanations whenever someone would express surprise at seeing him around Washington for so long. More significantly, he was beginning to

11. Stettinius to Harriman, December 13, 1944, *ibid.*, 1440.

suspect that neither Roosevelt nor Stettinius was being quite candid with him in explaining the United States' position vis-à-vis Poland. Both still sounded as if they intended to go to great lengths in securing Poland's independence, permitting no under-the-table deals between Great Britain and the Soviet Union at the expense of the Poles. Yet Lane detected enough signs of weakening of the American position to make him wonder about the eventual outcome of the crisis. He spelled out his thoughts at length in his December 20 memorandum, written presumably for circulation among the members of the American delegation about to depart for Yalta. He started by accusing Churchill, on the basis of the latter's speech in the House of Commons a few days earlier, of attempting to impose upon Poland—in accord with Stalin—a frontier settlement almost identical with the Molotov-Ribbentrop line. He praised President Roosevelt for his insistence on the independence of Poland but warned that "the practical view of our declarations will . . . depend on an interpretation of what is meant by 'independence.'" And he continued:

> If it is to mean that a minority under Russian influence is to be the nominal government of Poland, we will almost certainly have a repetition of the present situation in Yugoslavia and we shall be responsible, by acquiescing in Soviet and British plans, for setting a pattern in Europe which can only lead to the destruction of our prestige and possibly to future war. For the foregoing reasons, I urge that at the next meeting of the leaders of the United States, Great Britain, and the Soviet Union, we insist on the right of the Polish people to choose their own government without molestation from any external force and that such a government be permitted to govern the country as it sees fit. With the greatest army, navy, and air force in history at our disposal and in the light of the great material assistance we are giving to Great Britain and the Soviet Union, our views on this important matter should be given by the other parties the consideration they deserve. There is no threat implied in this statement regarding our present military force but it does emphasize that a basic American policy for which we have been fighting should not be disregarded by our allies.

Like most of the other material prepared in the State Department for the conference, this memorandum most probably was not read by either Roosevelt or any other leading member of the American delegation. Even if it had been read, the ideas expressed in it were so alien to the president that it would have had no impact whatsoever. It is a good guess that if Roosevelt by some chance had read this document, he would probably have appointed as his representative in Warsaw someone whose thoughts and attitudes were more compatible with his own: Lane was too old-fashioned in his beliefs and too forceful to be sufficiently accomodating in his future relations with the Polish communists and their Soviet backers.

On the other hand, Roosevelt would probably have had difficulty in finding a career diplomat (Warsaw was no place for a political appointee) much different from Lane in this respect. Most members of the foreign service of Lane's age and rank had a touch of Wilsonian idealism in their world outlook; very few of them had that kind of moral flexibility which seemed to be almost a necessity in the complex international situation as it formed at the end of the second world war. What aggravated the matter in this particular instance was the fact that Lane, unlike many of his colleagues, had been a confirmed interventionist since the early years of his career. He had always held to the belief that a more active role by the United States in European affairs could have prevented the outbreak of the war. Now, at the beginning of 1945, he felt that there could be no return to isolation for the United States and that, like it or not, it was destined to maintain the balance of power in the world. Therefore he was determined that his embassy in Warsaw was not to be a mere "listening post" where he would collect diplomatic gossip and dispatch his findings to a faceless and indifferent desk officer in the State Department. He convinced himself that Poland had become important to the United States; no less so than Mexico or Panama and perhaps more, since everything seemed to indicate that the international prestige of the United States was heavily involved there. Lane was going to represent in Warsaw the most powerful nation on earth, asserting American interests there, and making sure that the commitment to restoration of Polish independence made by his government was carried out. It was imperative not to betray the trust which the Poles had placed in President Roosevelt. Moreover, since the United States had already in effect abandoned the Polish government-in-exile, it was doubly important that the Polish nation have the opportunity, in Roosevelt's words, "to choose their own government without molestation from any external force," and that such a government be enabled to rule the country as it saw fit.

The discussions on the Polish question at Yalta consumed more of the participants' time than all other issues combined. Much as his hands were tied by his previous commitments (from Teheran on), Churchill defended Polish interests with vigor. Roosevelt, on the other hand, not officially commited, merely appealed to Stalin's magnanimity, saying time and again that although "the Poles were quarrelsome people not only at home but also abroad," it was important to give "some assurance for the six million Poles in the United States" that the envisaged elections in Poland would be freely held, so that "there would be no doubt as to the sincerity of the agreement reached here,"[12] Stalin remained singularly unimpressed by this argument. He refused to concede anything on the frontier question. He ruled out a fusion of the London and Lublin Poles as a basis for a provisional government in Warsaw, insisting that the Lublin Committee, already recognized by the Soviets as a de facto government, would merely accept several "democratic" leaders from Poland itself and from the Poles abroad, retaining its clearly pro-Soviet coloration. Grudgingly, Stalin accepted a formula that the new government thus formed "shall be pledged to the holding of free and unfettered elections as soon as possible on the basis of universal suffrage and secret ballot," elections in which all "democratic and anti-Nazi parties" shall have the right to take part. But he firmly turned down all suggestions for having the elections internationally supervised, and although he said (rather in jest) that the elections could be held within a month, he declined to specify any time limit in the text of the Declaration.[13] Unable to agree on the precise composition of the provisional government, the Big Three formed a commission to be seated in Moscow, consisting

12. FR, *The Conferences at Malta and Yalta, 1945*, 848.
13. For an analysis of the discussion of the Polish issue, see Herbert Feis, *Churchill, Roosevelt, Stalin* (Princeton, 1957), Chapter 54. In his report to the Congress on March 1, 1945, Roosevelt praised the agreement on Poland as "one outstanding example of joint action by the three major Allied powers," and described it as "the most hopeful agreement possible for a free, independent and prosperous Polish state."

of Molotov, Harriman, and Clark Kerr, the British ambassador to the Soviet Union, to "consult" with various Polish leaders "with a view to reorganization of the present [Lublin] government." No time limit was set for this task either.

The document entitled "Declaration on Poland," signed by Roosevelt, Churchill, and Stalin, which became the point of departure for United States policy towards Poland, Lane regarded as nothing short of a diplomatic disaster. To him, everything hinged now on the composition of the provisional government, a task entrusted to the Moscow Commission, and dependent on the ability of the Western Allies to ensure the "free and unfettered elections" to be carried out under the auspices of that government. It was hard for Lane to expect much success in either undertaking. He suspected that Roosevelt and Churchill had, in effect, conceded Poland to the Soviets.[14]

On March 14, 1945, one month after Yalta, Lane went to see Stettinius. As he recorded in a memorandum written the same day, the secretary appeared to be his most optimistic self as he talked about the progress of the Moscow Commission. Lane, who had followed dispatches from Moscow closely, pointed out that his optimism had no foundation in fact. Stettinius, who was not particularly interested in the Polish question, merely shrugged his shoulders. But noting Lane's unhappiness, he asked whether Lane thought he should perhaps take another post and let someone else go to Warsaw. Lane answered that "it would be a great mistake to take another post at this time, as it would be a public admission that the negotiations had failed." After a moment's thought, the secretary agreed.

It is difficult to reconstruct what exactly was on Lane's mind at this particular point. The main damage to the American position in Poland had been done and no review of this policy as laid down at Yalta was in sight. But as a practitioner of diplomacy, Lane probably hoped that not everything was beyond salvage, and that by giving the Declaration on Poland the

---

14. The reference to "free and unfettered elections" in the Yalta Declaration struck George F. Kennan (who himself was on the scene) "as the shabbiest sort of equivocation, certainly not calculated to pull the wool over the eyes of the Western public, but bound to have this effect." See his *Memoirs 1925-1950* (Boston: Little, Brown and Company, 1967), 212.

strictest possible interpretation and by insisting that it be carried out to the letter, the United States could retrieve at least
part of the loss. He may have hoped that the increasingly vocal
denunciations of the Yalta decisions would stiffen the official
attitude. The Poles in London, in the United States, and in the
Allied armies in Italy and elsewhere were, of course, most
bitter of all. More significantly, indignation over Roosevelt's
and Churchill's "betrayal" of the country which had lost six
million of its citizens since the beginning of the war, pronounced both in the House of Commons and in Congress, was
seconded by a great many Britons and Americans who had
never been friendly to the Soviet Union.

In addition to such general considerations, Lane's views
were doubtless affected by his growing knowledge of the deadlock developing among the Big Three over the crucial issue of
the Polish Provisional Government of National Unity to be
formed in accordance with the Yalta decisions. Stalin took a
position that the Lublin Committee, already recognized by the
Soviet Union as the Government of Poland, should form the
base of a coalition and merely invite a few acceptable Poles
from London and from within Poland to broaden itself. Churchill, exasperated by Stalin's *fait accomplis,* insisted that a
totally new coalition be formed, with the Big Three deciding
which Poles were to be added to the Lublin group. Roosevelt's
possition was closer to Stalin's. As he wrote Churchill on
March 29, "if we attempt to evade the fact that we place [at
Yalta] somewhat more emphasis on the Lublin Poles ... we
will expose ourselves to the charge that we are attempting to go
back to the Crimean decision."[15] The issue of Stalin's recognition of "the Lublin Poles" as a government did not appear to
him to be of importance. Counting on Roosevelt's acquies-
cence, Soviet foreign minister Molotov, presiding in the Moscow Commission, was adamant in insisting that the "reorganization" of the Warsaw government should be carried out without the Big Three having any say as to which non-communist
Poles must be added to it.

While the correspondence between Roosevelt and Churchill
on this sensitive subject still bypassed the State Department

15. FR, 1945, V, 189.

(Charles E. Bohlen, who drafted many cables for the president, although technically assistant to the secretary of state, was, in effect, on the White House staff), enough information was coming in to permit the picture to be reconstructed. Beginning with the end of February, Harriman, who was aware of Roosevelt's rapidly failing health and who was frustrated by the Soviet stalling tactics, directed more and more of his dispatches to the state department. With Stettinius engrossed in preparations for the United Nations conference in San Francisco, Acting Secretary Joseph C. Grew had undertaken the task of coordinating American and British moves in Moscow. Lane, who had a good working relationship with Grew, had full access to all the correspondence related to Poland and, for the first time since his appointment six months earlier, could make an informed judgment of the true state of affairs.

Predictably, Lane came up in favor of taking a tough line with the Soviets. In a long memorandum to the secretary of state of April 5, he warned that "appeasement or apparent appeasement can be as dangerous to United States interests in 1945 as it actually was in 1940 and 1941." Since Soviet actions in Poland and elsewhere and the deterioration of Soviet-American relations would sooner or later become fully known to the public anyway, it seemed advisable "to place publicly the responsibilities for the difficulties in the settlement squarely on the Soviet Government, where it belongs." Such a public statement, continued Lane, should indicate that the Soviets were not concerned with "the importance of effectively carrying out the terms of the Crimea agreement" and that they seemed to be intent—together with "the puppet regime now set up in Warsaw"—on preventing democratic Poles outside of Poland from taking part in the formation of a representative Polish government. In order to dramatize the situation, Lane recommended that he, as Ambassador to Poland, should resign; that his assembled staff be given other duties; and that further representation to the Government of Poland should be left in charge of Schoenfeld in London.[16]

16. For the full text of the memorandum, see Arthur Bliss Lane, *I Saw Poland Betrayed* (Indianapolis: Bobbs Merrill, 1948), 86-88. This book will be referred to as Lane's Account. Diplomatic correspondence related to the Polish question during this period is to be found in FR, 1945, V, 110 ff.

Stettinius, who, along with Roosevelt, believed that the United States should not display an excessive interest in the affairs of Poland, a country far removed from the traditional areas of American interest but of vital importance to the Soviet Union, left Lane's memorandum without reply.

The Polish Government is Formed

The impasse on the Polish question was finally broken later in the summer when Stalin abandoned his opposition to the Allies' determining the composition of the new government. This change was directly related to the uncertainties created by the death of President Roosevelt and Harry S. Truman's assumption of the presidency. Towards the end of April, Molotov, who initially did not plan to attend the San Franscisco Conference, suddenly changed his mind, and on the way to California stopped in Washington where he conferred extensively with Stettinius and Eden, and met President Truman. In a talk with Joseph E. Davies, an old and proven friend of the Soviet Union, Molotov confessed that the death of Roosevelt "threatened to bring complications because of the lack of full information" about Truman. While he intended "to support the Crimea decision one hundred percent, he feared differences of interpretations and possibly complications" because of Roosevelt's death. It was, after all, merely an executive agreement, not necessarily binding on Truman. In his talk with Davies, Molotov singled out the Polish problem as crucial. He felt it would have been resolved satisfactorily if Roosevelt had lived, but was now threatened by "wide disagreement."[17]

And threatened indeed it was. On the surface, there was near-complete continuity in the Administration; no new faces had yet appeared on the scene. But there was a vast difference between Truman and Roosevelt, and the climate in the White House was changing rapidly. Briefing Truman on April 20, Harriman, who arrived for consultations from Moscow, talked freely about a "barbarian invasion of Europe" and the deadly impact of Soviet control over East European countries. He hoped for a workable relationship with the Soviets, but only if there was a "reconsideration of our policy and the abandon-

17. *Davies' Journal*, April 23, 1945. The Library of Congress Collection.

ment of the illusion that for the immediate future the Soviet Government was going to act in accordance with the principles which the rest of the world held to in international affairs." He said that the Polish question would be most difficult to settle because "Stalin had discovered from the Lublin Poles that an honest execution of the Crimean decision would mean the end of Soviet-backed Lublin control over Poland." Truman replied "immediately and decisively" that unless the Polish question were settled along the lines of the Yalta decision ("we could not, of course, expect to get 100 percent of what we wanted but on more important matters, we should be able to get 85 percent"), the Senate wouldn't ratify the treaty of American adherence to the United Nations, adding that "he intended to tell Molotov just this in words of one syllable."[18]

At a meeting in the White House on April 23, Truman's advisers were divided. Secretary Stimson and General Marshall spoke against taking a tough stand. Secretary Forrestal and Admiral Leahy, the president's chief of staff, joined Harriman and General Deane, chief of the U.S. Military Mission in Moscow, in favoring a firm line on the issues related to the composition of the Polish government, even at the risk of a Soviet boycott of the United Nations Conference. President Truman declared that "our agreements with the Soviet Union so far had been a one-way street and that could not continue." It was now or never; Truman intended to go on with the plans for San Franscisco, and if the Russians did not wish to come, they could "go to hell." Later in the day, using rather blunt language, Truman told Molotov that "an agreement had been reached on Poland and that it only required carrying out by the Soviet Government."[19]

This was a drastic change from Roosevelt's time, and Ambassador Lane was elated. On May 4, he submitted another memorandum to the acting secretary, in which he quoted extensively from the April 5 memo ignored by Stettinius. He cited new instances of Soviet mistreatment of the democratic Poles, including the recent arrest of 16 underground leaders, some of whom Harriman and Clark Kerr had proposed as possible members of the future Polish government. He advocated

18. FR, 1945, V, 232-233.
19. *Ibid.*, 252-258.

"standing firm on our position," as the only way of obtaining concessions from Stalin. "Any deviation or compromise on our part will be interpreted as our weakness by the Soviet Government," wrote Lane, "and will merely serve to encourage it to make further demands or conditions. It would, furthermore, be disastrous to the prestige and interests of the United States." Lane concluded by stating that "it is only on the basis of the maintenance of this position that I could conscientiously continue in my present position."[20]

It became apparent in the following months that "standing firm" in dealing with Stalin was easier said than done. Rejecting endless British and American pleas, Stalin refused to free the arrested leaders of the Polish resistance or to modify his stand on the formation of the government. The latter question remained deadlocked until, late in May, Truman sent Harry L. Hopkins to Moscow to make arrangements for the Potsdam Conference and to discuss the outstanding issues. Hopkins and Harriman spent two days in conferences with Stalin and Molotov, pleading and arguing that the "Polish question had become a symbol of our ability to work out problems with the Soviet Union." In the end, Stalin agreed to let the British and the Americans recommend several non-communist Poles for inclusion in the Polish government, but categorically refused to yield on any other point. Upon returning to Harriman's residence after one session, the exhausted Hopkins summoned George F. Kennan, then counselor to the embassy. Kennan relates:

> He described to me Stalin's terms for a settlement of the Polish problem . . . and asked me whether I thought we could do any better. I said I did not. Did I think, then, that we should accept these terms and come to an agreement on this basis? I did not; I thought we should accept no share of responsibility for what the Russians proposed to do in Poland.
>
> "Then you think it's just sin," he said, "and we should be agin' it."
>
> "That's just about right," I replied.
>
> "I respect your opinion," he said sadly, "but I am not at liberty to accept it."[21]

---

20. *Ibid.*, 278-280.
21. *Memoirs*, 212-213.

We can only speculate on what moved Stalin—who concluded at Yalta, if not earlier, that the wartime alliance was doomed—to make this concession. Certainly it was not Hopkins' eloquence, and probably not even the toughness of Truman, which Molotov doubtless described to him upon his return from the United States. Most likely, with the war against Japan still to be fought, and on the eve of a crucial conference with Truman and Churchill, Stalin simply wasn't prepared to break with his Western partners over the emotion-laden Polish question, which, as he could see, had acquired for them great importance. Evidently reckoning that he was enough in control of the situation in Poland to be able to deal with the opposition there at a later date, Stalin overruled the Lublin group and cleared the logjam.[22] The meetings of the Moscow Commission were resumed and a compromise was quickly worked out: three Poles from London, led by Stanislaw Mikolajczyk, and five non-communists from Poland proper, were officially invited to join the thus "reorganized" Warsaw government. Prodded by Churchill (who was anxious to settle domestic political problems of his own), Mikolajczyk went to Moscow to be there in time to receive Stalin's ominous warning in the form of the public trial of his friends, the sixteen underground leaders from Poland.

Within a few days the distribution of the ministerial portfolios was worked out. Mikolajczyk received the posts of second deputy premier and minister of agriculture and land reform. Boleslaw Bierut, the new president of Poland, announced the make-up of the cabinet on June 28, 1945. Although all

---

22. His decision could have been influenced, among other things, by the hope of getting a loan from the United States, then being negotiated. It is not clear what amount was involved. Secretary of the Treasury Henry Morgenthau was prepared to give $10 billion. Other sources give figures of $6 billion and $3½ billion. The interest rate suggested by the Americans was supposed to be either 2 or 2½ percent, with the payments to start after nine or ten years. In the end, nothing came of it because the Soviets stubbornly insisted that the loan be interest-free. Another economic incentive at that time was straight aid. The Soviet Union received—after the termination of the Lend-Lease program—$244 million worth of goods not related to the war effort, for which it never paid a penny. The UNRRA aid to the Soviet Union (three-quarters of it paid for by the United States) amounted to $249 million. In addition, Stalin anticipated—and later received—very substantial reparations from the American and British zones in occupied Germany.

important ministries went to the Lublin group, and though it was obvious that Mikolajczyk was little more than a hostage in the communist-dominated government, the United States and Great Britain recognized it on July 5, 1945.

The American Ambassador Goes to Poland

In Washington, waiting for a settlement of the Polish question, Ambassador Lane was getting increasingly suspicious that both Truman and Churchill were desperate to settle for any face-saving solution of the Polish issue. There is no doubt that such was the case. Shortly after Harry Hopkins returned from Moscow, newly-appointed Secretary of State James F. Byrnes told Joseph E. Davies that "there was no intent [at the White House] that a new government was to be created independently of the Lublin government." Instead, the latter was merely to be reinforced with other representative democratic leaders among the Polish people. It was like a political compromise where the party in the commanding position, for the sake of cooperation, included other elements which were agreed upon. According to Byrnes, there was no justification under the spirit or letter of the Yalta agreement for insistence by Harriman and the British ambassador that an entirely new government should be formed.[23]

This interpretation differed vastly from the one prevalent in the State Department where most high officials still talked about a "strong position." Arthur Bliss Lane elaborated this necessity to President Truman on June 4. He emphasized the need for "our not compromising on the principles we had agreed on at Yalta." Lane expressed his apprehensions about the "Soviet obstructionist attitude" and his conviction that "we should under no condition appease the Soviet government" by letting the communists dominate the Polish government or "disrupt the Yalta commitments" otherwise. We do not know precisely what Truman told Lane, but the Ambassador recalled that he "came away from this conference satisfied that the president understood the situation and would pursue a course thoroughly in keeping with the American tradition of fulfilling international commitments."[24]

---

23. *Davies' Journal*, June 6, 1945.
24. *Lane's Account*, 115.

Not quite trusting Truman, Lane viewed Hopkins' trip to Moscow with great uneasiness. Its secrecy, and the fact that the State Department was again wholly bypassed in these negotiations, gave ample grounds to Lane's suspicions. And when he learned that the new government of Poland, instead of being a broad coalition of anti-fascist groups, represented merely a token expansion of the puppet Lublin Committee, and that Mikolajczyk had been forced to join it under the most humiliating conditions, Lane became alarmed. His first reaction—which he freely expressed at the department—was that the United States should refuse to recognize the new regime. When his arguments were brushed aside and recognition was extended in a hurry, obviously on President Truman's orders, he took it with such bitterness that on the eve of his already scheduled departure for Warsaw he seriously wondered whether it would not after all be wise to follow the suggestion Stettinius made to him in April to take some other post.

After several days of hesitation, unable to decide what to do, Lane went to see his old friend Ambassador Loy W. Henderson, recently reassigned to the department. Henderson listened sympathetically. His distrust of the Soviets dated back to the days of his service in Moscow under William C. Bullitt; even among the traditionalists in the foreign service he was known as a "hard-liner." A steadfast opponent of Roosevelt's "Great Design," Henderson had intense dislike for those presidential advisers who had been willing to sacrifice almost everything to the myth of Soviet-American friendship.

Henderson advised Lane to go to Warsaw. If he now relinquished his post, someone else, friendly to the communists, would most likely be sent there. Such a man, instead of salvaging whatever could be salvaged at this late date, would concede one position after another. Instead of insisting on "free and unfettered" elections that, after all, were specifically provided for at Yalta, such a man would whitewash the communists, thus contributing further to the American betrayal of Poland. Moreover, argued Henderson, as an experienced diplomat Lane would not be deceived by communist tactics and would be able to keep the president and the department fully informed, thus eliciting support for the fulfillment of the Yalta accords. Governments come and go, he said, but nations remain. It was essential for the Poles to know that the Americans had not abandoned them to their present fate, that the historical friendship between the two peoples continued. It was the duty of the ambassador to protect the long-range interests of the United States even in the current unfavorable political climate.

This line of reasoning appealed to Lane. The Soviet Union was receiving increasingly bad press in connection with its strong-arm techniques in ruling Eastern Europe. President Truman seemed capable of making up his own mind; the old White House crowd was on its way out. It was necessary to gain time, and since nobody had officially told Lane that Poland had been conceded to the Soviets, he could legitimately defend American interests there on the basis of the Yalta decisions as he interpreted them.

Lane wanted to discuss his future course of action with Secretary Byrnes, but Byrnes was about to leave for Paris and could not spare more than a few minutes during which nothing but generalities were exchanged. Lane attempted to see Byrnes once again in Paris where he arrived with his staff on July 6, two days after the secretary. It was a humiliating experience. Lane could not even get an appointment, and only on one occasion succeeded in saying a few words to Byrnes as he caught him on the way from his hotel room to the car waiting outside. Slamming the door, Byrnes said, impatiently, "Listen, Arthur, these things simply don't interest me; I don't want to be bothered with them."

Lane and his party spent over three weeks in Paris waiting for Soviet permission for their flight to Poland across Germany. The permission was finally granted, and on July 30, 1945, they arrived in Berlin. The Potsdam Conference was by then well underway. Since several leading members of the new Polish government participated in the discussions, Lane expected that he also would be asked to be present. To his great disappointment, Byrnes ruled against inviting Lane: Potsdam appeared to be an affair at which the spirit of wartime cooperation with the Soviet Union blossomed again, and Lane was regarded by some of Byrnes' advisers (such as Assistant Secretary James Clement Dunn and Director of the Office of European Affairs H. Freeman Matthews) as lacking flexibility and understanding in dealing with communists. After a few brief and very general conversations with several members of the American delegation, and largely ceremonial visits with Polish President Bierut and Vice Premier Mikolajczyk, Lane concluded that there was nothing to be accomplished in Berlin, and he left for Warsaw the next day.

Vexing Problems

In the summer of 1945 the Polish capital presented a grim picture. Most of the city lay in ruins, a tragic reminder of the uprising a year before. People were poorly clad, starvation was widespread, and Soviet soldiers were seen everywhere. Looting and raping were not uncommon; the Polish police (which had no jurisdiction over the Soviet troops) were barely able to maintain a semblance of order. Main thoroughfares were cluttered by horse-driven military convoys moving eastward, and by an endless stream of Polish refugees, expelled from what used to be eastern Poland, and moving westward to be re-settled in the "recovered" Oder-Neisse territories.

Ambassador Lane was extremely busy during his first weeks in Warsaw. To open the embassy for business was a much more difficult task in 1945 than it had been back in 1919. Because of the severe housing shortage, the embassy and its personnel, consisting of thirteen Americans, were lodged on one floor of the Polonia Hotel; residential rooms, including that of Ambassador and Mrs. Lane, often had to be used for receiving visitors and storing official files.

The lack of the most elementary comforts did not diminish the high spirits and enthusiasm of the Americans. Nobody complained about long and irregular hours and the staggering workload. From the day the embassy officially opened, consular officials were literally beseiged by hundreds of people who were coming from all over the country and patiently waiting in lines in the hotel corridors, ardently hoping to be admitted to the United States. Although many of them claimed American citizenship, few possessed the documents to prove it. But even the poor devils who were clearly concocting stories calculated to open the doors to America could not be dismissed, and the prescribed routine had to be followed in each individual case. The number of applicants mounted by the day, eventually reaching a total of some 15,000, assuring the staff plenty of work for months and years to come.

Correspondence was heavy. Poland had been cut off from the outside world for six years, and thousands of people in the United States — many of them influential — bombarded the embassy with requests to find out what had happened to their relatives and friends. There was little the embassy could do, but these letters could not be ignored and merely acknowledging them put a severe strain on the staff.

Arthur Bliss Lane, who had always attached importance to the maintaining of high morale among his aides, tried to alleviate working conditions as much as he could. He pressed the Polish authorities for more office space. He hired several English-speaking Poles as interpreters and secretaries. And he devoted much attention to the problem — which plagued the embassy throughout his stay in Warsaw — of securing equitable currency exchange rates for his staff. The official rate was 100 zloty for one dollar, but the runaway inflation in Poland made this rate completely unrealistic. The blackmarket rate, which reflected the actual cost of living, was already 200:1 when the embassy opened; within six months it reached 1,300:1. Faced with the danger of losing his staff (the State Department in those days did not have special hardship allowances or currency differentials), Lane resorted to the practice followed by all Western embassies in Warsaw of exchanging before each payday the necessary amounts of dollar currency, sent by pouch from Washington, for zloty at the blackmarket rate.

Vexing as they sometimes were, all such problems were of minor concern to Lane. They were tackled, if not solved, by his young and energetic aides, presenting them with endless challenges and testing their ingenuity and capacity for hard work. Lane's real and insurmountable difficulties were in his relations with Polish officialdom. From the very start these relations were cold and unfriendly. Before long they deteriorated to the point of an atmosphere of outright hostility, gravely affecting the ambassador's ability to function as an effective spokesman for his government.

It is true that Arthur Bliss Lane did not go out of his way to win friends and influence the men in the Polish government.

In his capacity as representative of the United States he did not feel a need for being solicitous and sympathetic in his dealings with the regime whose overall composition was determined by the increasingly hostile Soviet government. Nevertheless, he sincerely wished to keep channels of communication with the Polish officials open, knowing that without them he would not be able to exert any influence at all. In this, he was doomed to fail, for the atmosphere he had to operate in was unique in his experience. Much as he anticipated communist animosity, he could not have foreseen how total and pervasive it was going to be. In his past dealings with hostile governments, there had always been many influential individuals, not only outside official circles but also within the bureaucracy, with whom he could communicate on friendly terms. By cultivating them he could sometimes exert indirect pressure on the government, or, at the very least, be informed about what was going on. By working closely with visiting American correspondents, he could give the government adverse publicity in the United States of the kind which few countries could afford to ignore. At times, he had been able to exert economic pressure by negotiating grants or credits to be extended by the United States.

But the situation in Poland was such that none of the familiar means of diplomacy worked. He was accredited to a government which was full of sworn enemies of "capitalism" and which, moreover, in all its major decisions, was guided by another, much more powerful, government. Although formally bound by the Yalta and Potsdam agreements, and not yet ready to embark on an openly hostile course, the Soviets resented attempts by the United States to assert influence in Poland. Since Moscow-oriented communists (and, in many instances, actual Soviet citizens) occupied the top positions in Warsaw, there was no difficulty in circumscribing Lane's activities and in making both the ambassador and his staff feel uncomfortable in the Polish capital. There was no more talk about "traditional Polish-American friendship," no recognition of the fact that by helping to defeat Germany the United States had contributed to the liberation of Poland. The very generous UNRRA aid, for instance, to which the United States had contributed 72 percent, an offer of one thousand trucks from the American army surplus in Western Europe, and the substantial contributions of a number of American organizations were received by Polish officials without the faintest sign of gratitude. The members of the embassy were treated as representatives of an enemy state. Although they had relative freedom of movement in the country, they were at all times shadowed by the secret police, and there were reasons to believe that at least some of the locally-hired employees were impressed into regular reporting on their employers to the same insidious organization.

There were other irritants. Until Lane finally obtained his own radio-transmitter, his dispatches to Washington were sent via Moscow. The procedure took a week or longer, and many cables never reached their destination. Similar difficulties were experienced by American newsmen who managed to come to Poland—unless their reports were unfailingly favorable to the new regime. According to the Polish-American Treaty of Commerce, Friendship and Consular Rights of 1931, still theoretically in force, embassy representatives were entitled to visit all American citizens incarcerated by Polish authorities for whatever reason and offer them legal protection. But in several cases when this issue arose, Lane vainly tried to obtain the necessary permission from the ministry of public security, and in the end was told that the 1931 treaty was outdated. He had the greatest difficulty in obtaining exit visas for proven American citizens who had been caught in Poland during the war. On the other hand, the Jews, mainly destined to the badly overcrowded refugee camps in the western zone of Germany, were liberally granted Polish exit papers because the Warsaw government adopted a policy of ridding Poland of all national minorities. The requests of the State Department and of the American military government authorities in Germany to introduce some orderliness into this exodus were totally ignored by Polish officials, while Lane in Warsaw, for obvious humanitarian and political reasons, could not refuse stamping the papers of the Jewish refugees seeking asylum in the West.[25]

After having met most of the key officials on the cabinet and

---

25. The British were much more concerned with this problem. The accumulation of hundreds of thousands of Jews in the refugee camps of Western Germany had greatly increased pressure for admitting them to Palestine, then administered by Great Britain as a trustee of the United Nations Organization, severely aggravating British relations with native Arabs alarmed by a drastic change in the composition of Palestine's population.

subcabinet levels, Ambassador Lane concluded that they were a disagreeable, if not outrightly obnoxious lot. Their stiffness and constant guardedness left no room for normal, personal contact, and Lane quickly found convenient objects for his biting sarcasm. In a letter to Matthews, written in December 1945, he confessed that he had had "lots of fun" pulling the leg of Rzymowski, minister for foreign affairs. "Apparently he is considered even in Polish government circles," wrote Lane, "as the prize nitwit in the government, and at present it is never possible for any foreign diplomat, with the possible exception of the Russian, to see him alone . . . At my last conversation, when I had the most fun with him, three of his aides . . . were present."

There was only one man in the government of Poland who stood out in stark opposition to the graduates of the old Lublin Committee, and it was all but inevitable that the American ambassador and Vice Premier Stanislaw Mikolajczyk should gravitate toward each other. Although privately Lane referred to him as "Mikey," he had developed considerable liking and respect for the man who was rapidly emerging as the symbol of national opposition to the communist-dominated regime. Their relationship was a political liability to Mikolajczyk, and at least initially, Lane tried to exercise caution in his contacts with the Pole. Unlike his old friend, British Ambassador W. Cavendish-Bentinck, Lane considered it unwise to create the impression that the United States was backing the leader of the Peasant Party. "The obvious support which the British are giving to Mikey," wrote Lane in the same letter to Matthews, "drives the government people into a rage and makes the British even more unpopular with the government, if that is possible. Mikey has told me that he appreciates my being discreet in my relations with him as it would embarrass him if I were otherwise . . . If the impression got around that we were playing internal politics and backing Mikey's party to win the elections, I feel it would only hurt him in the long run." Whether Lane's discretion deceived Mikolajczyk's communist colleagues is doubtful, especially since the secret police kept a very detailed record of the movements and meetings of both. Even a purely social association between the American ambassador and the leader of the opposition was sufficient for them to draw far-reaching conclusions. But so long as Lane abstained from making any official representations on behalf of the Peasant Party, the communists could not make a public political issue out of this association.

It would be an exaggeration to say that Ambassador Lane was greatly saddened by his isolated position in the Polish capital. The United States sought nothing in Poland for itself. In economic terms, the Poles had everything to lose if their relations with America deteriorated. In political terms, Lane's function was not that of an ordinary ambassador. His strength derived from the fact that the United States had participated in recreating postwar Poland and was bound, by virtue of the Yalta and Potsdam decisions, to see to it that a permanent, democratically-elected government replaced the present provisional regime. This responsibility entitled Lane to intervene in matters of the purely domestic jurisdiction of the Polish government whenever he felt that the Big Three decisions were being violated. He did not hesitate to protest when the government imposed restrictions on the Polish press or tried to interfere with the reporting of foreign correspondents. Time and again, he insisted that all anti-fascist organizations, including non-communist and even anti-communist ones, had a right to function without police harassment. And he kept reminding Polish ministers that they were formally obligated to carry out free and unfettered elections on the basis of universal suffrage and secret ballot.

Lane was under no illusions. As early as August 28, 1945, he wrote to Matthews that the Soviet government would be unlikely to tolerate a less subservient regime in Poland. But this did not mean that the United States ought to go along with Soviet wishes. In his view, American policy could not be permitted to be dictated from Moscow, and he was in no mood for making the Soviet task easier.

During the fall and winter of 1945, the Soviet-controlled security forces launched a vicious campaign against former members of the anti-Nazi underground and against Mikolajczyk's Peasant Party. Mass-scale arrests, rigid censorship of all non-communist publications, and the elimination of opposition elements from lower levels of the government were a clear indication of the Soviets' determination to consolidate their hold on Poland. In assessing these developments, Lane tried to look beyond tomorrow. He put his thoughts down in a long letter which he wrote on March 1, 1946, to H. Freeman Matthews at the State Department. Having described the recent wave of terror in Poland, he pointed out that on the day elections were held, they would not likely be "free and unfettered elections" in the accepted sense of the term. "Not only will supporters of Mikolajczyk, such as members of the [anti-Nazi] underground movement, have been, through their imprisonment, deprived of the privilege of voting, but the example of their imprisonment will undoubtedly indicate to those who have been fortunate enough to escape the wrath of the security police the fate which awaits them in case they take an active political part against the government." And Lane continued:

The situation is no surprise to us. It is the logical sequence of the alliance between the Lublin communist group within the government and the Soviet Union. We have always felt that it is to the interest of the Soviet government that this puppet regime should remain in power to carry out the bidding of the Soviet government, both in political and economic fields. On the other hand, the Bierut regime can remain in power only with the protection of the Red army and the NKVD-controlled security police with its repressive and terroristic methods, to which I referred above. The understanding may not be based on mutual admiration but it is based on mutual advantage and I see no possibility at this moment that it will be dissolved.

From the foregoing you will appreciate that I consider Mikolajczyk's chances of winning the elections are virtually nil . . . I do not know by what means he will be defeated: it may be through expulsion of him and the ministers of his party from the government; it may be through the holding of rigged elections; it may be through an artificial creation of disorder which would require forcible measures to be taken, perhaps by the Red army; or, most tragically, it might be through the physical elimination of Mikolajczyk . . . With the recent death of Witos, Mikolajczyk is the only outstanding man of his party in the present government, and if he were eliminated some of the other elements . . . who have already been reported to have indicated a willingness to join a single list with the other five parties, might be willing to compromise, thus contributing to the perpetration in power of the communist group.

The question naturally arises as to what our policy should be. I do not feel that we should show our indignation through withdrawal of the American and British embassies. By withdrawing we would be merely playing into the hands of those in control, as our influence would disappear from the scene. Furthermore, the Polish people. . . . would feel themselves abandoned by the two best friends they have left—the United States and Great Britain. (Please, don't think that this recommendation is based on my desire to hold on to this job! Anyone who has been in Warsaw since the war will appreciate that this is not a bed of roses, and in fact there are few pleasant aspects connected with the post.)

I believe . . . there is very little which we can do here which will make itself felt except to continue to show sympathy for the Polish people and to maintain our firm position regarding American rights. If the Yalta decision should be flouted through the holding of fictitious elections or through the elimination of PSL [the Peasant Party] representation in the government, then I feel we should publicly make the facts known and abruptly terminate credit negotiations in Washington with Rajchman and his delegation. . . . I believe it essential for the Congress and for the American public to be informed regarding conditions in Poland, Yugoslavia, etc. Education of the public . . . will perhaps take a year or two. There will be attacks on us from the left-wing press . . . to the effect that we are endeavoring to bring about hostilities with the Soviet Union. Our stand should, in my opinion, be based not on ideologies but on determination to protect American lives and property rights.

All of this, of course, boils down in the last analysis to a decision as to what our policy is going to be towards the Soviet Union. My own feeling is that unless we give publicity to what is going on in Poland and other nations in an analogous position, we will not be able to use our influence in these countries either politically or economically. With the withdrawal of the greater part of our armed forces from Europe we have lost one of the few arguments which are effective with a power such as the Soviet Union. In answer to the criticism which would undoubtedly be made that we are courting war with the Soviet Union in making the unpleasant facts known, I should like to say that the American public has a right to know the truth; that unpreparedness nearly cost us the last war, due to the isolationist attitude of a part of the people of the United

States; that appeasement will be just as dangerous today as it was at the time of Munich; and that we run much more danger of war if we ignore the dangers of aggression than by honestly facing the facts.

This insistence on "making the unpleasant facts known" reflected Lane's keen awareness of the close relationship between trends in public opinion and the foreign policy of the United States. He knew that policies in a democratic society could not be reversed at will. Even if the government had reached a decision to take a firm stand in the face of Soviet challenges, it would be unable to carry it out so long as a large segment of the American public continued to regard the Soviet Union as a friend and ally. At the moment, the vast majority of influential newspapers and periodicals in the United States were critical of anything endangering Allied relations; many people were still fighting the enemy who was no more, and the powerful sentiments born in the war resulted in a highly biased press treatment of political developments in central and eastern Europe.

The success of the educational task contemplated by Ambassador Lane hinged above all on the appreciation of its importance by the men conducting the foreign policy of the United States, and it was there that Lane encountered most of his disappointments. Even those few in the State Department who essentially shared his views were restrained by considerations which had little to do with Poland. After all the pain and frustration of negotiating with the Soviets in the months following Yalta, there was no enthusiasm for a resumption of the battle over a country already under effective Soviet control. Poland was clearly off the Big Three agenda even from Truman's point of view. With all his forcefulness, he didn't expect anything more than holding the Polish—not the Soviet!—government responsible for the execution of the Yalta decisions. At the same time, there were a lot of influential men around who either questioned Lane's judgment or were annoyed with him for continuously bringing up the issues they wanted to forget.

Thus Arthur Bliss Lane—in his own mind, at least—was ultimately drawn into a form of two-front war. One, against the communists in Warsaw, he was prepared to lose, hoping only to win enough battles to make victory dear to the enemy. Another, against myopic policy-makers and appeasers of communism back home, he optimistically was determined to win. Being on the firing line in Warsaw, defending there American interests and prestige against self-proclaimed enemies of the United States, he expected his government to accept his recommendations and give him the diplomatic backing he needed. In actual fact, he received considerable support: from the Division of Eastern European Affairs, headed by Elbridge Durbrow; from Acting Secretary Acheson; and, on occasion, from Secretary Byrnes himself, busy as he was in Paris resolving European affairs. But in several important instances Lane was overruled, and, given the circumstances of his Warsaw struggles, he took these "defeats" particularly hard.

There were several major issues over which Ambassador Lane clashed with the Polish authorities during his year-and-a-half stay in Warsaw. Nationalization of American property, mistreatment of American citizens, freedom of movement for his staff and American newsmen, and the bothersome problem of currency exchange rates were legitimate areas of his concern in traditional terms.[26] But the Yalta and Potsdam agreements had empowered Arthur Bliss Lane, as the representative of the president of the United States, to intervene in

---

26. In retrospect, the attention Lane devoted to obtaining a more favorable dollar-zloty exchange rate for the embassy personnel may appear disproportionately great. But he had always been preoccupied with assuring for his staff a decent standard of living to enhance their morale and devotion to duty. With the "official" rate being 1:100 while the free market rate was, say, 1:500, the problem was felt most acutely, and found its reflection in Lane's dealings with the Poles and his correspondence with the Department. On one occasion, he dramatized it in a fashion peculiarly his own. Llewellyn Thompson, then a secretary at the embassy in Moscow, stopped in Warsaw on the way to Washington and was invited to take part in a poker party. All the players had piles of zloty before them. Obligingly, Lane offered to exchange Thompson's dollars for him at the official rate of exchange. At the end of the game Thompson found himself in possession of a sizeable amount of Polish currency and, before leaving, wanted to exchange it back into dollars. Lane, laughing heartily, said that the conversion of zloty into dollars is a privilege which nobody enjoys in Poland, but as a favor to a friend he was willing to do it—of course, at the free market rate of exchange. Thompson was not in the least amused, but Lane stuck to his guns; the story became for a while one of Lane's favorites, even though his relations with Thompson became somewhat strained as a result.

such internal Polish matters as freedom of the press and political parties, police persecution of democratic leaders and organizations, and the primary issue of holding free and unfettered elections to the Polish parliament. Once these elections were held and Poland was assured a freely elected democratic government, the signatories of the Yalta and Potsdam declarations would have ended their special role. The trouble was that the communist-dominated Polish government was determined to do all it could to prevent the American ambassador from discharging this special responsibility.

Since Poland was assumed to be an independent country, Lane had nowhere to go to complain about the difficulties he encountered. In carrying out his mission he could count on the goodwill of the Polish masses, increasingly hostile to the Soviets and their own communist leaders, and on Mikolajczyk's Peasant Party, which enjoyed enormous popularity because of its pro-Western image. But since the communists in the government commanded the loyalty of the powerful secret police and enjoyed the support of the Soviet authorities, this popularity—until election day—counted for little in Poland.

Under such circumstances, Ambassador Lane had come to believe that there was only one trump card the United States could effectively play in Poland: economic aid. After six years of war, the economic situation in the country was desperate. Industry and transportation facilities were either in ruin or at a standstill for lack of fuel and raw materials. There was an extreme shortage of food, aggravated by a radical land reform launched under Soviet auspices, and even the army and police were in rags. The Poles could not expect any help from the Soviet Union, whose own economy was in the worst condition since its revolution and civil war; on the contrary, the presence on Polish territory of large numbers of poorly disciplined Soviet troops accustomed during the war to living off the land, represented an additional drain on the meager resources of the country. Lane assumed that any government faced with such enormous difficulties—even a communist one—would be willing to modify its policy to accommodate the only great power capable of rendering significant assistance. He was determined to extract the maximum political price for this aid.

One of Lane's first recommendations to the State Department after he had arrived in Warsaw was to assure an equitable and nonpolitical distribution of UNRRA supplies in Poland—a program to which the United States eventually contributed over $300 million—by having it directed by an impartial, preferably American, administrator. This recommendation was turned down. At Moscow's request, UNRRA's Director-General, Herbert H. Lehman, put Mikhail Menshikov, the Soviet member of the UNRRA Council, in charge of the UNRRA mission in Poland and made it exempt from the normal control of the Council. Lane swallowed this pill bravely, rationalizing his defeat on humanitarian grounds. In a letter to Christian A. Herter on September 26, 1945, he wrote that "regardless of criticism, UNRRA must continue ... to furnish Poland with all the foodstuffs, agricultural machinery and livestock which is possible." He pointed out that "for reasons of humanity we cannot allow Poland to starve during the coming winter, and if for political reasons we should withhold supplies on the ground that they might find their way to Russia ... it would boomerang against us.... Even though UNRRA materials and livestock should be confiscated by Soviet troops ... we shall at least have done our duty and shall have obtained the credit from the Polish people for doing all in our power to help them under difficult circumstances."

Lane realized, of course, that UNRRA operations were autonomous and not subject to the State Department's direction. But there was another aspect to the developing American economic assistance program which he expected to be able to control in Poland: loans and credits, and the distribution of the army surplus materials administered by the United States government. A large portion of Lane's extensive correspondence with the State Department during his stay in Warsaw dealt directly or indirectly with the utilization of economic aid for the purpose of accomplishing political ends.

The Battle Over Credits

At a meeting on July 28, 1945, with several American delegates to the Potsdam Conference, a group of Poles, headed by Mikolajczyk and Minister of Industry Hilary Minc, presented an extensive list of items needed for the reconstruction of the

Polish economy. They asked for a credit of $380 million for the purchase of food and raw materials in the United States over a period of five years, half of which they promised eventually to pay back. In addition, they requested a long-term credit of $500 million for the purchase of capital goods for reconstruction purposes. These credits, the Poles explained, were above and beyond whatever Poland would receive in the form of reparations from defeated Germany.[27]

No decisions were taken at that time, but a month later the matter was brought up again, this time in Washington, by Dr. Ludwig Rajchman, one of the original participants in the Potsdam discussions.

A colorful and somewhat mysterious figure, Rajchman—a prominent bacteriologist—once headed the health section of the League of Nations and later went to Manchuria and China to study outbreaks of epidemics there. Although suspected by some of being one of the top Comintern agents (others believed that he was merely "a free-wheeling Marxist"), he surfaced in 1939 as an adviser to Chiang Kai-shek's government, probably thanks to T. V. Soong, Chiang's brother-in-law, whom he had known from the Geneva days.

In 1940, Rajchman rushed to Paris to offer General Wladislaw Sikorski his help in promoting Polish interests in the United States. His services accepted, Rajchman arrived in the United States with a Polish diplomatic passport, but soon ran into difficulties with the State Department (which questioned his diplomatic status) and joined the Chinese Embassy where Ambassador Soong appointed him chief of "China defense supplies." Through Soong, he met and developed excellent relations with many important Washingtonians. As one author put it, Rajchman was "a past master at collecting influential friends. His sophistication, his charm, and his tough-minded sense of history made him particularly popular among the young New Deal reformers who had suddenly found themselves, somewhat uneasily, reforming not only a nation but a world."

Rajchman's connections soon extended into the intimate circle of the White House; among his personal friends were such men as Harry Hopkins, Henry Morgenthau, Samuel Rosenman, Archibald MacLeish, Lauchlin Currie, and Felix

27. FR, *Conference of Berlin*, II, 455–458, 1532–1538.

Frankfurter. With the creation of UNRRA, he somehow became its first Polish delegate and got himself invited to Potsdam, where he became a close friend of Minc, the leading communist member of the Polish group. After the conference had ended, he briefly returned to Poland—for the first time since 1922—and was immediately admitted into the exclusive circle that included top-ranking communists such as Minc and Jacob Berman, under-secretary for foreign affairs. It was apparently decided that there was no better man than Rajchman to advance Poland's financial and other interests in the United States, and early in September, Rajchman reappeared in Washington.[28]

Rajchman presented the proposals of the Polish government regarding U. S. credits to the Office of Financial and Development Policy of the State Department on September 7, 1945. He did not get very far. Two weeks later, Dean Acheson—who then was getting his introduction into East European affairs—cabled Lane that "close economic relations between the United States and Poland will not develop, and financial assistance to Poland will remain small, unless Poland is prepared to give assurances that it will, after a reasonable period of transition, abstain from discrimination in trade and investment, and in particular to accord to nationals and corporations of the U.S. treatment as favorable as that accorded to nations of any other country with regard to all forms of commercial activity, consistent with the treaty of June 15, 1931; that it will not accord to any country exclusive positions in Poland's national economy . . . and that it will, in general, avoid the introduction of new barriers to trade." Authorizing Lane to inform the Polish government about these views, Acheson stressed that assurances alone would not be sufficient, and that "Poland's implementation of the assurances asked of her will

---

28. A few months later, his mission completed, Rajchman got himself appointed Polish delegate to UNICEF. Elected chairman of this international agency, he lived mostly in Paris. In 1957, when he came to New York on a visit, the Senate Internal Security Subcommittee, curious to find out more about his relations with Alger Hiss and Harry Dexter White, subpoenaed him to testify at its hearings. Rajchman chose not to appear, was cited for contempt of Congress, and quickly left the country. He died on the French Riviera a few years later. For a sketch of Rajchman, see Charles Wertenbaker, "The China Lobby," *The Reporter*, April 15, 1952.

naturally have an important bearing on the attitude of the U.S. toward any requests by Poland for further assistance." Acheson added that Rajchman asked ("under instructions from his Government, he says") for immediate credits of $190 million plus eventual reconstruction of $500 million more.[29]

It is not clear whether Ambassador Lane had received this cable before his two-hour talk with President Bierut on September 24, during which a very broad range of questions were discussed. At any rate, Lane expressed his opinion that U.S. aid and economic relations between the two countries would depend on many factors — not just those elaborated by Acheson. He mentioned the need for ending "economic chaos" in Poland and the arrests of persons for political reasons; he talked about the importance of having a free press and of ensuring "the right of parties opposed to the government to have equal rights in the elections." Not very tactfully, he told Bierut that "continuance of the Red army in Poland and incorporation of Russians into the Polish army were unhealthy conditions."

Bierut explained to Lane some of the complexities of the situation in Poland and the need for eliminating "fascists" (who, to Lane, were merely nationalists) from active political life. He said he had protested to Moscow against the leniency of Soviet authorities towards Soviet officers and soldiers "who had committed acts of violence" and that only 10 percent of the officers in the Polish army were Russian. Bierut also stressed that Poland must depend on its friendship with the Soviet Union. "At times this friendship is under strain due to pressure put upon Poland," said Bierut, but if this pressure "were resisted forcibly it would mean war and the extermination of Poland." Trying to establish some rapport with Lane, he also remarked that the "majority of Polish people desire to mold Poland on the U.S. pattern both economically and politically."[30]

The question of credits came up during the next interview Lane had with Bierut on October 3. Lane had come to complain about the lack of a reasonable rate of exchange of dollars into zloty for the embassy personnel, about restrictions upon the freedom of the press, and about the arrests, by security

29. FR, 1945, V, 376–377.
30. *Ibid.*, 376–379.

police, of American citizens. After promising to look into these matters, Bierut "referred to great benefits which would accrue to [the] U.S. through granting of credit" because of universal gratitude in Poland toward America for putting the Polish economy on its feet. Lane replied that his government would be favorably influenced in this matter if the abuses he complained of stopped, but added that he would not recommend the "granting of any credit which would be used for the benefit of the security police." In his dispatch, Lane concluded that "it was obvious from my talk, which was cordial throughout, that in addition to practical benefit this government is most desirous of obtaining a large credit to indicate to the Polish people its friendship with the U.S. government and thereby to solidify its position politically within the country."[31]

This was exactly what Arthur Bliss Lane determined to prevent from happening until the free and unfettered elections brought into being a very different kind of government in Poland. His knowledge of what was going on in Poland grew by the hour. He kept his channels of information as open as possible. In October, he undertook a trip to several Polish cities where he had meetings with liberal professors and local representatives of the Peasant Party; in Cracow he had a long conversation with Archbishop Sapieha, one of the leaders of anti-Nazi resistance and now in opposition to the regime. The overall picture of an emerging police state was so bleak that it is impossible to judge in retrospect whether Lane had real hope for a significant improvement. His recommendation to the State Department was "to take advantage of the Polish government's eagerness for a greater economic assistance and to use it as a lever," in order to "influence conditions for the better by taking a determined stand against any movement to stifle democratic life in Poland."

The Poles, on their part, had given up on Lane in their quest for credits and concentrated on lobbying in Washington, where Rajchman continued to play the leading role. For a while, Lane's repeated warnings against granting credits and the stream of unfavorable news about conditions in Poland blocked Rajchman's efforts. The situation began to change in November

---

31. *Ibid.*, 382–386.

when a high-level Polish mission headed by Vice Premier Mikolajczyk arrived in Washington to advance Polish economic interests.

Alone among the leading Poles, Mikolajczyk could take advantage of the feeling, common among British and American officials, that by being consigned to the Soviet sphere Poland had been let down by its Western friends. He was a forceful man, a good patriot, and a good politician. He believed that in addition to the direct benefits of American aid, his personal success in obtaining the credits would translate into an even greater popularity for his Peasant Party, simultaneously enhancing the image of the West in Poland at the expense of the Soviets. He told Durbrow that "the granting of credits by the United States would be one of the most important steps to insure that the Polish people could regain their independence." Being a practical man, he also scaled down the Polish request to $150 million. In a second, particularly confidential, conversation with Durbrow, Mikolajczyk assured him that "if elections were to take place now, the Communist Party would receive not more than 2 percent, while if the elections had taken place four months ago they might have received a maximum of 20 percent," adding that "unless the Soviet authorities decide to increase greatly the Red army forces in Poland and carry on a reign of terror and suppression, there is no possibility of Poland's going communist."[32]

On the same day, November 9, Mikolajczyk, accompanied by the Polish chargé d'affaires, was received by President Truman. Most of the discussion centered on the subject of credits. Truman was favorably impressed but didn't alter his overall view. On his instructions, Secretary Byrnes later in the evening cabled Ambassador Lane that he should "avoid linking political questions with credits except to imply that apart from the economic considerations, the granting of a credit may be seriously jeopardized if the record of the Polish government for the fulfillment of its obligations is impaired by a failure to adhere fully to its acceptance of the Yalta agreement and to its Potsdam commitment as to elections, and its further Potsdam commitment as to the freedom of the Allied press." The secre-

---

32. *Ibid.*, 405.

tary of state suggested that "it would be appropriate to observe in this connection that if the policies of the Polish government should create conditions under which free and unfettered elections would be an impossibility, and this fact became known to the American people, under our system it could not be ignored by this government when considering a Polish application for credits."[33]

Although this seemed like a pretty generous license for Lane to continue blocking the granting of credits, in the suggestion that political questions should not be linked to credits, he sensed a new note in Washington's attitude. Immediately, he responded with a series of forceful arguments as to why no credits should be given. "If we relax in our resistance," concluded Lane in his message of November 13, "and certainly the extension of credit would be interpreted as such, against the despotic rule which is now being perpetrated here, we shall not succeed in fulfilling our publicly expressed policy: the maintenance of a strong, free and independent Poland."[34]

Byrnes cautiously answered that as a result of his conversations with Mikolajczyk, he felt that a modest credit, not exceeding $25 million, should be extended "for the projects specifically approved by the embassy." But this was not a decision, added the secretary, and invited Lane's further comments.

And so it went. Time and again, as he reported political persecutions or other infringements on freedom in Poland, Lane returned to the belabored subject of credits, indicating his steadfast opposition to extending them. In the face of the increasingly bad press the Polish regime was getting in the United States, and in the absence of a conviction in the White House that this and other communist-dominated regimes of Eastern Europe could—or even should— be weaned away from Moscow, it was not easy for those who for one reason or another favored aiding Poland to overrule the strong-minded ambassador. Thus, attempts continued to gain his concurrence. On November 29, in a private letter, H. Freeman Matthews wrote Lane that the department was considering making at least some of the items Mikolajczyk asked for available to Poland. "If you

33. *Ibid.*, 411-412.
34. *Ibid.*, 412-414.

feel strongly that this would not be a helpful move," wrote the chief of the Division of European Affairs, "I would appreciate having any further arguments you want to make available to us . . . . Our thought here is that since Mikey thinks we can help him, we ought to go ahead and extend credits according to his plan."

Two weeks later, on December 11, Lane's personal friend and chief of the Division of Eastern European Affairs, Elbridge Durbrow, gently indicated to him that larger forces had been set in motion and that it might not be possible to hold the dike much longer:

> You will see (from the enclosed memoranda of conversations with Rajchman) that cold water was thrown upon the ambitious program that Dr. Rajchman has in mind. We have been working on this problem, trying to bring to the attention of all interested officials the various reasons why you, and the democratic leaders in Poland, feel that it would not be advisable to give large-scale credits to Poland at this time. While so far we have had success, I frankly do not feel that we can guarantee that things will remain this way since Dr. Rajchman has many friends, some of whom may be able to swing this away from the firm position we have all taken. In any event, we shall keep up the good fight from our end.

Had Ambassador Lane paid more attention to Durbrow's warning, he would have spared himself many unpleasant experiences. But he continued to persevere. The acute world-wide shortage of food compelled UNRRA to curtail its grain deliveries to Poland in January 1946, thus improving, in Lane's judgment, his bargaining position. He also counted on the adverse reaction in America to the Polish government's decree nationalizing industry (including foreign enterprises) and on the growing awareness of the public that communism was clearly getting the upper hand in Poland.

What Lane underestimated was the extent of Dr. Rajchman's influence in Washington, especially among some of the key officials in the Economic Division of the State Department, and with important Democrats known to him from the wartime years. Soon Rajchman and his aides, who knew that the American ambassador in Warsaw presented the major obstacle to the success of their mission, launched what amounted to a personal campaign against Lane. In this, they were aided by several press reports — planted by the Polish embassy in Washington to begin with — that Lane protested the nationalization decree and threatened that negotiations for a loan from the Export-Import Bank would be broken off because of it. The story was manifestly incorrect. Lane, who always talked to Polish officials on the assumption that Poland was a sovereign nation, and thus had every right to nationalize foreign property, did nothing of the kind. But on January 17, Minister of Foreign Affairs Rzymowski visited Secretary Byrnes in London with complaints about Lane. Byrnes cabled Acheson, requesting explanations.

Acheson replied on January 22, saying that "the Poles are deliberately misinterpreting remarks made by Lane to the Polish Foreign Minister." He informed the secretary of state that an Export-Import Bank credit of $40 million was under consideration, as well as a sale of $50 million worth of war surplus items (mainly the railroad equipment). The Poles, he wrote, asked for more money and even insisted that "political considerations should not be injected into economic negotiations." But, added Acheson bluntly, "we feel that we should not grant a large credit to Poland without obtaining further assurances . . . , particularly in view of clear indications that the Polish government may try to evade its obligations."

Simultaneously, Acheson instructed the chargé d'affaires in Warsaw (Lane was in Paris, attending a conference of economic advisers from American missions in Europe) to inform the Polish government that "the views expressed by Ambassador Lane regarding nationalization of property and zloty exchange represent the views of United States government," and to point out that "the tactics employed recently by the Polish government in its dealings with American officials cannot fail to have an unfortunate effect upon our relations with the Polish provisional government in general and upon the current credit negotiations in particular."[35]

This was tough language, tough enough to please Arthur Bliss Lane as he returned to his post. But no verbal toughness could offset the obvious fact that the United States government

35. FR, 1946, VI, 382–386.

was about to grant the Poles what they had been asking for. The amount had become immaterial. The issue had acquired, both to Lane and to the Polish communists, the symbolic significance of a major political battle, the outcome of which they considered crucial. Time and again Lane pleaded with the Department not to give in, as in his February 22 message: "We have reached the time when our policy towards Poland must remain completely firm and be conducted in such a way as to discourage the thought, not only of the present government in power but of their guiding authorities in the East, that [we do not intend] to be backed further against a wall." Lane further advised Acheson that, "Every move which we make which they can regard as a partial retreat will decrease the area in which we can operate and will encourage increasing optimism both politically and psychologically of those who oppose our principles."

Such thoughts, in application to the communists, were too novel for many people early in 1946. The prevailing feeling in the government was that the United States was too powerful a nation to be disturbed by the developments, however adverse, on the fringes of Europe and in the area which had been conceded to the Soviet Union anyway. There were also people who felt guilty for the mess Mikolajczyk had gotten into and who wished "to do something" for the Peasant Party leader—even though by that time he himself had changed his mind on the issue of credits. Finally, there were those who plainly sympathized with the communists and thoroughly disapproved of the great power play in Poland that Ambassador Lane was engaged in. The stream of Lane's messages, instead of gaining new adherents to the cause he was fighting for, tended instead to isolate him, to cast him in the role of a trouble-maker, if not a warmonger.

On April 18, 1946, the Department informed Lane that within a few days a formal credit agreement would be signed with the Polish embassy. The Ambassador responded immediately, literally begging his superiors not to take the fateful step. Byrnes, then briefly in Washington, replied with a curt message listing the considerations which had led to the decision.

Still unwilling to believe that the battle he had fought for so long against his own government had been lost, Lane reacted with a "Secret-Most Immediate-Urgent" dispatch, declaring that the decision to extend credits was "most discouraging" to him and indicating "either that the Department has little confidence in my evaluation during my nine months here of the situation in Poland or that for reasons of which I am unaware it does not wish to accede to my recommendations." And he went a step further, somewhat unconventionally stating his wish "to place on record my official protest as American ambassador in Poland" against granting of credits to the hostile Polish government. He sent this dispatch to Acheson in Washington, with a copy to Secretary Byrnes in Paris.[36]

On April 26, Ambassador Lane attended a meeting of the National Council of the Homeland, the quasi-parliament of the former Lublin Committee. Toward the end of it, Prime Minister Osobka-Morawski mounted the podium. Waving a sheet of paper and looking straight at the box where Lane was seated, he announced that he had just received information that the loans which the council had sought in Washington had been granted. Triumphantly he exclaimed: "This is the best evidence that the United States trusts the Polish government." The communist deputies and their allies cheered wildly. Ambassador Lane turned purple red. His hands were shaking and his speech was so incoherent that his interpreter (and assistant naval and air attaché), Lt. William J. Tonesk, feared that Lane had suffered a stroke.

The next day, the official government newspaper said in an editorial that the "Polish people received with deep satisfaction the news concerning the granting of a loan to us from the

---

36. *Ibid.*, 436-437. About the same time, the Department of State came under pressure from an unexpected quarter. On April 24, it was informed of an urgent telegram received from London by the British embassy in Washington with the expression of "dismay" on the part of Foreign Secretary Bevin that "the United States government had decided to grant credit to the Polish government since the promises we had extracted from that government were mere paper commitments which the Polish government most likely will not live up to." Bevin suggested that "if it was not too late, the embassy should immediately endeavor to induce the State Department to withhold granting of credit at least until a definite nearby date is set for the elections." It is quite possible that in this case Bevin acted on his own. On the other hand, Lane's close personal relations with Cavendish-Bentinck, British ambassador in Warsaw, may have been responsible for this last-minute effort to scotch the credit deal.

United States of America. We have no intention of belittling the significance of the material help received, but in our opinion the moral and, for this reason, the political side of the loan has an even greater meaning."

The Poles underestimated the tenacity of Arthur Bliss Lane. Taking advantage of the failure of the Polish government to carry out certain formal obligations arising from the credit agreement, Lane flew to Paris where, on May 6, he was received by Byrnes. Speaking with great eloquence, Lane succeeded in convincing the secretary that the Poles should not be permitted to get away with this failure to live up to the terms of the agreement. Byrnes instructed Acheson to suspend all of the deliveries of surplus equipment to Poland and told Lane to visit President Bierut and explain to him the motive for this suspension.

Once in Warsaw, Lane requested an audience with Bierut. He repeated this request several times but Bierut refused to meet with him. The ambassador was undismayed and even pleased that he had again emerged as the major stumbling block in the whole affair. His moment of triumph came when the influential Dr. Rajchman appeared in the Polish capital and, on June 12, called on him to discuss the terms under which the deliveries could be resumed. Describing this encounter two days later in a message to Acheson—whom he had come to blame for his initial defeat—Lane couldn't resist the temptation to mention that "Rajchman was adamant that even the law firm of Covington, Burling and Rublee had expressed desire to defend the Polish point of view on the grounds that the U. S. Government had defaulted on its agreement." The firm in question was, of course, the one Dean Acheson had been a member of, on and off, for many years, which put the acting secretary of state in a rather embarrassing position. But although Lane had a few disparaging things to say about Rajchman ("his lack of reliability should now be clear to the Department"), this conversation helped to untangle the situation. Probably on Rajchman's advice, Prime Minister Osobka-Morawski approached Lane at a British embassy reception and, with evident recognition of Lane's role in resolving the issue, earnestly gave him assurances that the Polish government would fulfill all the formalities it had undertaken under the agreement. Satisfied, and probably aware that this was as good a moment as any to get out of the tight corner gracefully, Lane cabled Acheson, requesting to be authorized to inform the Poles that deliveries were to be resumed. Acheson forwarded the telegram to Byrnes, who, on June 22, 1946, gave Lane the necessary authorization.

The issue of the Polish loans did not die easily. As the 1946 election campaign got under way in the United States, Republicans began to question the administration's policies in Eastern Europe. On July 15, 1946, Llewellyn E. Thompson, chief of the Division of Eastern European Affairs, complained in a letter to Lane that "the correspondents have been giving us so much trouble over the Polish loan business and it is in such a mess due to misunderstanding back here between the bank and various other agencies and individuals concerned that I will be glad when this thing goes through and we can forget it." One may guess that Lane felt little compassion for Thompson's discomfiture.[37]

Free and Unfettered Elections

The Declaration on Poland adopted at Yalta by Roosevelt, Churchill, and Stalin, having set the procedure for the creation of a "Polish provisional government of national unity," also specified that this government "shall be pledged to the holding of free and unfettered elections as soon as possible on the basis of universal suffrage and secret ballot. In these elections all democratic and anti-Nazi parties shall have the right to take part and to put forward candidates." A Statement on the Polish

---

37. In later years, when the cold war was already in full swing, the issue of the Polish loans came to plague Secretary of State Dean Acheson. In part because it was his law firm which had acted on behalf of Rajchman, he had to present lengthy explanations to the Senate Foreign Relations Committee, which considered his nomination in 1948. Bitter criticism was renewed during the McCarthy era when Acheson was depicted as a major appeaser of the communists. See Felix Wittmer, "Freedom's Case Against Dean Acheson" in the *American Mercury*, April, 1952, and the State Department's rebuttal in the press release of May 19, 1952. Although a full documentation of the episode is lacking, it seems that Achesons's involvement in the granting of the Polish loans was, at best, marginal, and that he approved them on the strength of the recommendations of the Department's economic division, and with the blessing of Secretary Byrnes.

Question signed by Truman, Attlee, and Stalin at Potsdam on July 31, 1945, repeated the same formula word for word, adding that "representatives of the Allied press shall enjoy full freedom to report to the world upon the developments in Poland before and during the elections." Although in many respects both documents were vague (Admiral Leahy, who attended both conferences, commented that "the Russians could stretch the agreement all the way from Moscow to Washington without breaking it"), and though Stalin's promise at Yalta that the elections would be held "within a month" was not taken seriously by anybody, the clause appeared specific enough to justify hope that Poland had not been lost to freedom. This hope was expressed not only in the editorials of liberal magazines and newspapers in the West, but could also be noticed in the private and official utterings of the more optimistically inclined American diplomats of the early postwar period. Ambassador Harriman, for instance, advocated the expansion of American aid to Poland on the grounds that it promised to assure "a far-reaching and permanent effect on the influence of the U.S. on the political scene in Poland and particularly on our influence in connection with . . . the holding of truly free elections."[38]

With the passage of time, the Yalta-Potsdam pledge for holding "free and unfettered elections" acquired special significance to those who, like Arthur Bliss Lane, had been watching the tightening of the communist grip on Poland. It was no

---

38. Harriman to the acting secretary of state, June 26, 1945, FR, *Conference of Berlin*, I, 786. It must be added that Kennan, Harriman's principal aide in Moscow, took strong exception to such a view, insisting that aid programs to East European states were only making it easier for the Soviets to establish their hegemony there while burdening the United States with a share of moral responsibility for the enslavement of these states. Generally speaking, in spite of some very basic differences in political philosophy, there were striking similarities in the approaches of Kennan and Lane to the postwar situation in Eastern Europe and to the question of the direction of American policy towards the Soviet Union. Lane, as a practitioner of diplomacy and ambassador to Poland, could not be as consistent in his views and actions as the much more detached counselor at the embassy in Moscow who tried to comprehend the significance of the developments he witnessed. Neither man harbored illusions on the crucial issue of postwar Soviet-American cooperation, but Lane was spoiling for a fight, while Kennan was ready to concede to the Soviets their newly acquired sphere of influence.

longer (if it ever had been) a test between the various political groupings within Poland, but a test between the Soviet Union and the United States and Great Britain. Like his British colleague V. Cavendish-Bentinck, Lane did not anticipate a victory for the West. But he intended to assert American interests in Poland to check the Soviet power insofar as possible. He was fully determined to utilize the forthcoming elections for the purpose of opening the eyes of the American public and government, by a demonstration of the implacable hostility of the communists towards all things Western.

In his undertaking, Arthur Bliss Lane had a friend and ally in Stanislaw Mikolajczyk. This shrewd peasant politician had belonged, before the war, to the left wing of Polish politics. In postwar Poland he was regarded by both sides as a "middle-of-the-roader." His own record was impeccable. Other Peasant Party leaders were likewise staunch democrats by conviction, and anti-fascists by definition. But since the establishment of Soviet hegemony in Poland, the Peasant Party had become a rallying point for all discontented and embittered Poles, including many of the nationalists of the Right, who under different circumstances would have viewed Mikolajczyk as a dangerous leftist and a traitor to the national cause. This motley following did not disturb Mikolajczyk: he was confident that he could control the nationalists if the "free and unfettered" elections brought him to power. He probably also realized that without this support the Peasant Party could command only a relatively small number of votes, perhaps insufficient to dislodge the communist-led coalition of left-wing parties. Viewing the situation realistically, he knew that even if he succeeded in getting a sizable plurality, the communist control over the election machinery would still deny him the fruits of victory.

Under such circumstances Mikolajczyk had no choice but to welcome support from any and all quarters. He knew that only in this way could he have a vast majority of the Poles on his side. By the middle of 1946, he knew that the Soviets would not let him head the new government. But he hoped that a show of overwhelming strength for his ticket at the polls might make the communists—and their Soviet backers—modify their tactics in imposing a full-fledged communist regime upon his country. With this idea in mind, he steadfastly refused communist suggestions to present a unified front to the voters in a common ballot on any but the most favorable terms. He demanded that his party by allocated 75 percent of the seats in the parliament—a condition obviously unacceptable to the communists and their allies.

Ambassador Lane, who continued to meet Mikolajczyk surreptitiously, felt that his friend was excessively optimistic and that nothing could deter the communists, backed as they were by the Red army and the vast secret police establishment, from grabbing power. But since Mikolajczyk's course of action did not interfere with his own strategy, Lane did not try to dissuade the peasant leader. On the contrary, the sharper the conflict between the Soviet puppets and the opposition became, the greater became the police terror and the more brazen the communist interference with the elections. But, Lane thought, the better would be his opportunity to convince the American public and government that the time for a drastic reappraisal of attitudes toward the Soviets had arrived.

The feeling that he was nearly alone in his struggle did not discourage Lane. He had several friends at higher levels of the department who shared (although perhaps less than he thought they did) his appraisal of the situation. There had been a barely perceptible shift in the attitude of the press, and Lane hoped that with the news becoming more spectacular by the day, the truth would sooner or later become known. Signs were pointing to a Republican victory in the congressional elections in November, and a number of Republican politicians were voicing criticism of the administration's continuing appeasement of the Soviets. Lane's immediate task was to extract a maximum political effect from the Polish elections. He was certain that, the mood of appeasement in Washington notwithstanding, the United States could not possibly back out of its Yalta and Potsdam commitments. Therefore, he could elicit all the protests he wished from the State Department against the repressive measures of the Polish regime as they related to the "free and unfettered" elections, and the more the United States went out on a limb protesting, the more resentment it would have to show once the elections were proven to be fraudulent. If the cause of democracy was to be defeated by the forces of tyranny, reasoned Lane, the defeat should at least have a certain educational value for Americans.

The official position of the American ambassador in Warsaw had become very weak. His relations with Polish officialdom had never amounted to a meaningful dialogue. After the fight over the credits, the Poles had no illusions whatever as to where Lane stood, and they treated him with calculated chilliness. It did not upset Lane, for he had come to accept this condition as normal. He knew that there was next to nothing he could do to impress the officials he dealt with; his formal protests had a diminishing impact. Lane suspected that this was due to the high-level contacts of Rajchman and Ambassador Lange in Washington. It was a bitter pill for Lane to swallow, but he felt that the fight was not over.

With official channels closed to him it was inevitable that Lane should draw closer to Mikolajczyk. He abandoned all pretense that he was not backing the Peasant Party. Both men concluded that a pro-American label could no longer hurt the party in the atmosphere of spreading police terror. But Lane made no promises of assistance to Mikolajczyk, and the latter was too wise not to see that he was essentially on his own in the developing struggle.

The first test of strength came on June 30, 1946, in a referendum carried out in Poland on three relatively insignificant constitutional issues. The government coalition urged the voters to vote in the affirmative on all three points, the Peasant Party (and the Christian Labor Party, allied with Mikolajczyk) endorsed only two. Since this was regarded by everybody as a preview of the future parliamentary elections, Lane mobilized all the members of his staff to observe the procedure in various electoral districts of the country; a large number of American newsmen joined forces with the embassy to provide even wider coverage. This operation revealed a number of irregularities: mass arrests of opposition party members had preceded the voting; the government had virtually monopolized all means of propaganda and deprived the opposition of a chance to spread its message; the voting was not secret; and most importantly, the tabulation of ballots everywhere, except in Cracow, was done in the absence of opposition representatives. When the results of the referendum were officially announced, the government appeared to have scored a victory by a 2:1 majority on the issue challenged by Mikolajczyk. But in the city of Cracow, where the ballots were tabulated before the boxes were removed to the communist-run election headquarters, the ratio was about 6:1 *against* the government.

Communist leaders, both Polish and Soviet, doubtless knew the real figures and could easily surmise that if the forthcoming national elections were conducted according to democratic procedure, the opposition led by Mikolajczyk would obtain a majority. This they were firmly resolved to prevent. Their actual decisions remained, of course, secret, but in the ensuing weeks the pressure upon the Peasant Party increased so much that Mikolajczyk came to the conclusion that direct British and American supervision of the elections was imperative if his party were to survive as a political force. Lane, with whom he discussed the idea, rejected it out of hand on the grounds that such a supervision was not practically feasible, and that a direct intervention on the part of the Western powers would be likely to hurt the Peasant Party's standing with the voters. Although the British supported Mikolajczyk perhaps even more energetically than Lane, Cavendish-Bentinck voiced similar objections.

In the meantime, the Polish government was faced with a difficult dilemma. While putting the screws on the internal opposition, it somehow needed to improve its image in the United States. Economic conditions were going from bad to worse, and America was the only possible source of help. A new delegation headed by Hilary Minc prepared for departure to Washington, but in view of the news stories about referendum frauds and secret police activities, the friends of the "new Poland" in the United States found it hard to act on the delegation's behalf. In order to neutralize adverse American reaction, an attempt was made to discredit American representatives in Poland.

President Bierut gave an unprecedented interview to W. H. Lawrence—published in the *New York Times* on July 20—in which he expressed his government's resentment at American meddling in the internal affairs of Poland. He attacked Ambassador Lane personally, saying that Lane "could not or would not endeavor to understand the Polish people"; that while some Americans have no difficulty in comprehending the situation in Poland, Lane had "a psychological problem" which prevented him from similar comprehension. Simultaneously, the Poles planted a story in the London *Observer* hinting that the Polish government might request that Ambassador Lane be recalled for violations of the rules of diplomatic behavior. As one State Department official recorded, it all pointed "to a definite campaign to discredit Ambassador Lane," not unlike a previous attempt in January when the Polish foreign minister visited Byrnes in London to complain about Lane's alleged encroachments upon the sovereignty of Poland.

Since Bierut came very close to declaring that Lane was *persona non grata,* his challenge could not be left unanswered. On August 4, 1946, Acting Secretary Dean Acheson, with the full approval of Secretary Byrnes, issued a most unusual statement in which he expressed great "surprise" at Bierut's remarks. "Ambassador Lane," said Acheson, "is an experienced diplomat who has represented this government in many parts of the world. His reports from Warsaw have always indicated great sympathy for Poland and the difficulties she is facing. Ambassador Lane continues to enjoy the complete confidence of his government." The Associated Press carried an extensive commentary, underscoring that Byrnes and Acheson "threw their full support behind U. S. Ambassador Arthur Bliss Lane . . . in what appears to be a bitter undercover struggle with President Boleslaw Bierut of the communist-dominated government of Poland." The Associated Press further explained that "in this struggle, which is essentially between Moscow and Washington-London, Ambassador Lane is the American spearhead. The available evidence here indicates that policy is being determined primarily in the State Department, though with Lane's full support."

In order to further impress the communists with the futility of efforts to drive a wedge between the State Department and the ambassador in Poland, Acheson instructed Lane to present a strongly-worded note regarding the June 30 referendum, warning the Poles that the fraudulent techniques they had employed in this case must have no place in the forthcoming national elections, as this would violate the principles proclaimed at the Yalta Conference. The note stated that there should be no arrests or threats of arrest during the election campaign; that all the parties should be represented when the ballots were counted; that results of the voting were to be immediately published by local districts; and that there should be an adequate system of appealing election disputes.[39] The final text of the note was worked out in telegraphic consultations among Acheson, Byrnes, and Lane, after which the ambassador delivered it to the foreign ministry.

There was no official reply, then or later, to this document: that is, none except for a statement which the Polish embassy in Washington released on August 27, declaring that the note was "being regarded by the Polish government as infringement upon Poland's sovereign rights and interferences in her internal affairs." Taking issue with the American declaration of its obligation to assure the free and unfettered elections, the embassy insisted that there was no provision in either the Yalta or Potsdam agreements "for a foreign supervision before the elections" and accused the United States of an "open interference with completely internal party politics in Poland" and of taking sides "by giving open diplomatic support to those parties known to be in disagreement with views and decisions on election problems of the majority in the government coalition."

The Setback

Ambassador Lane was extremely pleased with Acheson's statement, the note of protest, and the attention it received in the United States. For a change the shoe was on the other foot, and Lane reckoned that, having received this rebuke, the "Moscow Crowd" in Warsaw would think twice before assailing him again. To be sure, Lane did not anticipate more than a temporary respite. But for the moment it looked as if valuable time had been gained, and Mikolajczyk's resurgent hopes had acquired a more solid foundation. There also appeared to be a slow-down in the communists' drive against the Peasant Party. Poland was getting increasingly bad press throughout the Western world; many quarters formerly friendly to the Bierut

---

39. For the text, see Department of State Bulletin, August 18, 1946.

regime voiced disapproval of its bullying tactics, and references to the "Iron Curtain" in Europe were appearing with
increasing frequency in newspaper editorials and political
speeches. Surveying these developments, Arthur Bliss Lane
revised his earlier pessimistic expectations. He began to hope
that the communists might be put on the defensive in connection with the forthcoming elections, provided they were
held within a couple of months as was then anticipated. With
still more luck, the government formed as a result of the elections might show an improvement in the position of the Peasant Party, thus postponing the consolidation of communist
power in Poland.

Lane's hopes were shattered on September 6, 1946. On that
day Secretary Byrnes delivered a speech in Stuttgart before an
audience which for the first time since the beginning of Allied
military rule in Germany included a number of Germans. He
questioned the finality of Poland's western frontier and of its
acquisition of the so-called Oder-Neisse territories. Strictly
speaking, there was nothing new in the position which Byrnes
took on this issue: he merely reminded his audience that these
territories were given to Poland at Potsdam for temporary administration, pending the final peace settlement with Germany.
By bringing the matter up at that time and place, Byrnes hoped
to put a damper on French demands for a permanent dismemberment of Germany and to counteract the recent Soviet
efforts to pose as the champions of German interests. It was
feared in Washington that the miserable conditions in the western zones of occupation would enable communist influence to
spread there with grave consequences for the future of Europe.
In making a bid for the allegiance of the German people,
Byrnes was only vaguely aware of the Polish interest involved.
To him, Poland was beyond salvation, and the probable reaction to his statement there—if he thought about it at
all—appeared of distinctly minor importance.

The reaction in Poland was immediate and violent. Practically every Pole, regardless of his political views, had come to
consider the "Recovered Territories" as an integral part of the
country.[40] A large part of the indigenous German population

---

40. For the official Polish position, see FR, *Conference on Berlin*, I, 757–777.
Very few Poles (such as Arcieszewski, who still headed the powerless gov-

had fled before the Red army's advance. The remainder was being driven out by the Polish authorities who were employing means of remarkable cruelty in clearing out the cities, towns, and villages for the millions of Poles who were being transferred there from the eastern part of prewar Poland, now incorporated into the Soviet Union, and from the overpopulated areas of central Poland. The entire operation was directed by the Polish communists, working in close cooperation with the Soviets and enjoying the power of patronage in distributing German spoils. There was a great deal of uncertainty in the air, and fears that one day the Germans might demand their lands back were widespread. It was precisely because of these fears that any suggestion that the western frontier was a subject for reconsideration evoked universal resentment and indignation in Poland.

Ambassador Lane, who was thoroughly familiar with the enormous sensitivity of the issue—and was in no way involved in the complexities of the German problem—was furious as he read news reports about Byrnes' speech. From his vantage point, it was not the Germans but the Poles who were natural allies of the United States in the developing struggle with the Soviet Union. He believed that Poland was entitled to a generous territorial compensation for its contribution to the allied cause in the war and for its loss of the eastern provinces. What outraged him the most, however, was the timing of the Stuttgart address. With the Polish elections a few months away, the emergence of the United States in the role of defender of the hated Germans meant, in his view, a political death-warrant for Mikolajczyk's Peasant Party, which had become identified in the public mind with the Americans. He felt that "the United States had suffered a severe setback in standing and prestige with the Polish people generally, whose friendship had been so important to us in the past and might be a critical fac-

---

ernment-in-exile in London) opposed such an expansion at the expense of Germany on the grounds that it would forever tie Poland to the Soviet Union, which alone could protect it against the German revisionism, in the future, thought to be inevitable.

tor ... should we be unfortunate enough to participate in another war in Europe."[41]

Lane's expectation that the communists would seize this opportunity to pose as the sole protectors of Polish interests quickly materialized. Utilizing all means of propaganda, they did their best to distort Byrnes' statement to show the Americans as joining hands with the Germans in forming a crusade against the East, and to brand the Polish friends of the United States as traitors to the national interest. Mass protest rallies were held throughout the country. A communist-led mob attacked the Peasant Party headquarters in Warsaw, beating up several officials and destroying all the records and furniture in the building. A mass demonstration was also staged in front of the Hotel Polonia, the seat of the American embassy. Newspaper editorials loudly demanded that Mikolajczyk immediately repudiate the American "supporters and protectors of Germany." Taking advantage of this atmosphere, the communists summoned a meeting of the National Council of the Homeland and pushed through their version of the electoral law, providing no safeguards for a fair tabulation of the votes and thereby dooming the last chance for the Peasant Party to win the elections.

Much as the whole episode distressed Arthur Bliss Lane, he refrained from putting his feelings on record. His appraisal of the Polish reaction, cabled to Byrnes on September 17, sounded almost optimistic. "Regardless of the ephemeral irritation, which I am impelled to report your remarks have provoked in Poland," wrote Lane, "I am confident the Poles as a people have greater confidence in our friendship than that of any other nation." Ten days later, he reported that "while the Secretary's Stuttgart speech had hurt Mikolajczyk politically, from an overall diplomatic viewpoint the effect of the speech was not unfavorable to Polish interests." On October 3, he vigorously defended the American position in a long talk with Prime Minister Osobka-Morawski, but his dispatch about it did not sound dramatic at all. He concluded the interview by asking rhetorically whether in the event that the Polish frontier

41. *Lane's Account,* 265–266.

were moved east of the Oder and Neisse Rivers the gainer would be Germany or the Soviet zone in Germany. "In answer," reported Lane, "Osobka merely laughed."

On the Way Out

The absence from the official record of expressions of the extreme indignation Arthur Bliss Lane felt during the weeks following Secretary Byrnes' unfortunate address is readily explainable. One reason was that he was ready to depart on an extensive home leave. Expecting to learn more about the prevailing winds upon his arrival in Washington, he saw no point in getting into another fight which could only complicate his relations with the colleagues he was soon to see. Another reason was that Lane realized that his protracted battle was becoming nonproductive. He did and said all he could, but the impact upon the machinery of the Department was minimal. His attempt to enlist the aid of the British — who were now pressing Washington for a harder line toward Polish communists — was backfiring. At the end of September he received a telegram from Byrnes specifically directing him not to reveal to the British ambassador in Warsaw the contents of official communications, a clear sign of the Secretary's annoyance.

But there was a more fundamental reason for Lane's reticence. Having taken stock of the situation as calmly as he could, he reached the conclusion that the damage done to his mission in Poland was irreparable. The state of affairs being what it was, the current assignment held no more appeal for him. He blamed the failure of his mission on those in the State Department and elsewhere who continually refused to support him in his strategy and, in fact, did a great deal to make his task impossible.

Lane was still in top form and too young to retire. Yet the immense strain he had been laboring under since his arrival in Warsaw was telling on him. Now that he had had all the challenges any ambitious career diplomat could wish, Arthur Bliss Lane was beginning to think that a quiet post in some attractive European capital would be more to his liking. He had had enough of Poland, of dealing with an implacably hostile government, and of living in a city which held no attraction whatsoever. He found it increasingly difficult to face the mounting frustrations in the performance of his mission. He had no intention of resigning. A resignation before the elections was out of the question: this would have been an admission of weakness and defeat, and Lane still was a fighter, defending even on the firing line the cause of freedom and the honor of the United States. But the tension was so unrelenting that even temporary relief was welcome. When, early in October, he received permission to leave Poland for two months of vacation and subsequent consultations at the State Department, he could not conceal his delight.

Lane's first stop was Paris, where the peace conference was still going on. The large American delegation was deeply involved in intricate negotiations over the peace treaties to be signed with the former enemy nations. Lane did not see Secretary Byrnes but spent some time in conversations with Matthews, Dunn, and Bohlen, trying to figure out where and how Poland fit into the overall foreign policy of the United States. It did not take him long to discover that the fortunes of that country were of minimal concern to the Americans, while Germany loomed more important than at any time since the war. He communicated his findings regarding the background of the Stuttgart speech to his chargé d'affaires in Warsaw, Gerald Keith. In a letter dated October 17, Lane wrote that according to the members of the American delegation, Byrnes had made his speech "deliberately to smoke Molotov out on the [presumed] Soviet plan to give western Polish territories to Germany. The Soviets had been working on this plan for over six months and the secretary's speech was apparently such a surprise that Molotov did not comment, nor did the German communist newspapers, for a week." As the Americans surmised, it was at this point that the Soviets decided to support the Polish position rather than the German. But insofar as the United States was concerned, "there has never been any intention on the part of the secretary to oppose the Polish demand for territory at the peace conference." Since it appeared certain that the Soviets would stall on discussing the German treaty, Lane concluded that the question of Poland's western frontiers would not be decided for some time.[42]

---

42. Shortly before his resignation, on January 13, 1947, Lane addressed to General George C. Marshall, the new secretary of state, a long message

Lane was very encouraged by the growing determination of the leading American diplomats in Paris to stand up to the Soviets. As he wrote to Keith in another letter: "A general policy has been set up and the Department was instructed by the secretary to give no economic assistance to any governments which are not friendly with us. The Czechoslovak situation was a case in point and I am sure .... that similar action will take place with respect to Poland. ... The general attitude has stiffened a great deal since last June, in part due to all the insults the Americans have had to take from the communists lately."

Lane's brief vacation on the Riviera and in Rome was sufficient to put him in a more optimistic mood. Arriving in Washington on November 5, he energetically plunged into discussions of Polish affairs. To his disappointment, Lane found that, unlike the members of the American delegation in Paris, these officials were reluctant to take a hard line in dealing with the Soviet Union and its satellites in Eastern Europe. Acting Secretary Acheson was "characteristically noncommittal" in listening to Lane's admonitions to suspend further

---

wholly devoted to the question of the Polish western frontiers, which was expected to be discussed at the Moscow conference of foreign ministers. In it, he presented his arguments against returning the disputed lands to Germany: (a) the consent of the Big Three at Potsdam to deport the German population from these lands and the negative reaction which a revision of this decision was likely to evoke among the Polish people; (b) the need for compensating the Poles for the lost territories in the East; (c) the political gains which the Soviets would be likely to score in Poland if they emerged as the sole defenders of Polish interests; (d) the practical unfeasibility of effecting such a transfer of territories in view of the Soviet control over the eastern part of Germany.

There were two responses to Lane's presentation. One was from Robert Murphy, who was then the senior political adviser to General Lucius D. Clay in Germany. In a personal letter of January 24, 1947, Murphy expressed his belief that "something should be done" in the way of returning at least a part of the Oder-Neisse territories to Germany, if it were to be self-sufficient in food production (at that time, the Americans were still trying to see the occupied country as a single economic unit), and that at least some of the expellees should be allowed to return to their native land. Another reaction came from General Walter Bedell Smith, ambassador to Moscow. In a brief note dated February 1, written on the eve of the conference, Smith stated that "the vital question is one of Germany versus Poland," and that from his own point of view it seemed "more important to keep Germany headed West than to prevent a general turn to the East on the part of Poland."

financial assistance to the Polish government. Similar pleas at the Department's economic division and in the Export-Import Bank fell on deaf ears.

This was discouraging, but by now Arthur Bliss Lane cared much less. What was happening in Poland was merely one element in a picture dominated overwhelmingly by the emergence of the Soviet Union as a dynamic, aggressive, and hostile power. The American public seemed to be awakening to this danger: the Congressional elections — which gave the GOP the majority in both houses for the first time since 1932 — reflected considerable dissatisfaction with the administration's foreign policy. Important ethnic groups of East European origin were clearly deserting the Democratic Party to which they had been attached since New Deal days. As Lane saw it, the task was to accelerate this trend by educating the public to the realities of the postwar world, thereby forcing a re-examination of foreign policy by the government.

This education, logically, had to start with the press. In spite of noticeable stiffening in the attitudes of many periodicals on the issue of the communist menace, Lane found the press coverage of the latest events in Eastern Europe quite unsatisfactory. In an effort to enlist further support for his line of thinking, he undertook a vigorous one-man campaign. He saw and talked at length with a number of members of Congress. With the State Department's reluctant permission, he held a press conference in Washington at which he urged sending trained observers to Poland to cover the elections. He made a special trip to New York where he spent a few days meeting with the publishers and editors of several periodicals.

Lane's success in this endeavor was apparently mixed, or, perhaps, the editors he talked to promised him more than they were prepared to deliver. In his letter of December 10, written while on his way back to Poland to C. Burke Elbrick of the Department's Eastern European Division, Lane said that he had received "some rather disquieting reports of Sydney Gruson, the *New York Times* man in Warsaw," who apparently had been "pretty well taken in by the Poles." He absolved Mrs. Gruson (Flora Lewis) of the same sin, pointing out that according to his information she disagreed with her husband's views of the Polish regime, and expressing doubt "whether Henry

Luce would keep [her] on if she also had a Red complex."
Lane was not completely sure that Sydney Gruson was in fact
"deliberately playing the Red game," but promised that if he
discovered that such were the case, he would immediately
communicate his findings to Arthur Sulzberger.

"Free and Unfettered"

There is no need to describe here the political conditions in
Poland on the eve of the elections and the circumstances under
which they were held. The story has been told many times
before: by Arthur Bliss Lane himself; by Mikolajczyk and other
Poles who eventually found themselves in exile; and by a
number of detached and not-so-detached American and foreign
observers and scholars.

Ambassador Lane, upon his return to Warsaw, concluded
that there was no way to prevent the communist victory. The
Soviet Union in its bid for absolute domination in Eastern
Europe was not going to tolerate anything but a completely
subservient regime in Warsaw. Moscow was still acting by
proxy through the Polish communists and the other political
groups which allied themselves with the communists in the
"government bloc." But there were persistent rumors circulating in the Polish capital — rumors given wide credence — that in
case of a Peasant Party victory in the elections, the Soviet
government would order the Red army to occupy Poland and
subject the country to the kind of military rule which had been
established in the Soviet zone of Germany. Since not even the
Polish communists wished to see this happen, the Bierut government made an all-out bid for power, launching a campaign
of intimidation and outright terror against the opposition on a
scale that dwarfed everything Poland had experienced since
the war.

Much as they had been battered, Mikolajczyk and his comrades-in-arms not only refused to give up, but became more
optimistic by the day. The support for the opposition among
the Polish masses was stronger than ever. The communists
were widely regarded as stooges of an alien power which had
implanted itself in the country, and the old spirit of resistance

ran high. So pervasive and omnipresent was the dislike of all things Russian that even the skeptics were carried away. A belief that at least for the time being the communists would not dare to grab power in open defiance of the West was widespread. The romantic Poles, in their ardent desire to remain independent, grossly exaggerated the influence which the United States could—or indeed was willing to—exert upon the outcome of their struggle.

Arthur Bliss Lane did nothing to encourage these expectations. He was convinced that the communists would stop short of nothing, and that the enormous Soviet backing would assure them victory. He also knew that his own government was not going to do anything, aside from monotonous protests, to prevent this victory from taking place. Nevertheless, it was impossible for him to stay on the sidelines. He continued to see Mikolajczyk who, in fighting for the political survival of his party, was losing all sense of reality in his expectations of support from the West. Lane tried to bring him into a more sober frame of mind and discourage him from carrying out some of his wilder schemes—such as addressing a "note" to the signatories of the Yalta and Potsdam agreements (including the Soviet government) with a request to intervene in Poland, stop police terror, and assure the "free and unfettered elections." Lane's admonitions were to no avail; Mikolajczyk simply would not listen.

The elections took place as scheduled, on January 19, 1947. Although many voters appeared intimidated, there was no violence. Few foreign observers recorded any irregularities at the polling places, but in the tabulation of ballots, representatives of the opposition were excluded in all but thirty-six precincts out of a total of 5,200. Under these circumstances the official results, announced a few days later, were not surprising: the government bloc secured 394 seats in the parliament, the opposition parties 50, with 28 going to the Peasant Party. Mikolajczyk was shaken by this outcome, but he could point to the fact that in the thirty-six precincts where the tabulation was done in the presence of opposition representatives, the Peasant Party scored majorities ranging from 65 to 85 percent. And he soon learned from a trusted personal friend (who was a leader of the Socialist Party and therefore had access to the high councils of the government) that in the country as a whole the Peasant Party had collected 74 percent of the total votes cast.

The fraud was obvious and few foreign correspondents were deceived by the official figures. Ambassador Lane, who took particular pains to facilitate the widest possible press coverage, must have been pleased. With rare exceptions, the American press sympathetically reported the sad plight of the democratic opposition in Poland. Great Britain and the United States did not fail to declare that the Polish government, having resorted to "measures of coercion and intimidation" against bona fide anti-fascist elements, had failed to live up to its solemn obligations.

Arthur Bliss Lane did not have to wait until the election results had been announced to realize that the game was over. The goodwill toward the West, so widespread among the Polish people, did not help the United States retain a position of influence in Poland. The communists were unrestrained in their rapid consolidation of power and establishment of a totalitarian state. Observing the imposition of rule by a small Soviet-sponsored minority over the vast majority of the vehemently anti-communist people, Lane could not accept the idea that this outcome was inevitable from the start. It was convenient to blame the Bierut regime for the violation of its obligations but, as Lane saw it, it was primarily the United States which had let the Poles down by failing to fulfill its solemn commitment. If the steps he had advocated for the last year and a half had been taken, he was sure that the state of affairs in Poland would have been vastly different; the communists, both Polish and Russian, would not have dared to proceed toward their goals with such unheard-of brazenness; and the balance of power in Europe would not have been in such a shambles.

Since he did not question his own judgment, Lane blamed his superiors in Washington for their inability to understand the stakes involved in the struggle in Eastern Europe, and for their failure to employ political and economic leverage—which he considered to be of great potential—in the defense of American interests. He knew that the government could not act without public support, but he also believed that it could have mobilized public opinion if, instead of suppressing information unfavorable to the Soviets, it had launched a massive educational program of the kind he had suggested in his letter to H. Freeman Matthews on March 1, 1946. During his previous visit to the United States, he had noticed considerable stirrings among the public. But the government, as a body, was clearly lagging behind the people, still bent on following the old discredited course in its relations with Moscow.

With the passage of time, Arthur Bliss Lane found it increasingly difficult to serve a government whose policies he judged erroneous. He had less and less patience with the Department's bureaucrats, who from his vantage point seemed not to understand the basic facts of life. Many times during his thirty years in the diplomatic service, Lane had followed his instructions while disagreeing with them. He did not always do it happily, and certainly not indifferently, but he knew the rules and carried out official policy to the best of his ability. But what he had lived through in Poland was unlike anything he had experienced before. He found himself at loggerheads with his government on every major issue. He fought for his views with greater tenacity than ever before, and he lost. It was, to him, much more than a personal defeat. Although a very proud man, Lane possibly could have learned to live with a deep sense of humiliation, watching the Polish communists laugh at him as they succeeded with the aid of their agents in the United States. What made the situation unbearable was Lane's conviction that the United States had suffered in Poland a devastating blow to its international prestige, a blow which could have been avoided.

Arthur Bliss Lane found himself at the crossroads of his career. He was tempted to resign and carry on his fight outside of the government. On his last trip home, he had enjoyed meeting various interesting and important men in domestic public life. He remembered the satisfaction he felt whenever he succeeded in influencing their thinking by drawing attention to the crucial problem of the communist menace. He had found others who were, indeed, ahead of him in the realization of this danger and who could add a great deal to his knowledge and understanding of the postwar world. The congenial environment of such associations and the prospect of joining a crusade unhampered by official regulations appeared attractive.

On the other hand, resignation seemed too drastic a step to take. The diplomatic service had always been more than just a career to Arthur Bliss Lane. In spite of its recurrent frustrations, it was a way of life, rich and rewarding in experience and accomplishment. The world of international politics and diplomacy, full of people of power and influence, was his world; he knew no other. He was financially independent, but attached little importance to money; his own life was meaningful because he represented the United States abroad and was entrusted with the implementation of his president's policies.

At this juncture, however, the old criteria did not seem to apply any more. Lane knew that he simply could not remain in Poland after the communists had entrenched themselves, and although nothing had been said, or even intimated, he sensed that his superiors in Washington would be relieved if he left Warsaw. He still could serve at some other post. But if he were to choose one, he would not look for glory or prestige. After all the strain and tension of the preceding months, he wished to be in a quiet and undemanding place.

About four weeks before the election in Poland, Lane heard the news that Myron C. Taylor, the personal representative of the president to the Pope, intended to retire. This looked like a unique opportunity. The post at the Vatican was a minor one, but perfectly respectable, and a transfer from hated Warsaw to Rome, the city he knew and loved so well, appeared immensely desirable. Without giving the matter a second thought, Lane wrote, on December 23, 1946, a letter to Secretary Byrnes, requesting to be considered as Taylor's successor. "Because of the health of my wife, who suffered three heart attacks in the autumn, I do not feel that I can subject her indefinitely to the rigorous life which exists in Poland today," wrote Lane. "For the same reason, I would prefer not to serve at a post where the social life is a strain on the wife of the chief of mission. As my wife and I both speak Italian . . . and as we are both personally acquainted with the Pope, I feel that we can be of real usefulness to our government." Lane added that neither he nor Mrs.

Lane were Roman Catholic, and concluded by saying: "As this is the first request for a post which I have made in my thirty years of service, I trust that you will forgive me for intruding on your very active life."

Byrnes did not reply. Within one week he himself was replaced by General Marshall, and, as usual, the ensuing changing of the guard in the State Department interfered with the normal flow of communications. On January 13, 1947, Arthur Bliss Lane wrote another letter, this time to Selden Chapin, director general of the foreign service. He mentioned his letter to Byrnes and reiterated his desire to be transferred to a "less rigorous post," either to the Vatican or to Berne, Switzerland, another position which was then expected to become vacant. Chapin did not answer either, but on January 24, Dean Acheson, now under-secretary of state, wrote Lane a one-paragraph, "My Dear Mr. Ambassador" letter, saying that "although Mr. Taylor is not now in Rome, there is no expectation that he will give up this position in the near future." There was no reference to the post at Berne.

However, before Acheson's message reached Warsaw, Arthur Bliss Lane had made his decision to resign. He had concluded that the scandal of the Polish elections would attract greater attention in America and elsewhere if he emphasized this inglorious event by his resignation, thus killing two birds with one stone. On January 23, he sent a telegram to Secretary Marshall. He referred to the Polish elections as "a mechanical routine to indicate a legal justification for the puppet regime to continue in power," and expressed the opinion that "only through the exercise of American public opinion can the Soviet government be prevailed upon to ease its policy of domination of European countries and to refrain from further imperialistic expansion." And he continued:

> For all practical purposes my mission to Poland is ended. I believe I could do more by educating American public opinion as a private citizen than I can by remaining in Poland, where my continued presence would be considered as tacit acquiescence in the recent fraudulent elections. I should, therefore, appreciate it if the Department would permit me to retire from the Foreign Service.
>
> I believe that now is the time to state our policy clearly and

emphatically and without diplomatic evasion or reserve, for I feel
that the situation which has just culminated in the elections is
potentially one of the most far-reaching in its implications insofar
as American foreign policy and the possible subsequent creation of
military hostilities are concerned.

In all likelihood, the secretary of state read this communication with relief. It was Marshall's (and Acheson's) belief
that Ambassador Lane suffered from a bad case of "localitis,"
tending to become too involved in the internal affairs of Poland
and repeatedly putting the United States in the uncomfortable
position of helpless protest over matters which, in the opinion
of many high officials, it had no practical way of influencing.
The State Department, however, did not announce Lane's resignation from the foreign service at this time for precisely the
same reason that motivated Lane to submit it. The controversial Polish elections were still very much in the headlines, and in Marshall's considered judgment, the ambassador's
dramatic gesture could only add fuel to the fire. Since the
procedure required that ambassadors submit their resignations
directly to the president (which Lane, at that point, had not
done), the secretary of state merely instructed Lane to come to
Washington "for consultations," with the understanding that he
would not return to Warsaw thereafter.

On February 15, Ambassador Lane called on the new Prime
Minister, Cyrankiewicz, to establish official relations with the
new government of Poland and to inform him of his own imminent departure. Lane spoke candidly and at length. He listed
all American efforts to aid Poland and pointed out that the
Polish government had not reciprocated by trying to improve
Polish-American relations. It was a short-sighted attitude, said
Lane; his belief was that once the Polish lack of cooperation
became known, the United States would be unlikely to continue its assistance. Cyrankiewicz remarked that if such was going
to be the case, Poland would have no choice but to become
totally dependent on the Soviet Union.

A week later, on Washington's birthday, Arthur Bliss Lane
held a reception for the American and British colonies of Warsaw. He bade a sorrowful farewell to all his friends and colleagues, warmly thanking them for their cooperation and devotion to the common cause, and expressing his hope that he

would accomplish more in the United States for the Polish people than he could in Warsaw. On February 24, 1947, the Lanes left the Polish capital.

Washington, where Lane arrived on March 6, was quite different from what it had been when he visited there a few months earlier. The political atmosphere was changing. The State Department, Congress, and the White House were busy with preparations for a major change in American foreign policy that was to become known as the Truman Doctrine. Replacing the waning British power, the United States was emerging on the international arena as the undisputed leader of the Free World, seemingly determined to contain communism politically, economically, and militarily.

This visible departure from the old attitudes toward the Soviet Union did not impress Arthur Bliss Lane sufficiently to make him change his decision to resign. The men in power in Washington were still the same, and he not only mistrusted their ability to cope with the unfolding crises, but also questioned the sincerity of their conversion. The change in their views had not come from within, through a re-examination of past errors. Instead, it had been brought about by outside pressures and by the need to accommodate domestic public opinion. It did not take Lane long to discover that even in the new circumstances neither Marshall nor Acheson was particularly anxious to retain his services. He could not get the post at the Vatican—which Truman wanted to abolish anyway because of the objections of some Protestant groups—and nothing else interested him at that point.

President Truman received Lane on March 21. He listened sympathetically to Lane's explanation that he could do more in strengthening the American position vis-à-vis communism if he reverted to the status of a private citizen, able to "speak and write openly, without being hampered by diplomatic convention." Truman approved Lane's course of action and, on March 25, sent him a formal letter, expressing his deep appreciation of the ambassador's "vigorous efforts" in Warsaw and the great reluctance with which he accepted Lane's resignation.

VI

Epilogue

The transition to his new status was not easy for Arthur Bliss Lane. There was no embassy to run, no reports to be written, no important appointments with foreign officials to be kept. Whatever he had to say he said now as an individual, even if he was identified as the former ambassador of the United States to Poland. He did not have to weigh each word as he did before, and he could speak much more forcefully. But he was not speaking for the United States government.

Shortly after he resigned, Lane suffered a personal tragedy. His daughter Peggy, who had married an Air Force pilot two years earlier, suddenly died of pneumonia while the Lanes were visiting her in California. The loss of his only child accentuated the drastic transformation in his life, somehow adding to his desire to prove to himself and to others that he still had an important mission to perform. In the subsequent months and years, private citizen Lane seemed to be busier than ever before. He held press conferences, gave interviews, addressed scores of audiences across the country, and wrote articles for newspapers and magazines. He obtained Dean Acheson's permission for unrestricted access to the official files of the Department, and after one year of hard work published a book, *I Saw Poland Betrayed*, a vivid memoir of his last mission that quickly became a best seller. He carried on extensive correspondence with emigrés from East European countries and maintained contact with prominent figures of both parties identified with ethnic group politics. He was active in the Paderewski Fund and in the Katyn Massacre Committee which collected evidence of the mass slaughter of Polish officers perpetrated by the Soviet authorities in the Katyn Forest on the eve of the German invasion. He became a member of the board

283

of the National Committee for a Free Europe, headed by Joseph C. Grew. In 1951 he took a plunge into partisan politics. He joined the Republican National Committee, assuming charge of its foreign language group activities. In the presidential campaign of 1952 he offered advice to all Republican contenders; his own preference for the presidency was Senator Robert Taft.

Anticipating a GOP victory, Arthur Bliss Lane did all he could to effect a radical change in American foreign policy. He tirelessly advocated the abandonment of Truman's policy of containment and its replacement by a more dynamic policy aimed at the eventual liberation of all nations enslaved by communism. Lane was convinced that a reiteration of the lofty principles of the Atlantic Charter and a repudiation of the Yalta agreement would attract many hyphenated Americans to the Republican banner. In the charged atmosphere of the Korean War this reasoning sounded convincing, and Lane was gratified when both positions were accepted at the Republican national convention. The 1952 GOP platform promised to "repudiate all commitments contained in secret understandings such as those of Yalta which aid communist enslavements" and anticipated "genuine independence" of the captive East European nations.

In his political fights, Arthur Bliss Lane always sought specific targets: he had never liked abstractions. Such targets still abounded in a country with vivid memories of its recent past. There were plenty of people—many of considerable influence—who still regarded the Soviet Union as a friend and ally, who blamed Truman for the cold war and the growing tensions in Soviet-American relations, and who liked Mao Tse-tung and hated Chiang Kai-shek. There were others who had accepted the Iron Curtain as a fact of life and insisted on non-interference in the Soviet bloc's internal affairs, either because they subscribed to the concept of "spheres of influence" and hoped that the Soviets, with their hands full in Eastern Europe, would leave the West alone; or because they feared to provoke another global conflict. His convictions and temperament being what they were, Lane regarded all these people as political adversaries.

In the relentless struggle of the 1950s, the lines became

sharply drawn. Many of Lane's former friends and colleagues who had remained charter members of the "liberal establishment" (which continued to dominate the foreign service under the Eisenhower administration), viewed him as an "extremist." By the law of natural political gravitation, Lane rapidly moved towards the opposite pole, associating himself with the most determined foes of communism in public life, such as Herbert Hoover, Douglas MacArthur, Robert Taft, and Styles Bridges. As his frustrations multiplied, he tended to blame the "liberals" in the government and elsewhere for the inability of the United States to check communist encroachments upon the Free World's positions. Inexorably, this tendency prompted him to make common cause with the most militant anti-communists of the era and, notably, with Joseph R. McCarthy.

The GOP triumph of 1952 did not bring about the kind of reappraisal of United States foreign policy that Arthur Bliss Lane had so anxiously sought. The Party plank promising to roll communism back was quietly and speedily forgotten. Under a barrage of criticism and charges of warmongering, the new administration adopted essentially the same defensive policies vis-à-vis the Soviet Union that had been followed under the Democrats. Even though he expanded the meaning of containment and identified communism as the principal enemy of the United States, John Foster Dulles did not depart greatly from the basic concepts of Dean Acheson.

Arthur Bliss Lane received no reward for his contribution to the GOP victory. For a short while he was considered for a minor post, but politically he was by then too far removed from the mainstream of his time. He was disillusioned with the new leadership and sharply questioned its ability to protect the vital interests of the United States and its allies. Because of Lane's total inability to compromise on the central issue of communist menace, his relations even with political friends in the administration deteriorated. His growing abrasiveness and hot temper (which he found more and more difficult to control) considerably reduced the circle of people who found him congenial. His view of the future after the Geneva summit meeting of 1955 became deeply pessimistic. True to himself, he regarded the spirit of *détente* as a tragic compromise with evil which boded no good for the United States. He was realistic enough to see that his crusade was doomed, and he abandoned his struggle as futile. He died in 1956 of cirrhosis of the liver at the relatively young age of 62.

Conclusion

Having surveyed Arthur Bliss Lane's career, we may appropriately ask whether he was in fact a successful diplomat, that is, whether he accomplished in the line of duty as much—or more—as a foreign service colleague might have accomplished in his place. The answer to this question is necessarily affirmative, for both in the performance of his routine functions and in his handling of critical situations Lane's record was quite outstanding. His singular dedication to his office, his perfectionism and ability to extract maximum effort from his subordinates, and his readiness to act forcefully, relying on his own judgment, saved him from being a "typical" career diplomat. A good administrator, Lane possessed unusual intelligence and an ability to grasp complicated issues and reduce them to manageable essentials. He did not "specialize" in any geographic area or in a specific set of problems: in his time tradition held that a good diplomat, given adequate general experience, should be able to cope with any situation. By the time he had become a head of mission, Lane rarely solicited anybody's advice.

Nor was this all. In spite of the many years he spent abroad, Arthur Bliss Lane seldom lost touch with political trends in the United States as they affected the country's foreign relations. For the most part he was successful in sizing up the frame of mind of the leading officials in the State Department and the White House. His reports from the field were rarely profound, but rather carefully tailored to the level of knowledge and understanding he could expect of those who read them. Lane's effectiveness was further enhanced by his uncanny knowledge of human nature and ability to exploit the weaknesses of the individuals he dealt with.

Lane's life was not one of untarnished success. But many of his failures—or what he considered to be failures—resulted from his outstanding ambition and his intense desire to accomplish more than was feasible under existing circumstances. No American envoy, no matter how wise or skillful, could have prevented Anastasio Somoza from seizing power in Nicaragua in 1936 unless, of course, the United States government had been willing to intervene with military force. Nevertheless, Lane succeeded in delaying the showdown. More importantly, he seems to have been chiefly responsible for discouraging Somoza from resorting to a traditional bloodletting in his drive for power. This in itself was no mean accomplishment.

Similarly, under the conditions that existed in Yugoslavia in 1940, no diplomacy could have persuaded the Belgrade government voluntarily to commit suicide by openly challenging the Axis. But here, again, Lane's efforts helped to delay Yugoslavia's adherence to the Tripartite Pact by several crucial months. His part in the overthrow of Prince Paul's regime was not a glorious one, and faced with the consequences of the coup d'état, he went through a period of painful anguish. He could justify what he did, for he had followed the wishes of his president. But he did it against his better judgment and for reasons which appeared to him of questionable validity.

It might be said that Lane's struggle in Poland was doomed from the outset. Given the unwillingness of the United States and Great Britain to clash with the Soviet Union over the issue of Polish independence, there was nothing that Lane, or anyone else in his stead, could do to enforce the Yalta agreement. Lane himself became fully aware of the essential hopelessness of the cause of Poland's freedom within weeks after his arrival in Warsaw, and, in fact, he set for himself a much more realistic goal: to preserve insofar as possible among the Polish masses the image of the United States as a nation that opposed their enslavement by the communists; and to make the American government and public aware of the magnitude of the communist menace by forcing the outstanding issues to a point of open confrontation with the Warsaw regime. Although he cannot be credited with accomplishing this combined goal single-handedly, his contribution was significant. Lane's achievement was recognized—and resented—by many high officials in Washington, who loathed to face the unpleasant realities of the postwar era. Many a Soviet apologist called Lane a warmonger, a reactionary, and an extremist.

On many occasions in his career Arthur Bliss Lane acted upon his own political interpretation of the developments with which he had to deal. He was something of a Wilsonian idealist and even a romantic; perhaps because of his long experience in Latin America, he tended to have an exaggerated view of the power and the might of the United States which he, as ambassador, represented in foreign lands. Yet in the performance of his daily duties he remained essentially a pragmatist. He did not expect that diplomacy would alter fundamental power relationships existing in the world at any given moment. Because of his ambition and almost unlimited self-confidence, Lane tended to set his sights too high and suffered frustrations when he failed to achieve his goals. In the excitement of a crisis, many persons of greater experience and larger responsibilities than Lane's have adopted such hopes and tried for too much.

In spite of his obvious accomplishments, Arthur Bliss Lane enjoyed only a limited popularity among his colleagues in the foreign service and in the State Department hierarchy. In part it was because he combined strongly-held views with a generally combative disposition. Most successful careers in the foreign service are molded by men who studiously avoid the spotlight, stay away from controversies, and exercise caution in stating their views. They display a near-perfect efficiency in carrying out even the most contradictory and illogical instructions, and they unfailingly (and cheerfully) subordinate their own judgment to the decisions of their superiors. A "good" diplomat must know his place in the establishment. In situations where sharp disagreements arise at the policy-making levels in the department, or between the department and the White House, a career-minded diplomat avoids taking sides. And under no conditions does he attempt to influence policy through by-passing established channels or carrying his case—however discreetly—outside of the executive branch.

In view of such prerequisites for a successful career, one may wonder how Lane ever managed to reach the top rungs of the ladder. As one of his old friends, Ambassador John C. Wiley, once remarked, the chief trouble with Lane was that he had "never accepted the principle that a diplomat should learn to tolerate his own government." Toward the end of his service

Lane defied many other conventions of diplomatic behavior with increasing frequency, and few of those who knew him were surprised when he finally abandoned his service to the government and joined the opposition.

It is possible, as so many people who knew Arthur Bliss Lane have suggested, that he was not temperamentally suited to be a diplomat—that he would have been more successful, and certainly happier, in politics or journalism. But then, we may ask, how many men in the foreign service of the United States truly belong there? All we can reasonably hope for is that at least some of them possess enough skill and experience to be able to handle their jobs adequately, and that they retain presence of mind in critical situations. By these standards, Arthur Bliss Lane passed the test well, standing out among his contemporaries, remembered—if not exactly admired—for his unorthodox ways and for the sheer force of his colorful personality.

Index

A

B

G

H

R

T

U